D0078202

AFTER THE

HOLOCAUST

Rebuilding

Jewish Lives

in Postwar

Germany

Michael Brenner

Translated from

the German by

Barbara Harshav

PRINCETON UNIVERSITY PRESS • PRINCETON, NEW JERSEY

First published in Germany under the title *Nach dem Holocaust: Juden in Deutschland 1945–1950* © C. H. Beck'sche Verlagsbuchhandlung (Oscar Beck), Munich, 1995

English translation © 1997 by Princeton University Press
Published by Princeton University Press, 41 William Street,
Princeton, New Jersey 08540
In the United Kingdom: Princeton University Press,
Chichester, West Sussex

Library of Congress Cataloging-in-Publication Data

Brenner, Michael.
[Nach dem Holocaust. English]
After the Holocaust : rebuilding Jewish lives in postwar Germany /
Michael Brenner ; translated by Barbara Harshav.
p.   cm.
Includes bibliographical references and index.
ISBN 0–691–02665–3 (alk. paper)
1. Jews—Germany—History—1945– 2. Holocaust survivors—Germany.
3. Germany—History—1945–1955. 4. Germany—Ethnic relations.
I. Title.
DS135.G33B7513   1997
943'.004924—DC21   97-1149   CIP   r97

This book has been composed in Dante

The publication of this work has been subsidized by Inter Nationes, Bonn

Princeton University Press books are printed on acid-free paper and meet the guidelines for permanence and durability of the Committee on Production Guidelines for Book Longevity of the Council on Library Resources

http://pup.princeton.edu

Printed in the United States of America

10 9 8 7 6 5 4 3 2

To the memory of my grandparents Lippmann and Malka Brenner, my aunt Jadwiga Brenner, and my uncle Meir Brenner. For all of them the liberators came too late.

Contents

Preface to the English Edition

As this book appears, the German-Jewish community is undergoing its most significant transformation in the postwar period. Within the last five years this community has doubled in size, and an end to the immigration of Jews from the states of the former Soviet Union is not in sight. In fact, Germany, which half a century ago launched the attempt to create a Europe without Jews, is today the only European country showing a steady increase in its Jewish population. Alongside the statistical changes come challenges to the internal structure of the Jewish communities in Germany. Reform and Conservative Judaism have recently made inroads into a community previously characterized by East European–style orthodoxy. The trend toward religious pluralism has perhaps found its most visible expression in the 1995 installation of the first woman rabbi in a German-Jewish community.

The last section of this English edition incorporates those most recent changes, which have occurred since the appearance of the German edition in 1995. The main body of this book, however, remains unaltered. It deals with the very foundations of the German-Jewish postwar community between 1945 and 1950, the study of which is even more relevant in light of its present expansion. Only a few details have been revised. Annotations were added if thought necessary for the English reader. I would like to thank Dr. Juliane Wetzel of the Zentrum für Antisemitismusforschung in Berlin for her valuable remarks on the German edition; my translator, Barbara Harshav, for her thoughtful comments much beyond pure translation issues; my editor at Princeton University Press, Dr. Brigitta van Rheinberg, for her assistance throughout the editing process; and Lauren Lepow for her meticulous review of the manuscript. I would also like to take this opportunity to express my gratitude to my colleagues and students at Brandeis University and the Tauber Institute for the Study of European Jewry, where most of this book has been written. I am especially indebted to Sylvia Fuks Fried, with whom I had the pleasure to plan a conference on Jews in postwar Europe.

As I complete this English edition, I feel more attached to the topic than ever before. Having received an invitation to become the first incumbent of the newly created chair for Jewish History and Culture at Munich University, I will return to Germany after spending over a decade studying and teaching in Israel and the United States. Thus in contrast to the German edition I can no longer speak of the "secure distance" from which I undertook this study, but should rather express my hope that I may be able to add my modest share to the rebuilding of the German-Jewish community from within.

Whether the five decades of Jewish life in postwar Germany were merely a brief epilogue to a glorious past or the beginning of a new, albeit modest, chapter in Jewish history remains to be judged by future generations.

Lexington, Massachusetts
October 1996

AFTER THE

HOLOCAUST

LIBERTY, the improbable, the impossible liberty, so far removed from Auschwitz that we had only dared to hope for it in our dreams, had come, but it had not taken us to the Promised Land. It was around us, but in the form of a pitiless, deserted plain. More trials, more toil, more hunger, more cold, more fears awaited us.

—PRIMO LEVI, *The Reawakening*

Introduction

TEN YEARS after the beginning of the "Thousand Year Reich," Joseph Goebbels declared Berlin "judenrein" [free of Jews]. By this time, over half a million German Jews had either left Germany or had been deported to death camps in the East. Those who remained were either in hiding or (still) protected by "Aryan" spouses or parents. During the last years of the war, Jewish life in Berlin and the rest of Germany was nonexistent. The few thousand "illegal" Jews or those protected by "mixed marriages" could expect to be discovered any moment and wrenched away from the protection of their relatives.

After the war, the legacy of Mendelssohn and Heine, Freud and Einstein remained without heirs; the ruins of synagogues were to give way to parking lots and lawns. In terms of quantity, even half a century later, the Jewish community in Germany is not equal to one-tenth of its prewar population; in terms of quality, the comparison is even more striking. Yet 1943 did not mark the end of the visible presence of Jews in Germany once and for all. In the first postwar years, some quarter of a million Jews lived in Germany; most of them were East European survivors of the Nazi terror. In many places that could not be rendered "judenrein" by the Nazis since no Jews had ever lived in them, Jewish schools and sports clubs now emerged. In the provinces of Lower Bavaria and North Hesse, in the cities of Berlin and Munich, and near the Bergen-Belsen camp, these "remnants" (in Hebrew: *she'erit ha-pleyta*) created an unfamiliar Jewish culture in modern Germany. They established several yeshivas and printed hundreds of Yiddish newspapers; they elected their political leadership and initiated theater groups, historical associations, and Jewish soccer leagues.

These activities produced only an ephemeral phenomenon, which came to an end when two sovereign German states replaced the Allied administration. For most Jews, the blood-soaked soil of Germany was only a stopover on the way to Israel or the United States. Nevertheless, in many respects, this brief, and so far last, chapter of Jewish creativity in postwar Germany has far-reaching significance. The fact that Jewish survivors were firmly entrenched on German ground—and, as the *Exodus*

affair showed, were forcibly returned to Germany—had an impact on the
United Nations, which was discussing the creation of a Jewish state. For
the survivors themselves, the psychological effect of these years was
often long-lasting, since many of them were denied the experience of full
liberation. They continued to be confined in camps, behind barbed wire,
supervised by uniformed guards. Finally, this chapter also forms the foundation for the restoration of a Jewish community in West Germany—a
foundation laid amid shards and debris, tears and ashes.

This book reviews the first five postwar years in terms of their
significance for the restoration of Jewish life in Germany, and consists of
two levels. The first part presents a concise overview of the situation of
the Jews in postwar Germany using contemporary sources as well as
subsequent research. In the second part, the eyewitnesses speak for themselves. This group of fourteen persons was not chosen as a typical sample
of Jews in postwar Germany. Instead, I was interested in interviewing the
few persons still alive who played an active role in the restoration of
Jewish life in Germany immediately after the war and remained leaders
of Jewish communal life thereafter. I could therefore select only from a
very small group, which unfortunately includes few women. In other
respects, however, my interviewees represent a broad spectrum of background and experience. They include German Jews who returned from
exile and East European Displaced Persons, a member of the Jewish Brigade within the British army and a Polish Jew whose life was saved by
Oskar Schindler, a cantor from Salonika and a rabbi who was among Leo
Baeck's last students in wartime Berlin, the leaders of Germany's largest
Jewish communities and organizations and those who rebuilt and led tiny
Jewish communities, the founder of the only German-Jewish weekly and
a representative of foreign aid organizations who remained in Germany
after fulfilling his mission.

If, for most of the surviving Jews, the period between their liberation from the concentration camps and the establishment of the Central
Council of Jews in Germany [*Zentralrat der Juden in Deutschland*] consti-
tutes only a transitional phase of their flight from Europe, for a minority
it marked the beginning of a long-term restoration of Jewish life in Germany. This perspective demands that the experiences of Eastern European Displaced Persons and those of German Jews, which are usually
considered separately, be studied in tandem. Leaders of both groups laid
the foundation for the establishment of new Jewish communities in postwar Germany.

On this topic, it is particularly tempting to resort to "oral history," for many witnesses who played an active role in the restoration of
Jewish life are still able to present their views in this area. Not to gloss
over the problematic nature of memories as historical sources, these ac-

counts will serve not as a basis for the historical survey but rather as illustrations of the events described in the first part of the book. Therefore, they are printed separately as a second part.

Along with the many archivists and librarians who facilitated my research with their support, I am grateful above all to my interlocutors. Four of them—Heinz Galinski, E. G. Lowenthal, Julius Spokojny, and Wolf Weil—passed away before this book was published, and are mentioned here in memoriam. This book originated in the home of my parents, who exemplify both the Eastern Jewish and the German-Jewish traditions, and who played an active role in the restoration of a small Jewish community in postwar Germany. Their influence sharpened my view of German-Jewish postwar society, as did my subsequent study at the College for Jewish Studies in Heidelberg and my service on the executive board of the Jewish Students Association in Germany. I am indebted to my friend and colleague Stefan Rohrbacher for a critical examination of the manuscript. Although I have been out of the German-Jewish milieu for years, its problems have continued to preoccupy me even more from the safe distance of a scholar. This book, then, is also a product of the historian's interaction with his own history.

I.

Historical Overview

1. Liberated—But Not Free

January 18, 1945, in Auschwitz seemed to be a day like any other in this vestibule of death: pillars of smoke rose over the camp; inmates prepared for roll call. But they soon realized that this day was to be different from all previous days. The clouds of smoke didn't smell like burned flesh. All indications of the murder that had taken place here, telltale remains of files and documents, were turned into ashes. And that evening, when the inmates were once again assembled on the *Appellplatz* [parade ground], it was the first time they were lined up not by blocks but haphazardly. With cannon thunder in the background heralding the approach of Russian troops, there could be no more doubt that this was the beginning of the end.

"The entire camp was in a turmoil of excitement, with prisoners seized by alarm and euphoria at one and the same time," one former inmate recalled the withdrawal of the SS on January 18.[1] But the euphoria of the Auschwitz inmates was premature. A few days later, when the Russians reached the site of the genocide, they found only a few sick and weak inmates. Most of the approximately sixty thousand survivors had been forced to leave the camp with their guards on January 18 and were driven westward. The word "evacuation," used by the Nazis to characterize the removal of the concentration camp inmates, is a euphemism in view of the real circumstances; people were not taken out of the war zone and brought to safety, but were driven to death by the thousands. At a time when German troops were increasingly hemmed in, when the defense of any remaining German territory was becoming increasingly desperate, when countless German soldiers were being obliterated by bombs, the SS apparently had nothing more urgent to do than organize death marches from the annihilation camps of the East. In past years, millions of Jews from all over Europe were deported to the East in freight and cattle cars; now, the small remnant of survivors moved westward mostly on foot, toward the concentration camps in Germany, which had been declared "judenrein" in 1943.

The Long Way to Freedom

The SS drove the half-starved, emaciated prisoners from Auschwitz and its auxiliary camps to Neuengamme and Ravensbrück, Sachsenhausen and Bergen-Belsen, Buchenwald and Flossenbürg, Dachau and Mauthausen. Weakness, illness, and freezing cold made the several hundred kilometers of the march the last straw for many of them. One survivor described the death march from Auschwitz in these words:

> The snow was quite high, and after three hours, there were the first victims. They couldn't keep up with the pace at which we were driven, kept falling back, wound up in the rear rows, fell down, got up again, and tried with their last bit of strength to go on. We supported them, but soon we couldn't anymore. By now, it was terribly hard to drag yourself forward in the snow. They remained behind, and the last SS man shot them down. . . . Food was out of the question. Before we could force the bag open with our frozen fingers to take out the ice cold bread, the column started moving again. It was so hard to drag this kilo of bread and most of us threw it out on the way. We simply had no more strength.[2]

The Buchenwald chronicler Eugen Kogon recorded a similar description of the death march from the East:

> In endless columns the wretched host rolled over the countryside, day after day, often for weeks, without food, without adequate clothing. Those who could go no farther were shot down by the SS or those armed prisoner minions, or simply left by the wayside. . . . More centrally located camps had to make room for thousands upon thousands of evacuees who reported stories of unrelieved terror. The picture was one of chaotic disintegration, studded with harrowing incidents.[3]

Those who reached the destination were still weeks and months away from liberation. For most of them, these weeks constituted the most dreadful torment of their imprisonment in concentration camps. The concentration camps in Germany were extremely overcrowded; hygienic conditions defied all description; food was even scarcer than in the previous years. But even under these circumstances, the "evacuation" continued, constantly claiming new fatalities. As the ring of Allied troops around Germany grew tighter, the death marches were accelerated into the remaining German territory and adjusted to the changing front lines. The survivors were driven from Stutthof to Ravensbrück, from Gross-Rosen to Flossenbürg, from Nordhausen to Bergen-Belsen, from Buchenwald to Theresienstadt, from Flossenbürg to Dachau. The description of the situation in Dachau was also characteristic of other camps in these last weeks of the war:

The circumstances were always the same: dead tired people, who had come through days and sometimes weeks of marching on foot or crammed into railroad cars, suffering from cold, hunger, and disease, trudged into the camp. But in Dachau, there was no appropriate provision for them; their arrival aggravated conditions that were already catastrophic and made the death count rise even higher.[4]

Until the final days of the Nazi regime, the Jews experienced special treatment. In Dachau, on April 23, 1945, the camp leadership separated the 2,000 Jewish prisoners for evacuation from the camp three days later; in Buchenwald, the same thing happened on April 6 with the 6,000 Jews there.[5]

Even without systematic gassing, the brutal conditions of the final weeks claimed thousands of human lives. In Bergen-Belsen, where the camp population had risen from 18,000 to 60,000 in the first four months of 1945, as inmates arrived from the East, 18,000 prisoners died in March 1945, and another 9,300 in the first two weeks of April. For comparison: in all of 1944, the death count amounted to "only" some 2,000 prisoners.[6] In Dachau, by January 1945, 3,000 people had fallen victim to a typhus epidemic. The mass evacuations overcrowded the Dachau camp again, and more than 12,000 people perished in the three months before the Liberation.[7]

In the final weeks of the war, the Flossenbürg concentration camp in the Upper Palatinate became a terminal point for several death marches from the increasingly constricted territory of the Reich. Ever since summer 1944, Flossenbürg and the external units subordinate to this camp were constantly filled with concentration camp inmates from the East, including many Jews. Of the approximately 30,000 deaths in Flossenbürg and its external camps, about three-fourths occurred during the last nine months of the camp's existence. The death rate in February 1945 was especially high: in the main camp, an average of 59 people died per day (in January, the figure was 28).[8] In mid-April, the evacuation from the Flossenbürg concentration camp itself began. As American troops kept getting closer, the inmates were to be taken to Dachau, but in fact only one transport with 2,000 of the 16,000 inmates got there. The survivors of most of the other death marches were liberated on the way by the Americans.[9] One Jewish inmate, who had survived the Warsaw ghetto, Maidanek, Auschwitz, and Gross-Rosen, felt that the last weeks in Flossenbürg were the most terrible chapter of his time in the camps: "We slept four to a bed, like sardines. In addition, the *Kapos* and the SS poured water in the beds. If anybody had to use the toilet, he couldn't get out. You had to pull him out. . . . For 'food,' we got water a butcher had cooked sausages in."[10]

As the situation in the concentration camps became increasingly desperate, Allied troops were moving inexorably closer. For the concentration camp inmates, that advance was a life-and-death race with time. For thousands of survivors it came too late. In the first weeks after the Liberation, in Bergen-Belsen alone, 14,000 people died, most of them Jews, as a result of their imprisonment in concentration camps.[11] When the camp gates opened at Buchenwald on April 11, Bergen-Belsen on April 15, Flossenbürg on April 20, Dachau on April 29, and Mauthausen on May 3, only very few were able to express their joy, which could hardly be put into words; after four, six, or even twelve years of camp life, a life in freedom was now to come. A contemporary report from Dachau reflects the enthusiasm of those days:

> The Americans are here! The Americans are in the camp! Everyone is moving. Sick people leave their beds, the almost healthy and the block staff run to the block streets, jump out of windows, clamber over board walls, run to the parade ground. From far and near you hear the shouts and cheers. Shouts of joy. . . . We kiss each other like brothers and congratulate each other. Many have tears in their eyes. We shake each other's hands: Free, free![12]

But after the first shouts of joy subsided, the Jewish survivors became aware of the limits of their joy. Most of their families were murdered; their communities were destroyed; their material existence was precarious. They had all longed for this day of liberation, and countless times they had dreamed of those first days in freedom. Yet the reality did not have much in common with their dreams. For the time being, they remained on the hated German soil, behind barbed wire, controlled by uniformed guards. The historian Wolfgang Benz judged the situation in Dachau after the Liberation:

> Externally, for most, the situation after April 29, the day of the liberation, was not much different from the previous condition. Although the threat from the SS had ceased, there was still mortal danger from typhus and typhoid fever, from the horrible sanitary conditions, from the corpses lying all around, which were still being removed even a week after the liberation. And the liberation had not yet brought freedom either, at least not the freedom to leave the camp grounds.

In early May 1945, the commander of the American Liberation Army announced to the survivors, "Anyone found outside the camp without a permit will be shot."[13]

In view of this stipulation, it is no wonder that a French report of autumn 1945 summarizes the situation of the concentration camp survivors in these words: "We were liberated, but we are not free."[14] President Truman assigned Earl G. Harrison to examine the situation of the Jewish survivors in the camps in the American Occupation Zones of Germany and Austria. Harrison's judgment was even harsher. In his report of August 1945, which made quite a sensation in the American administration and public, Harrison criticized the lack of food and clothing in the camps, as well as the barbed wire fences around many camps, which remained from before. He went so far as to compare the American army with the SS in terms of their treatment of the Jews. "As matters now stand, we appear to be treating the Jews as the Nazis treated them, except that we do not exterminate them. They are in concentration camps in large numbers under our military guard instead of SS troops. One is led to wonder whether the German people, seeing this, are not supposing that we are following or at least condoning Nazi policy."[15]

From Concentration Camp to DP Camp

After the war ended, citizens of Allied countries who remained outside their homelands were designated as Displaced Persons (DPs). The approximately 50,000 liberated Jews were part of some eight million Displaced Persons who lived in occupied Germany and Austria shortly after the end of the war.[16] The 50,000 Jews shared with these eight million the fate of being driven from their home by the war. But unlike most non-Jewish DPs, the Jewish survivors no longer had a home to return to. They usually spent the first postwar years in so-called DP camps near the site of their liberation, which often also housed Nazi collaborators from the Baltic States, the Ukraine, Hungary, and other countries. The presence of former Nazis and their collaborators in the DP camps led to violent protests among the Jewish survivors.

In the Neustadt camp on the Baltic Sea, for example, only 800 of the 4,000 DPs were Jews. The French report quoted above mentions the presence of Germans, who were still walking around in their old Wehrmacht uniforms, as well as Latvian and Lithuanian Nazi collaborators, who were granted the same rights in the camp as the former concentration camp inmates. Sick Jews preferred to remain in their barracks without any medical facilities rather than go to the hospital where they would be treated along with German patients by German doctors. In Neustadt they were also forbidden to leave the camp for several days without written permission. This restriction of freedom of movement was particularly painful for concentration camp survivors, since their first concern was to search for any members of their family who might still be alive.[17]

Even after the Liberation, the traditional tension between Jews and Poles still operated. Thus, in May 1945, non-Jewish Poles in Dachau threatened the violent disruption of a Sabbath service if it were held in the main square of the camp. A soccer game between Jewish and Polish

The Jewish police in Föhrenwald (Yad Vashem Photo Archives)

DPs ended in a stabbing when the Jewish team won. In Hohne-Belsen, Polish DPs demolished the Jewish prayer house, destroyed the Torah scrolls, and fired shots at the rabbi.[18]

Given this situation, the creation of separate Jewish camps was particularly urgent. The first purely Jewish camp was in Feldafing in Upper Bavaria, where Jews liberated near Bad Tölz had been brought in late April. (See interview with Ernest Landau.) By July, non-Jewish Hungarians were taken to other camps and Jews liberated in Dachau were moved to Feldafing. A few months after the Liberation, Feldafing's 6,000 inmates were almost exclusively Jewish. The creation of this first Jewish DP camp was due to the cooperation of the American camp commander, Lieutenant Irving Smith, and the American Jewish chaplains Max Braude and Abraham Klausner.[19] A broad autonomy could be established in the Jewish DP camps, ranging from a Jewish camp administration to Jewish courts and Jewish camp police. This Jewish police force was the first thing that struck a visitor to the DP camp Berlin-Tempelhof: "The entrance to the camp was guarded by a camp police force composed of inmates; the white American MP helmet bore a blue Star of David. Their patrols were everywhere in the streets of the camp, maintaining law and order."[20]

Along with the demand for Jewish camps with an autonomous administration, there was an urgent need to deal with hygiene in the camps. The American major Irving Heymont, who was in charge of the DP camp in Landsberg am Lech with up to 6,000 DPs (approximately 5,000 of them Jews), reported in September 1945: "The camp is filthy beyond description. Sanitation is virtually unknown. Words fail me when I try to think of an adequate description."[21] Heymont indicated how difficult it was for camp inmates to adjust to normal life after years in concen-

Kosher soup kitchen in Feldmoching (the Hebrew and Yiddish writing means "Good appetite") (Yad Vashem Photo Archives)

tration camps. In another camp, an American Jewish chaplain reported that many women who had been treated disrespectfully for years by the Germans in the concentration camps had lost all sense of shame: "From time to time, when my duties took me to their barracks, they went on dressing or undressing, as if I weren't even there."[22] Nor were external living conditions in the DP camps likely to ease integration into a normal life. Many camps were hopelessly overcrowded. The Zeilsheim DP camp, a housing development on the outskirts of Frankfurt, was generally considered one of the better DP camps, yet here too living conditions were intolerable, as a contemporary American Jewish chaplain noted:

> Originally set up for 1,800 DPs, at the time of my visit [October 1945] it was bursting at the seams with 5,500 men, women and children. Living conditions were beyond description. In a two bedroom flat, three families, 7 persons were living. One couple for each bedroom and one couple with a 16-year-old boy in the living room. Whenever a friend of this boy would come to visit him, they set up a cot for him in the kitchen. This was a typical flat for Zeilsheim.[23]

The Yiddish camp newspaper, *Undzer Hofenung* [Our hope], of Eschwege in Hesse reported in December 1946 on the DP camp of Babenhausen: "Housing conditions are horrible. These used to be stalls for the horses of the cavalry of the Third Reich; now they are flats for the surviving Jews. The Jews did not want to leave the trains so as not to have to move in here."[24] In the DP camp of Türkheim, 450 Jews lived behind a fence that was still electrified.[25]

In Berlin, too, the surviving Jews were assembled in DP camps. The German-Jewish newspaper *Der Weg* [The road] described the DP camp at Berlin-Tempelhof thus:

> The camp itself is housed in several large, connected new buildings, which are bordered by a square. At first glance, one has the impression of terrible overcrowding. The streets are teeming with people, who are all dressed alike and who look rushed. An average of six to eight persons sleep in a room of four by five meters. The kitchens are also occupied. Only seldom did I see a closet, and never a table or a chair.

And an American Jewish chaplain described a Jewish old people's home in Berlin:

> I have seen Displaced Persons camps. I have seen places where a large number of Jewish survivors huddled together waiting for better times to come. But I have never, never seen—before or after—a place more depressing than that home in Berlin in 1945. People were too weak to stand on their feet; too cold to walk around; therefore, covered with rags and rugs and anything they could find to add a little warmth, they stayed in bed. Their rooms had wooden boards in place of windows, and hope in the future took the place of heat![26]

The fact that many Germans at this time lived under housing conditions just as bad was cold consolation for the Jewish survivors. They had hoped that the end of the war would bring about a change in their situation: the victim was now to be granted the easy life many of the murderers had been leading for years. But in reality, the victims were still living in camps in a cramped space, without any privacy. It must be emphasized, however, that not all DP camps were in such a dreadful condition as those described above. The most varied housing possibilities were used as DP camps, from former stables to barracks and apartment houses to convents, schools, hotels, and sanitoria.

Even under better material conditions, however, there was still another obstacle to "normalization": the mental condition of the liberated people. After years of humiliation and persecution, after the murder of most of their family, integration into society was a difficult process. Thus the correspondent of the *Manchester Guardian* characterized the general atmosphere in the Jewish camps as "one of apathy, greyness, and despair."[27] Irving Heymont used similar terms to describe the atmosphere among the DPs in the Landsberg camp he commanded: "With a few exceptions, the people of the camp themselves appear demoralized beyond hope of rehabilitation. They appear to be beaten both spiritually and physically, with no hopes or incentives for the future."[28]

The policy of the Allied occupation forces was intended to return the DPs to their countries of origin as soon as possible, which
pleased most of the non-Jewish Displaced Persons, who had been
driven out of their homelands by force. By May 1946, 88 percent—that
is, almost six million Displaced Persons—had left Germany and were
repatriated in their homelands.[29] Others, who had collaborated with the
Germans or who simply rejected the Communist rule of their homelands, feared repression after their return and preferred integration into
German society. For the great majority of the Jewish DPs, however,
both staying on hated German soil and returning to Eastern Europe
were out of the question. When the commander of the Third American
Army, General George Patton, who pursued an indiscriminate policy of
immediate repatriation of all DPs, wanted to transport the Jews from
the DP camp of Buchberg to Poland in July 1945, these Jews refused to
obey the order and were ultimately supported by Earl Harrison, envoy
of the American president.[30] Patton's anti-Jewish attitude can be clearly
seen in his diary entries. Thus, in September 1945, he noted: "We entered the synagogue which was packed with the greatest stinking bunch
of humanity I have ever seen. . . . Either the Displaced Persons never
had any sense of decency or else they lost it all during their period of
internment by the Germans. My personal opinion is that no people
could have sunk to the level of degradation these have reached in the
short space of four years."[31] The resistance of the liberated East European Jews in Germany was expressed by their representative, Jacob
Olejski, at the "Peace-Victory Rally" in Landsberg on August 24, 1945:
"No, we are not Poles, even though we were born in Poland; we are
not Lithuanians, even if our cradles may once have been in Lithuania;
we are not Romanians even if we first saw the light of day in Romania.
We are Jews! . . . We demand that the gates of Palestine be opened
wide for us so we can live there as a free, independent, and self-reliant
people."[32]

Flight into a Cursed Land

Olejski spoke not only for the Jewish DPs living in Germany but
also for the majority of Jewish survivors who were still in Eastern Europe.
The Jewish communities of Eastern Europe were destroyed in World
War II, and often the non-Jewish population of these states had partici-
pated actively in this destruction. Worse, even after the war was over,
Jews returning primarily to Poland found that their lives were not safe.
Traditional antisemitism, nourished by the recent wave of annihilation,
as well as the fear that the surviving Jews would demand the return of

their property, led to regular pogroms from 1945 to 1947, in which over 1,000 Jews lost their lives, more than in the decade before the war. The most violent pogrom, which occurred in Kielce in June 1946, claimed at least 47 lives.[33] It is understandable that, in 1946, a report on Jewish refugees and Displaced Persons in Europe reached the conclusion: "It can frankly be stated that eighteen months after liberation the war is not yet over for European Jewry."[34]

Of the approximately 80,000 Jews still living in Poland in August 1945, hardly any wanted to remain there. Most declared their desire to immigrate to Palestine to help establish a Jewish state. But the British government balked at Jewish immigration to Mandatory Palestine. Many of the Jewish survivors immigrated illegally to Palestine through the organization *Berihah* (Flight), which was an important chapter in the annals of the Jewish state. But even those who could not or would not immigrate illegally to Palestine tried to leave Eastern Europe as soon as possible. As a stop on the way to Palestine or the United States, they used the American Occupation Zone in Germany, where they could join with Jews liberated on German soil in the existing Jewish camps.

It is surely one of the ironies of history that it was Germany, of all places, that became a haven for Jewish refugees in the first years after the war. Unlike the non-Jewish DPs, who had mostly left Germany by 1945, the number of Jewish DPs in the American Occupation Zone in Germany increased during 1946 from just 40,000 to over 145,000.[35] In the summer of 1947, about 182,000 Jewish DPs were living in Germany. Over 80 percent of them came from Poland, followed far behind by Hungarian, Czech, Russian, and Romanian Jews.[36] In the American Occupation Zone, several large camps were formed, each with some 5,000 inhabitants. These included the camps in Feldafing, Föhrenwald, Pocking, Landsberg, and Leipheim in Bavaria; as well as Zeilsheim, Wetzlar, and Eschwege in Hesse. About one-fourth of the Jewish DPs lived outside the DP camps in German cities. For a time, Munich, with up to 7,000 Jewish DPs, formed the center of Jewish life in postwar Germany. But smaller towns near the Czech border, where the refugees flowed in, also became temporary refuges for thousands of Eastern European Jews. Places that had never before had a Jewish population now became short-term Jewish centers.

In the British Occupation Zone, there was no significant increase. Unlike the American occupation policy, Great Britain refused to grant official recognition to Jewish nationality, since that would have been an indirect admission of the right of a Jewish state to exist. This could have had comprehensive political effects on the development in Palestine, which was still administered by the British.

DP camps in southern Germany with more than two thousand Jewish inmates, 1947 (John Hollingsworth, Indiana University)

On the basis of political motives, the British administration re-fused to allow Jewish refugees into the zone of Germany under their occupation. Furthermore, the camp structure in the British Occupation Zone assumed a different configuration from that in the American Occupation Zone. While in the American Zone several large camps had been formed and many Jews lived outside the camps in cities, the problem of the Jewish DPs in the British Zone was limited mainly to the Hohne-Belsen camp, a former armored SS barracks, which sheltered prisoners liberated from Bergen-Belsen. In mid-June 1946, more than 9,000 of the 12,000 Jewish DPs in the British Occupation Zone were in Hohne.[37] In the French Occupation Zone, the problem of Jewish refugees never reached the dimensions it did in the two other Western zones: in 1947, when more than 150,000 Jews were living temporarily in the American Occupation Zone, only 1,281 Jews were in the DP camps of the French Occupation Zone.[38]

2. CULTURE BEHIND BARBED WIRE

The destruction of East European Jewry meant not only the murder of millions of people but also the violent end of a venerable culture with its own language, religious traditions, and a broad spectrum of secular forms of expression in literature, music, and art. Unlike the German Jews, who were largely acculturated, the roughly eight million Jews of Poland, Romania, Hungary, the Baltic States, and the Soviet Union were, for the most part, separated from non-Jews by language and culture. They were considered an ethnic minority, and after World War I they demanded recognition of their cultural autonomy with religious freedom as merely one component. On a secular level, the cultural independence of East European Jews was expressed in the establishment of Yiddish- and Hebrew-language schools, in a multitude of Yiddish and Hebrew daily and weekly newspapers, in book publishing, and in a broad network of Jewish cultural and sport associations.

In Eastern Europe itself, this flourishing Yiddish and Hebrew culture did not survive the war. Unabated antisemitism and Communist leveling in the Soviet satellite states, as previously in the Soviet Union itself, ensured that no Jewish culture could exist anymore among the few Jews remaining there. Nor was there any revival of East European Jewish culture in the countries of immigration; in the United States, most immigrants considered integration into the American melting pot to be inconsistent with the preservation of their own language and culture; and for decades in Israel, Yiddish culture had been portrayed as the embodiment of a ghetto mentality and was condemned as a disagreeable rival of the Hebrew renaissance. It is one of the many ironies in the chapter of the Jewish DP communities in postwar Germany that, for a brief span of time, this place became the scene for an epilogue of prewar East European Yiddish culture in miniature.

For a few years, in the DP camps between Belsen and Landsberg, Feldafing and Zeilsheim, an autonomous Jewish culture came back to life; its conditions were totally different from those in prewar Europe, but its forms of expression were taken from the destroyed shtetl. By constructing a Jewish society clearly distinguished from the German environment, the Jewish DPs lightened the psychological burden of being held in Germany after the Liberation. Jewish schools, theater groups, newspapers and magazines, sports clubs, libraries, and historical committees allowed many Jewish DPs to forget, at least for a while, that they were living in Germany. One of the principles of most committees representing the Jewish DP camps was that Germans were not permitted to enter the camps and German officials were not called in on administrative matters. The comments of Josef Rosensaft, chairman of the Central Committee for Displaced Persons in the British Zone, looking back at the Hohne-Belsen camp, apply to most Jewish DP camps: "Belsen remained a kind of extra-territorial unit inside Germany to its last day, which was September 6, 1950."[1]

The Written Word

The Jewish press was especially significant in the cultural activity of this extraterritorial entity. Between 1945 and 1951, over a hundred newspapers and magazines—often short-lived—existed in the DP camps and among the Jews living outside the camps. The overwhelming majority were in Yiddish, but there were also Jewish publications in Polish, Hungarian, German, Romanian, Lithuanian, and Hebrew. Most of these newspapers were established in the same way: in the first days after the Liberation, handwritten carbon copies were distributed in individual sheets; a bit later, the still handwritten "newspapers" appeared as carbon copies or photocopies. When the first printing presses were brought into the camps, professionally produced newspapers could appear, which, however, usually represented yet another twist: in the first months after the war, the Hebrew letters used for Yiddish writing could not be obtained in Germany, so most of the Yiddish newspapers were initially in Latin letters. With the help of American Jewish welfare organizations, the first presses with Hebrew letters reached Germany in late 1945, allowing the publication of a regular Yiddish and Hebrew press.

The significance for the Jewish survivors of publishing their own journals should not be underestimated. For more than five years, these people had been deprived of news on a regular basis; and in the concentration camps, their only source of information had been the "oral broadcasting network." At a time when both local and regional events in occupied Germany as well as international political developments in the Middle East were enormously important for them, Jewish newspapers were a personal necessity for those survivors. But news was not the only important aspect; the press also devoted a great deal of space to publishing the experiences of the survivors. Finally, serial novels and feature supplements carried on the tradition of the destroyed prewar Jewish culture, which still lived in the memories of many Jewish DPs. But, for most of them, another section was of paramount interest: the lists of surviving Jews and announcements for family and friends. The rapid appearance of the first Yiddish DP newspapers immediately after the war can be attributed not least to the great interest in these lists.

The first Yiddish newspaper with the Hebrew title *Tehiat Ha-Meytim* (Resurrection of the dead) appeared in the Buchenwald concentration camp on May 4, 1945, three weeks after the liberation of the camp and four days before the war ended. It was handwritten and, in this respect, also served as a precursor of subsequent Yiddish newspapers of the Jewish DPs, like the Belsen camp newspaper, *Undzer Shtime* [Our voice], whose establishment was described by Josef Rosensaft:

> We had no printing plant, no typewriter, no duplicator, no newsprint, not even ordinary paper. Yet, the three Chaverim [fellows] who undertook to implement the fantastic idea of a Jewish newspaper in Belsen, of all places, produced it! They worked day and night: one of them wrote the whole paper in longhand; another went off to look for paper; and the third went to some place near Brunswick where he hoped to find a duplicator.[2]

And the historian Lucy Dawidowicz, who worked for American Jewish organizations in Germany, recalled how the Yiddish newspapers succeeded in commandeering the printing press of the former Nazi paper *Der Völkische Beobachter* for its first edition.[3]

The titles of the newly founded papers generally symbolized the situation of the Jewish DPs: along with *Tehiat Ha-Meytim*, such titles as *Bafrayung* [Liberation] (Munich), *Untervegs* [On the road] (Zeilsheim), *A Heim* [A home] (Leipheim), *Frayhayt* [Freedom] (Lampertheim), or *Ibergang* [Transition] (Munich) were especially prominent. The first Jewish newspapers appeared in the two large Bavarian DP camps, Feldafing and Landsberg, in October 1945. While *Dos Fraye Vort* [The free word] from Feldafing was still produced on a typewriter, the *Landsberger Lagertsaytung* [Landsberger camp newspaper] was printed, although initially in Latin letters.[4] It was in *Dos Fraye Vort* that the conflict among the various political factions first surfaced. After long deliberation, an editorial board was formed of representatives of the three major political factions: Zionists, socialist Bundists, and religious Orthodox.

One week after the first issue of the Landsberg camp newspaper came out, the first Yiddish journal printed with Hebrew letters appeared in Munich. The weekly *Undzer Veg* [Our road] was the organ of the Central Committee of Liberated Jews in Bavaria, hence one of the few regional newspapers of the Jewish DPs. The first edition of October 12, 1945, contained three Yiddish pages and one summary page in English. During the five years it appeared, it focused primarily on public an-

The newssheet "Landsberg Mirror" (Yad Vashem Photo Archives)

nouncements and reports of immigration to Israel, as stated in the first issue: "*Undzer Veg* intends to guide the *she'erit ha-pleyta* to the last stop on the road to our destination."[5] In 1947, *Undzer Veg* appeared biweekly with a circulation of 7,500 copies. Regular columns on Jewish life in Bavaria as well as on developments in the Middle East were as much a part of the paper as were literary contributions and search lists.

Most of the local Yiddish periodicals were established after the immigration of East European Jews during 1946. The newspaper *Undzer Hofenung* [Our hope], published in the DP camp Eschwege in Kassel, appeared for the first time on June 4, 1946. Like other DP newspapers, *Undzer Hofenung* is historically significant for its early documentation of the war years. In the very first issue, survivors reported on their fate. Eyewitness accounts like *My Escape from Maidanek*, *The Uprising in Treblinka*, or simply *Camp Memories* were often published in installments.

By late 1946, under the directive of the military authorities, the Yiddish press in the American Occupation Zone was centralized. The numerous local newspapers had to cease their operation and were replaced by one central newspaper in Munich (*Undzer Veg*) and five regional newspapers in Landsberg, Regensburg, Bamberg, Frankfurt, and Eschwege. Party and organization newspapers, however, were allowed to continue.[6]

The publications of the *she'erit ha-pleyta* were not limited to newspapers alone. Jewish survivors also published monthly illustrated magazines, cultural journals, volumes of poetry, novels, prayerbooks, and topical supplements to Jewish religious law. The Central Committee of Liberated Jews in the British Zone compiled a list of fifty-eight Jewish publications in this area between 1945 and 1949, including the picture book *Undzer churbn in bild* (Our destruction in pictures), the Yiddish *Samlung fun Kazet- un Gettolider* (Anthology of songs from camps and ghettos), and the German-language cultural journal *Zwischen den Zeiten. Jüdisches Leben—Jüdisches Wissen* (Between times. Jewish life—Jewish knowledge).[7] In 1947, the publication department of the Central Committee of Liberated Jews in the American Zone issued 168,000 copies of thirty-six different books. Lists of surviving Jews were particularly important, like, for example, the several thousand names and locations of surviving Warsaw Jews in the *Liste fun di lebngeblibene Warszewer Jidn in der US Zone in Dajczland* (List of the surviving Warsaw Jews in the U.S. Zone in Germany).[8] In April 1946, JOINT (American Jewish Joint Distribution Committee) representatives historians Koppel Pinson and Lucy Dawidowicz discovered some 25,000 books in the Offenbach archive warehouse where the Nazis had stored the confiscated Judaica, and contributed them to libraries in several DP camps.[9]

Education and Religious Life

The survivors were particularly concerned with the children who had received no systematic schooling during the war. Some fifty textbooks for the extensive school system of the *she'erit ha-pleyta* appeared in Germany.[10] By July 1, 1945, a Jewish elementary school with 200 students was established in Belsen. The main pedagogical difficulty was that both students and teachers came from various countries and spoke different languages, such as Yiddish, Russian, Hungarian, or Polish. On September 17, 1945, a high school with 60 students opened, whose curriculum included Jewish subjects like the Bible, Talmud, and Hebrew, along with physical education, natural science, general history, anatomy, and archaeology. Instruction was in Yiddish, Polish, and Hebrew. Initially, no textbooks were available and the teachers—some of whom belonged to the Jewish Brigade[11]—had to teach from memory.[12]

Very few children survived the concentration camps; the age groups in the DP camps reflected the annihilation policy of the Nazis: children and old people had practically no chance of survival. According to a census conducted by the Institute of Jewish Affairs, of 25,000 Jewish survivors in Germany and Austria in July 1945, almost 90 percent were between 16 and 45 years old, while only 3.6 percent were under the age of 16, and 7.3 percent were over the age of 45.[13] The number of students

Jewish kindergarten, Ulm (Sedan Barracks) (Yad Vashem Photo Archives)

was correspondingly small at first. In Belsen, there were 200 students in the elementary school, 60 in the high school, and another 60 in the kindergarten. With the influx of refugees in 1946, however, the number of children increased rapidly, from about 7,400 children under 18 in the American Zone in March 1946 to 20,000 by the end of the year.[14] This demographic development was also due to the enormously high birthrate among the Jewish DPs, in sharp contrast with the declining birthrate among the non-Jewish population. In 1945, the birthrate of the Bavarian population was 5 births per 1,000 persons, while the rate per 1,000 Jewish DPs in Bavaria a year later was 14.1. The number of students also increased. In the U.S. Occupation Zone in January 1947, over 10,000 students were registered in day schools and another 3,000 children attended religious schools.[15]

The statistical analysis of the Jewish population in the small Bavarian town of Weiden illustrates the unusual age structure with a local example. Of the 944 registered Jewish DPs in the first postwar years, only 3 were over 60 years old at the time of the Liberation, and only 22 were between 45 and 59. Almost all Jewish survivors belonged to the younger generations, between 30 and 44 years old (202), and between 16 and 29 (547). During the Holocaust, the survival rate of children born in the 1930s or 1940s was as low as that of the older generation. On the other hand, the number born between 1945 and 1949—137 out of a total of 944—was disproportionately high.[16]

Because of the years when education was impossible, the vocational training of adults and older youth constituted an important enterprise. In the American Occupation Zone in 1947, 235 Jewish night

The Maccabi Föhrenwald soccer team (Yad Vashem Photo Archives)

schools with 5,000 students were established.[17] In late 1946, some 500 Jewish DPs attended the Landsberg "Popular University," which offered courses in history, literature, geography, English, and Hebrew. A library with 2,000 volumes was set up in Landsberg, named after the Hebrew national poet, Chaim Nachman Bialik, and housed in the office of the former Wehrmacht commander. Instead of portraits of Hitler, the walls were now embellished with pictures of Bialik and the Yiddish writer Sholem Aleichem, as well as of Roosevelt and Eisenhower.[18] Instruction in the vocational school included practical language study as well as technical training.

The sport activities of the Jewish DPs in postwar Germany have sunk into oblivion today, even though they provide a particularly significant illustration of the active autonomous life of this society. In Bavaria alone, two soccer leagues of Jewish DPs were formed. In the Lower Bavaria–Upper Palatinate League, for example, "Hapoel Neunburg vorm Walde" played "Kadima Deggendorf," and "Maccabi Marktredwitz" played "Hakoah Schwandorf." Other sports, like table tennis and boxing, were also actively pursued. In Hohne-Belsen alone there were six different sports associations: *Ha-Tikvah* (Hope), *Kokhav* (Star), *Ha-Gibor* (Hero), *Ha-No'ar Ha-Zioni* (Liberal Zionists), *Betar* (Revisionist Zionists), and *Ha-Shomer Ha-Tsa'ir* (Left Socialist Zionists). A contemporary list includes 169 Jewish sport clubs in postwar Germany.[19]

Religious groups built their own educational infrastructures in the larger camps, thus continuing institutions that had existed in Eastern Europe before the war but had disappeared in Germany by the nineteenth century because of the strong acculturation trend among German Jews. The most prominent were the yeshivas established in Belsen,

Yeshiva in Leipheim (Yad Vashem Photo Archives)

Eschwege, Feldafing, and Landsberg. In many places, the revival of Jewish religious life meant the brief resumption of a tradition that had been discontinued for a century. For example, in Bavarian Fürth, where there had been a famous yeshiva until the beginning of the nineteenth century, Talmud study was resumed after 1945 under the direction of the distinguished Rabbi David Kahana Spiro, who had been a leading rabbinic authority in prewar Warsaw. In February 1946, Rabbi Alexander Rosenberg, who investigated the religious situation in the DP camps for the American Joint Distribution Committee, mentioned the existence of 4 yeshivas, 18 rabbis, 16 kosher slaughterers, and 4 circumcisers in the American Zone. At that time, the JOINT had distributed 2,000 sets of tefillin, 1,000 tallises, 10,000 prayer books, and 50 Torah scrolls.[20] In Bavaria in 1947, there were a total of 2,000 Jewish students in religious schools.[21] In Munich, the city with the only complete preserved Talmud manuscript in the world, a new edition of the Babylonian Talmud was prepared shortly after the war by Rabbis Samuel Abba Snieg and Samuel Jacob Ros. The reproduction appeared in 1949 in Heidelberg with a drawing of the concentration camp and the road to Israel as a frontispiece.[22]

However, only a minority of the DPs were religious, and the years of persecution had left obvious scars on them too. An observer of DP life reported on their religious activity: "While there may be formal observances and official symbols there is little true piety. In no Jewish DP camp, for example, is it possible to experience the real feeling of the traditional Sabbath, the kind of spirit that hovered over the small towns of Galicia, Poland and Lithuania on the last day of the week."[23] In Landsberg, there were reports of constant friction between the minority of 1,500 Orthodox Jews and the majority of some 4,000 secular Jews over religious observance in the camp; but the Orthodox group finally prevailed with their demand for a general observance of the Sabbath rest in the camp.[24]

Religious life among the Jewish DPs was organized by the rabbis among the survivors, who came largely from Hungary or Slovakia, where the annihilation of the Jews began only in late 1944. In many camps, the East European rabbis obtained support from American Jewish chaplains who had come to Germany with the Allied soldiers. Rabbinates and rabbinical courts were set up in the various occupation zones. The rabbis' first task after the Liberation was to bury the dead and provide emotional consolation for the sick and the weak. Another difficult rabbinical activity was issuing *heterim* (permission to marry) for those whose spouse was missing and who wanted to remarry. Weddings were one of the joyous experiences in camp life and were hardly rare events. Most of the survivors were young men and women between the ages of twenty and forty who could only dream of having their own families while they were in the concentration camps. Soon after the war ended, many couples formed to build a future together. In Belsen, there were over a thousand marriages between 1945 and 1947.[25] An item in the Eschwege DP newspaper, *Undzer Hofenung*, indicates the frequency of marriages: in August 1946, it was reported that a bridal gown was available to be lent for weddings in the camp. But even weddings could not obscure the tragic situation of those who had just been saved. The ceremony under the traditional wedding canopy usually began with the memorial prayer for the murdered parents of the couple. Only in rare cases were surviving family members present at the wedding. (See interview with Ernest Landau.)

Additional functions of the rabbinate included establishing ritual baths (*mikvehs*) and supervising ritual slaughter (*shehitah*). During the years of persecution, along with physical torment, religious Jews also experienced the humiliation of not being allowed to live according to their religious laws. It was particularly hard to give up the rules concerning food (*kashrut*), and thus the rabbis were especially interested in restoring *shehitah* after the war. Kosher meat could often be slaughtered in municipal abattoirs, as in Regensburg from December 1945 on. Another religious stipulation that could not be followed in the concentration camps was the circumcision of newborn males. In Belsen alone, some five hundred circumcisions were carried out by 1947.[26] For those DPs living in cities outside the camps, the Jewish holidays presented another problem. Since the synagogues were usually destroyed, adequate space to hold services for several hundred or, in some places, even thousands of Jewish survivors had to be found. In Munich, the first Hanukah celebration in freedom took place in the Prinzregententheater in December 1945. In other cities, cinemas, courtrooms, and theaters were rented for the High Holidays for the Jewish DPs. Only in very few cases could intact synagogues be used for their original purpose, as in Lower Bavarian Straubing. In nearby Landshut, a prayer house was inaugurated in February 1946—the first since the destruction of the Landshut Jewish community in 1450, when the medieval synagogue had been converted into a church.

Passover, commemorating the exodus from Egypt to the Land of Israel, from slavery to freedom, had special symbolic meaning for many of the liberated Jews. The Haggadah, the traditional Passover liturgy, emphasizes that each generation should celebrate this festival as if they themselves had come out of slavery into freedom. For the Jewish survivors, this empathic response was certainly not difficult. However, in a *Pessach-Buch—Zum ersten Befreiungs- und Frühlingsfest der Überreste Israels in Europa* [Passover book—for the first celebration of freedom and spring of the remnant of Israel in Europe], published in 1946, Samuel Gringauz, chairman of the Jewish camp committee in Landsberg am Lech, also stated one essential difference between Egyptian and German oppression:

> The exodus from Egypt brought the immediate freedom of the people. The end of slavery also meant the beginning of freedom. . . . Quite different after the exodus from Nazi slavery. The end of slavery does not yet mean the beginning of freedom. The liberated remnant of the Jews finds the way to the Promised Land closed. All other lines of movement are also closed to the Jewish people.

Gringauz concluded his introduction with the appeal: "Given permission by no one—yet we will go. Led by no one—yet we will march. Taught by no one—yet we will create."[27]

Eating matza (unleavened bread) is one of the regulations for the Passover. In Berlin in the spring of 1946, matzot were baked in the Sarotti chocolate factory.[28] The commandment *zakhor* (remember) always had an especially important significance in Jewish history: Passover commemorates an event that took place three thousand years ago, and Hanukah celebrates the victory of the Maccabees over the Greek occupation of Palestine more than two thousand years ago. The Hebrew Bible contains several purely historical books, and medieval Jewish chronicles continue the tradition of recording historical events. Thus the first task of the liberated Jews was to record their personal suffering so that none of it would pass into oblivion. In Belsen and Munich, central historical committees were formed that systematically collected the reports of the survivors and composed questionnaires, which were later bequeathed to Yad Vashem, the central Holocaust memorial in Israel.[29] The journal *Fun letstn Khurbn*

[From the recent destruction], published in summer 1946 by the *Historische Kommission der befreiten Juden in der amerikanischen Zone* [Historical Committee of the Liberated Jews in the American Zone], is particularly significant. Like current "oral history," important eyewitness accounts of the survivors were collected for posterity. The Historical Committee preserved altogether 2,500 testimonies, and over 1,000 photographs, as well as statistical and folkloric material.[30] While still in the DP camps, the Historical Committee began the special training of questioners to interview children without causing them too much psychological pain.

Most of the children in the DP camps had grown up in concentration camps and had miraculously weathered their first years. They knew no life outside the camp fence and confronted violence and death every day. Even after the Liberation, those experiences remained in the consciousness of both adults and children. UNRRA (United Nations Relief and Rehabilitation Administration) officials were shocked to discover that Jewish kindergarten children in the Hohne-Belsen DP camp were informed of the details of Nazi crimes and that pictures of heaps of bodies, gas chambers, and crematoria were shown to them.

The Shadows of the Past

This proximity of death and persecution appeared in another cultural institution of the DP camp. Following the rich tradition of theater in the East European Jewish world before the war, Yiddish theaters were founded after 1945 in several DP camps and German cities with Jewish DP populations. These theaters did not generally carry on in the often comic tradition of the prewar repertoire but rather reflected the tragic events of the war years. The plays performed by the *Dramkrays Hazomir* in the DP camp of Landsberg am Lech illustrate the connection with the immediate experience of suffering. *Kiddush Hashem*, the term for Jewish martyrdom, was the name of one play; while another was titled *Yizkor*, the Jewish prayer for the dead. The *Münchener Jüdische Theater MIT* performed the Yiddish play *Ich leb* (I live), another stage presentation of suffering in the concentration camp. The "Heroic Drama in Three Acts" begins in an "assembly camp in a cemetery" and portrays the escape of Jewish prisoners, who join the partisans. Jewish survivors played the parts of SS men, Gestapo officials, Ukrainian camp guards, and Jewish *Kapos*.[31]

Not all theater performances dealt with the immediate past. The *Kazett-Theater* in the Belsen camp debuted in September 1945 with a play by the Yiddish classic writer Sholem Aleichem. The play had to be largely improvised, as its director, Samy Feder, recalls: "We had no book, no piano, no musical scores. But we could not wait for supplies from outside.

"Kazett [concentration camp] Theater," Bergen-Belsen, 1945. (Yad Vashem Photo Archives)

There was a need to play and an eager public. . . . Somebody remembered parts of a play; somebody remembered a song which we could write down." At the premiere, director and cast were overwhelmed: concentration camp survivors walked many kilometers on foot to see a play again for the first time in years. "I have never played to such a grateful audience. They clapped and laughed and cried."[32] The *Kazett-Theater* soon had to give guest performances in Hanover, Braunschweig, and Kassel, as well as in Belgium and France. In the two years it existed, the *Kazett-Theater* played forty-seven performances. In Belsen itself, another theater group was set up: the Workers' Theater of the leftist Zionist *Poaley Zion*. In the American Occupation Zone, the Jewish DP theater frequently gave guest performances. In Föhrenwald, which had its own theater group, the visits of the Feldafing Yiddish theater were especially popular.[33]

Music was also widespread in the DP camps. In the larger camps, the musicians among the DPs founded their own orchestras. Regular concerts of the "house orchestra" as well as visits from neighboring Jewish musicians complemented the entertainment program.[34] In smaller camps, like Neunburg vorm Wald in Bavaria, there was an attempt to produce at least the illusion of a happy daily life through dances, but the lost normality could not be reproduced with entertainment.[35]

Those who wanted to escape the past and establish a new life in Germany were often faced with the hopelessness of their enterprise. The best examples of a conscious reorganization of Jewish life were the *Hakhshara kibbutzim*, agricultural settlements built right after the war by Jewish survivors in Germany. According to Zionist ideals, these were to provide practical preparation for a life of agricultural labor in Israel. But as long as kibbutz members still lived in Germany, the illusion of Jewish communal life in the kibbutz could not drive out the shadows of the past, a paradox probably most obvious to the members of one kibbutz near Nuremberg, built on property that had once belonged to Julius Streicher, editor of the vulgar antisemitic newspaper *Der Stürmer*.[36]

But members of other kibbutzim also had to realize that the ground under their temporary new homes was not the earth of the Holy Land of their dreams. Thus just as the DP camp of Hohne-Belsen remained "Bergen-Belsen" for the survivors, most members of a kibbutz who were liberated from Buchenwald called their new residence "Kibbutz Buchenwald," even though it was not in Buchenwald but in Geringshof near Fulda. A contemporary report shows the gap between the ideal of the kibbutz and the reality of Kibbutz Buchenwald even more clearly:

> Visitors think that life in a Kibbutz is happy—and thus it seems at first glance, if nobody tries to look deeply in those sick and miserable faces. Those people can never be happy: their happiness was buried together with their closest relatives. They desperately tried to revive their happiness: they touch the earth with their fingers, but the earth is their own tear and their own bloody heart.[37]

3. AUTONOMY AND EMIGRATION

Political Organization

Right after the Liberation, Jewish survivors began organizing politically. On April 18, 1945, only three days after the Liberation, a committee of former Jewish prisoners was formed in Bergen-Belsen and elected Josef Rosensaft chairman. Rosensaft outlined his four major tasks as the search for family members, the physical and psychological rehabilitation of the survivors, and the struggle for their rights.[1]

The committee's most urgent political task was to obtain separate housing for the Jewish survivors. Recognition of the Jews as an inde-

Josef Rosensaft speaking at the Second Congress of Liberated Jews in the British Zone, Bad Harzburg, July 1947 (Beth Hatefutsoth—The Nahum Goldmann Museum of the Jewish Diaspora, Tel Aviv, Israel)

pendent group was the first demand of camp committees everywhere, because liberated Jews were initially classified by their country of origin as Poles, Hungarians, or Romanians. The demand for tolerable housing conditions was another function of the committee. When some of the inmates liberated in Bergen-Belsen were to be removed from a barracks in Hohne to Lingen and Diepholz to make room for the British army, they mounted an effective resistance against the move, citing the impossible living conditions. They were supported by the committee, as reported by Josef Rosensaft:

> The buildings given us in Lingen and Diepholz were bleak and cold, without light or water, quite unsuitable for human habitation. We demanded that the British rescind their decision. Meanwhile, one transport was already on its way to Lingen and Diepholtz and another one was getting ready to move. We stopped the second transport from moving out of Belsen and brought the first one back. Those who came back re-occupied the Belsen buildings which were designated for the troops.[2]

The political organization of the liberated Jews in the British Zone made progress in the summer of 1945 against the opposition of the British occupation troops, who kept refusing to acknowledge Jewish nationality. The first congress of the liberated Jews in the British Occupation Zone was finally held in Hohne-Belsen on September 25–27, an event that had an impact far beyond the British Occupation Zone of Germany and was considered a sign of life of the *she'erit ha-pleyta* by Jews everywhere. Seventy correspondents from all over the world reported on the congress, whose participants included delegates of Jewish organizations from the United States, England, and Palestine. It was only after the endorsement of the congress by international Jewish organizations that the Jewish Central Committee in the British Zone was granted political recognition.

In 1947, in one of the first sociological studies of the life of Jewish DPs in Europe, the American historian and director of the JOINT office for educational issues at the time, Koppel Pinson, wrote: "The Jewish DPs are a marvelous example of a society without an elite. The elite of European Jewry were the first to be exterminated. . . . The present leadership of Jewish DP's is, but for a few exceptions, made up of people who have little experience in social planning or social responsibilities."[3] This harsh judgment by a contemporary observer certainly applied to several local DP camps, but not to most regional leaders of the DPs, who had emerged by 1945.

In the British Occupation Zone, where most of the Jewish DPs lived in one camp (Hohne-Belsen), all the threads of the political organization were in the hands of the chairman of the Central Committee, Josef Rosensaft. No matter how Rosensaft's political acts were judged, his personal commitment to the interests of the Jewish DPs in the British Occupation Zone was acknowledged by all sides. Rosensaft, the former owner of a foundry in Polish Bendzin, achieved recognition of Hohne-Belsen as a Jewish camp, organized a functioning camp structure with a multitude of cultural activities, tended to the Jewish education of children, and founded a health department in the camp. He ruled the Jews in the British Occupation Zone with almost dictatorial powers but was repeatedly reelected democratically and did everything to improve the condition of "his" Jews. He was assisted by Norbert Wollheim, a German Jew and Auschwitz survivor, who represented both the DP camps and the reestablished Jewish community in Germany. Wollheim, who had been active even before the war in German-Jewish community work, was also entrusted with the role of intermediary with the authorities.[4] (See interview with Norbert Wollheim.)

In the American Occupation Zone, with its many, widely scattered Jewish DP camps, a single leading personality was able to achieve essentially less than in the British Zone, but the danger of a dictatorial administration was also correspondingly lessened. In large camps with several thousand Jewish DPs, local self-government played a decisive role; and regional committees of nearby DP camps took shape. In North Hesse, such a regional committee, representing over 20,000 Jewish DPs from Wetzlar, Fulda, Eschwege, Hofgeismar, and other camps, was formed in November 1946 because the central offices in Frankfurt and

Munich were too remote.[5] Similar attempts at regional committees were recorded in Württemberg and Bavaria. The regional committee for Lower Bavaria and the Upper Palatinate served 6 camps, 31 Jewish communities and committees, 5 *hakhsharot* (kibbutz training camps), as well as 4 sanitoria and hospitals, with a total of about 18,000 Jews.[6]

Nevertheless, there was also a "Central Committee" in the American Occupation Zone whose representatives were elected democratically, as in the British Zone. Even if no individual figure à la Josef Rosensaft emerged, it is still legitimate in a certain sense to speak of an oligarchy comprising an elite of Lithuanian Jews, who constituted only 3 percent of the Jewish DPs but were their most important leaders. Of the 15 members of the "Central Committee," 8 were Lithuanian, 4 were Poles, and 3 were Romanians.[7]

The chairman of the "Central Committee," the thirty-three-year-old physician Zalman Grinberg from Kovno, can best be understood as a counterpart to Josef Rosensaft. Grinberg combined moderate Orthodoxy, enthusiastic Zionism, and the West European culture he had come to know in his studies in Basel. He was prominent in the first organized activity of the Jewish DPs on May 27, 1945, a performance by the surviving members of the Kovno ghetto orchestra in the St. Ottilien DP camp hospital, an evacuated Benedictine monastery. After the national anthems of the four Allied nations—the United States, Great Britain, France, and the Soviet Union—Grieg's "Song of Solveig" and works by Ravel rang out. The finale was the national anthem of the future Jewish state, "Hatikvah."

Grinberg was president of the Central Committee of Liberated Jews in Bavaria, which was formed on July 1, 1945, and expanded in January 1946 to the Central Committee of the Liberated Jews in the American Zone. He retained this position until he emigrated in July 1946, and was succeeded by David Treger.[8] Grinberg's closest associates were his former comrades-in-arms from the Kovno ghetto: the journalist Levi Shalit and Samuel Gringauz, a former judge in Memel, postwar chairman of the camp committee in Landsberg am Lech and president of the Council of Liberated Jews in the American Occupation Zone of Germany.[9]

In large DP camps, democratic elections were held within a few months after the Liberation to prevent the old leadership class of the concentration camps from becoming a new elite in the DP camps as well. In Landsberg am Lech, the city where Hitler wrote *Mein Kampf* in prison, free Jewish elections took place on October 21, 1945. Two slates of candidates fought a fierce election campaign. The *Ichud* (Unity) slate, led by Samuel Gringauz, which eventually won, was supported by the old Lithuanian leadership class. It was challenged by a group composed primarily of Polish Jews led by the chief of the Jewish camp police. Election posters

Election posters (with portraits of David Ben-Gurion and the founder of Revisionist Zionism, Vladimir Jabotinsky) for the Zionist Congress of 1947, in the
Pocking-Waldstadt DP camp (Yad Vashem Photo Archives)

were made for the campaign, and on election day special curtained voting booths were available. The election itself was modeled largely on the
American system, as camp commander Irving Heymont reported home
on election day: "We are all very proud of our success in reproducing the
mechanics of an American election."[10]

Initially, the leading figures in the DP camps tried to avoid split-
ting into various parties and were largely successful. In June 1945, the
founding assembly for a United Zionist Organization took place among
the liberated Jews in Bavaria; its main objective was to overcome the political conflicts that had characterized the prewar Zionist movement and act
together during this time of crisis.[11] But, given the increasing gravity of the
situation in Palestine, as well as the influx of Jewish DPs from Eastern
Europe in 1946, political unity could no longer be maintained. Even without outside help, incipient political parties were formed in the large DP
camps based on the model of the prewar Jewish communities in Europe.
The Zionists did indeed become the most significant political group among
the emerging parties, but they did not succeed in achieving unity even
within their own ranks. (See interview with Julius Spokojny.)

Neither the shared suffering nor the standard inmate garb could
eradicate all the prewar social and ideological distinctions. What often
appeared as a unified group to an outside observer was in reality an
extremely differentiated society, forced to live together only by external
circumstances. Internal oppositions between religious and nonreligious

groups, between Zionists and Bundists, as well as between various leadership cadres often consisting of Baltic Jews and the masses of Polish Jews all emerged in every camp soon after the Liberation. Within Zionism, the DPs continued the traditional distinct trends, which ranged from rightist Revisionists who favored a Greater Israel, through liberal General Zionists, to socialist Ha-Shomer Ha-Tsa'ir. But non-Zionist parties, like the socialist Bund advocating Yiddish culture and the religious Agudath Israel, also existed in the political spectrum of the DP camps.

Outside Help

The initiative for political unity on a regional basis within the American Occupation Zone originated with a young American reform rabbi, who had come to Germany as a chaplain with the American troops. In May 1945, Rabbi Abraham J. Klausner entered Dachau, and over the following weeks he became familiar with the situation in the Bavarian DP camps. Klausner helped organize the first meeting of some fifty representatives of Jewish DPs from the American Occupation Zone on July 1, 1945, in Feldafing. The next day, a temporary office in the Munich antiaircraft barracks was obtained until rooms were made available in the German Museum on July 11. Meanwhile, on July 25, 1945, the first conference of Jewish survivors from all parts of Germany took place in St. Ottilien. The primary function of this conference was to publicize the demands of the survivors, which was done with a sensational event on the evening of July 26: after the discussions ended, the ninety-four delegates set out for the Munich Bürgerbräukeller, where, on the symbolic site of the rise of Nazism, amid profaned Torah scrolls scattered on the floor, they demanded permission to emigrate to Palestine.[12]

The Jewish leaders of the American Occupation Zone were striving for a platform for all Jewish DPs in Germany regardless of the borders between the zones. Such a joint platform, however, ran into the opposition of Rosensaft, who saw his dominant position endangered. In late 1945, the influx of Jewish refugees to the American Occupation Zone began, and the Jewish population in that zone increased rapidly, while it stagnated in the British Zone. Right after the Liberation, there was about the same number of Jewish DPs in both zones; but two years later, the American Zone had ten times as many Jews as the British Zone. Josef Rosensaft and the Central Committee of Liberated Jews in the British Zone would have had to accept a subordinate role in a general organization and preferred to remain independent. No general organization of liberated Jews in Germany was ever established prior to the mass emigration of the Jewish DPs.

Aside from Rabbi Klausner, Jewish DPs received support from another unexpected source: the Jewish Brigade, a unit of the British fighting forces composed of 25,700 Palestinian Jews in September 1944, which saw combat in Italy shortly before the end of the war. Their primary unofficial task, however, was organizing the illegal immigration to Palestine and supporting the Jewish DPs in Germany, Austria, and Italy. Representatives of the Jewish Brigade set out from Italy for Germany in June 1945 to investigate the situation of the Jewish survivors. As they headed north, the envoys came upon several Jewish DPs and were confronted with their current problems. In a few cases, the representatives of the Jewish Brigade managed to obtain from the military authorities separate Jewish camps and better living and housing conditions for the Jewish survivors.[13] (See interview with Arno Hamburger.)

The Jewish survivors greeted the members of the Jewish Brigade enthusiastically. All of a sudden, they were facing fellow Jews who had not suffered in the concentration camps but had participated actively in the victory over Germany. Moreover, they brought news from Palestine, the land Jewish DPs could only dream about for now. This joy at the appearance of the Jewish Brigade, however, was dimmed by the increasingly clear perception that they were once again abandoned and forgotten by the whole world. For, aside from the small delegation of Jewish soldiers in British uniforms, the world seemed hardly to be aware of the Jewish fate. Foreign and international welfare organizations entered the scene only relatively late. UNRRA (United Nations Relief and Rehabilitation Administration), created in 1943 to help the Allies cope with civilian problems, was not active in the Jewish DP camps until a few months after the Liberation.

But representatives of Jewish aid organizations like the American Joint Distribution Committee (JOINT) and its British counterpart, the Jewish Relief Unit, the Hebrew Immigration Aid Society (HIAS), the Organization for the Promotion of Work among Jews (ORT), and the World Jewish Congress were not seen in the DP camps either during the first two months after the Liberation. The main reason for their delay was the disapproval of the American government, which feared conflicts of authority in the administration of the DP camps. This explanation, however, could hardly mute the indignation of the liberated Jews about the absence of foreign Jews and international aid organizations. Josef Rosensaft expressed the opinion of many Jewish DPs when he stated in retrospect:

> So there we were, liberated at last. But many months went by before the first signs of effective help appeared. It is a fact that in the whole of Jewry there was not one famous children's specialist, surgeon or gynaecologist,

who was willing to come and work with us, even for a short time, despite all our appeals. We had to accept the help of German doctors and nurses whom the British sent into the camp.[14]

Given this feeling of desertion, visits of prominent Jewish politicians, especially Zionist politicians from Palestine, were particularly important. The high point was the visit of David Ben-Gurion, later the prime minister of Israel, to the Jewish DP camps of Landsberg, Feldafing, and Zeilsheim in October 1945. The American camp commandant in Landsberg reported on his visit there:

> To the people of the camp, he is God. . . . The first I knew of his coming was when we noticed the people streaming out to line the street leading from Munich. They were carrying flowers and hastily improvised banners and signs. The camp itself blossomed out with decorations of all sorts. Never had we seen such energy displayed in the camp. I don't think that a visit by President Truman could cause as much excitement.[15]

Immigration with Obstacles

No subject roused the feelings of the Jewish DPs like the demand to immigrate to Palestine and rebuild a Jewish home. The issue of immigration was the core of all conferences of Jewish DPs. In April 1946, when an Anglo-American committee asked 138,320 DPs in the three Western occupation zones which country they preferred to immigrate to, 118,570 answered, "Palestine."[16] Even those who did not want to immigrate to Palestine themselves shared the conviction that only the establishment of a Jewish state could prevent a new catastrophe for the Jewish people. Hence Jewish survivors greeted the British ban on Jewish immigration to Palestine with incomprehension and indignation. Like the members of the Jewish Brigade, the Jews in the British Occupation Zone of Germany were faced with a strange paradox: they had welcomed the British as liberators and owed their survival to British steadfastness during the war; but now, the former allies in the struggle against Germany had become bitter enemies in the struggle for Palestine. As during the long years of persecution, now too the Jews felt pressed into the role of a powerless object of history, this time by British policy. Nowhere was this powerlessness expressed more strongly than among the DPs held in Germany, waiting impatiently to leave the land of their tormentors.

The tragic affair of the refugee ship *Exodus 1947* revealed to the world the difficult situation of the Jewish DPs kept in Germany. The

Inmates of the Pocking-Waldstadt DP camp demand the dissolution of the DP camps and free immigration to Palestine (Yad Vashem Photo Archives)

Exodus was a worn-out American cruise ship brought over the Atlantic by the Jewish military organization *Haganah* (the precursor of the Israeli army) with the help of the Jewish Brigade. Official papers to transport 4,500 refugees to Columbia were obtained; but in fact, the flag with the Star of David was hoisted, and the ship left Marseilles in July 1947 heading for Zion, with 5,000 Jewish DPs on board—including children, women, old, and sick people—who wanted to build a new life in a new state. It was a risky voyage, and when the ship reached the coast of Palestine, it was hit by a storm and was discovered by British destroyers. After a grim struggle that claimed several casualties and inflicted serious damage on the *Exodus*, the crew and passengers of the refugee ship gave up their resistance. They were billeted in three British ships to await the fate of all immigrants stranded before the coast of Palestine: British internment camps on Cyprus.

But England's foreign minister, Ernest Bevin, who strictly maintained the ban on immigration to Palestine, intended to teach these refugees a lesson; he ordered the passengers of the *Exodus* returned to Germany. Under protests of world opinion, the three refugee ships set sail for the West; and after a three-month odyssey, they put into port at Hamburg in September 1947. Only the old and the weak voluntarily stepped onto German soil; many of the younger people had to be dragged off the ship by force. As in the past, they were once again forced into German trains. The correspondent of the *Lübecker Zeitung* reported: "Never have I seen such railroad trains. Only a narrow door for every car. Windows and doors are barred with wire mesh. Inside, no place of any kind to

Exodus refugees back on German soil (Yad Vashem Photo Archives)

sit. . . . Infinite bitterness shows clearly in the faces. Food, brought to them on the train by the Red Cross, flies back out through the bars onto the tracks."[17] After a brief stay in the internment camps of Am Stau and Pöppendorf, they were transferred to the barracks in Emden and Wilhelmshaven in November 1947. The Jewish DPs in Germany demonstrated their solidarity with the men and women of the *Exodus* in several ways. After the ship was ordered to return to Germany, they went on a hunger strike. When the ship reached Hamburg, they organized a large protest demonstration. As a show of solidarity with the returnees, the Jewish DP organizations arranged for special food rations to be delivered to the people stranded in the internment camps.[18]

The desperate situation of the Jewish DPs in general and the spectacular case of the *Exodus* in particular played a role in the diplomatic recognition of the Jewish state, which was finally confirmed by the UN decision in November 1947 to partition Palestine. In May 1948, when the State of Israel was declared, the new citizens of Israel included DPs from Germany who had reached that country illegally. What awaited them there was not the peace they had long yearned for, but another war declared by five Arab states against Israel on its first independence day. After years in German concentration camps and in British or American DP camps, the Jewish survivors were now fighting for the independence of the Jewish state.

Not all the survivors were strong enough to serve as soldiers in a still underdeveloped country in the Middle East so soon after their liberation. They sought other, more peaceful and comfortable homes, and found them in Australia, South America, or Canada. Aside from Israel, however, the major country of immigration was the United States, where, by 1952, some 80,000 Jewish DPs had found a new homeland.[19] Many of them had friends or relatives there, and they saw their best economic and political prospects in America.

The prevailing Zionist ideology among the leaders and the masses of DPs often made it difficult for the emigrants to choose places other than Israel. In many camps, those emigrants were stoned and cursed as traitors as they left the DP camp. To indicate the proper destination, the Central Committee of Liberated Jews in the American Occupation Zone issued a poster showing Jewish DPs turning their back on a European city skyline and going toward a scene of palm trees. One clear sign of the official rejection of places of immigration other than Israel was the refusal of the Central Committee to allow a group of orphans to accept an invitation to well-to-do homes in England and France.[20]

With the establishment of the State of Israel, the DP camps and communities in Germany embarked on a phase of dissolution. In 1948 and 1949, several Jewish institutions withdrew from what was once again a Germany governed by Germans; Jewish newspapers ceased operation; the DP camps emptied out. In April 1948, about 165,000 Jews were still living in Germany; five months later, they had already shrunk to less than half of this number.[21] What the publication of the Central Committee of Liberated Jews in Bavaria, *Undzer Veg*, had announced back in September 1946 had now become reality for most Jewish DPs: "The next year will be the last year on cursed German soil."[22] When this hope had been expressed, the Jewish population in occupied Germany was still growing because of the influx of East European Jews. It took three more years for the editors to venture another prediction in their final edition: "It is now clear, even for the old, the sick, and the greatest skeptics, that the German Diaspora will not last much longer." In a few months, they went on, there would be no trace left in Germany of the Jewish refugees who had been forced to stay there. Nevertheless, they did admit that there was a small group that did not want to leave Germany: "Those are people who will someday realize that they have committed a terrible error, both for themselves and for their families . . . it will be too late—and no one will be able to help them anymore."[23]

Nine months later, the editors of *Undzer Veg* understood that they had misjudged the situation. In January 1950, a considerable number of Jewish DPs were still in Bavaria, and the former editors decided to revive the newspaper, arguing that the Jews who were still in Germany during this last phase of the dissolution should not remain without a Yiddish newspaper. The attitude of the editorial staff toward the issue of emigration had not changed: "To remain in Germany when everything is dissolved and everyone has departed means in fact to be lost to the Jewish people."[24] On December 28, 1950, *Undzer Veg* finally ceased publication.

As of 1952, some 12,000 Jewish DPs still remained in Germany.[25] Many of them, who could not integrate into Israeli society or who could not obtain an economic foothold there, had returned from that land. Others had stayed in Germany for various reasons: because they were sick and weak or had to take care of ailing relatives; because they had built an economic life for themselves in Germany; or because they had married German women. They were members of the Jewish communities newly formed in many cities and, at least officially, could no longer be considered "Displaced Persons." The last chapter of the Jewish DPs was set in the DP camp of Föhrenwald in Upper Bavaria, where, in 1954, there were still 1,400 Jewish DPs who had been under the control of German authorities since 1951. They refused to leave the camp, preferring isolation to integration into German society. When the camp was evacuated in the winter of 1956/57 and the last camp inmate left Föhrenwald on February 28, 1957, the history of the DP camps in Germany was concluded.

4. YEKKES AND OSTJUDEN

While the closing of Föhrenwald brought to an end the history of Jewish DP camps, the fate of Jewish DPs in Germany continued. Most (492) of the last 1,000 or so residents of Föhrenwald moved to nearby Munich and other German cities, like Frankfurt or Düsseldorf. In Munich and Frankfurt, the Jewish DPs were housed in the same neighborhoods where, even without the existence of a camp, they often lived isolated from the non-Jewish environment.[1] In the larger German cities, they found well-organized Jewish communities, which had often been set up by other Jewish DPs in the first postwar years. The establishment of so-called DP communities or *Jüdische Komitees* [Jewish committees] was necessary outside the camp where there was no formal Jewish organization. Like the DP camps, these communities were originally considered only transitional organizations that would dissolve by themselves as the Jewish DPs emigrated. However, in the early 1950s, when it turned out that a small portion of the Jewish DPs wanted to stay in Germany, these communities became permanent organizations and considered themselves successors of the prewar Jewish communities.

The Reestablishment of German-Jewish Communities

In the reestablished communities, the 12,000–15,000 Jewish DPs of East European origin encountered an equal number of German Jews who had survived the war in concentration camps or in hiding. Most of them were spouses or children of mixed marriages and had survived for much of the Nazi regime under the protection of their non-Jewish family members. Of the 7,000 German Jews registered in the Berlin Jewish community in 1947, about half were in what the Nazis designated as "privileged mixed marriages," while a quarter were "nonprivileged" and had to wear the yellow star. One thousand four hundred and sixteen Berlin Jews had survived the war as "illegals" in hiding.[2] Half the Jewish population in Berlin in 1946 were over fifty years old, while only 6.8 percent were under eighteen.[3]

Most German-Jewish inmates of concentration camps who survived the war were liberated in Theresienstadt, but there were those who hoped to return home from other concentration camps at the end of the war. The Auschwitz survivor Hans Winterfeldt, who was liberated in Mauthausen, waited in vain for a quick return to Berlin:

> I really had imagined liberation differently. We were free, but nothing more. . . . I was strongly convinced that former concentration camp inmates would be taken home and now hoped it would soon be my turn, for I had been in the barracks for at least fourteen days and no one was concerned about us. We were free and could go, but where? . . . I mistakenly assumed that the outside world had stood still. . . . I didn't know that transportation was crippled all over Germany, that there was no mail, telephone, or railroad contact, that Germany was now divided into four zones, that you couldn't travel as a civilian into the Russian Occupation Zone, where my uncle lived and where I had to return, because Berlin was there.[4]

The years of oppression had also been years of isolation. Behind the gates of the concentration camps, the inmates often received no news of the fate of their families. In their hometowns, almost all the survivors went through the same experience: except for those who had managed to get out in time, they were the only survivors of their families. The report of one concentration camp survivor from Haigerloch in Württemberg is characteristic of the first impression after their return home: "When I climbed the stairs now, I thought good friends and family would come to me from all the houses. I couldn't control myself. The houses are still intact. . . ."[5]

In smaller cities, for the most part, only a few individual members of the original Jewish population had survived the war. The 50 survi-

✡ Jüdisches ✡
Krankenhaus Berlin
Wir ehren die toten
Opfer d. Faschismus

Representatives of the Jewish Hospital at "Victims of Fascism—Rally" in the
Berlin Lustgarten, September 14, 1947 (Bildarchiv Abraham Pisarek, Berlin)

vors in Mainz, who had been classified as Jews by the Nazis, were almost
exclusively from Christian-Jewish marriages, and only half regarded
themselves as Jews. Three of them had worn the star; one survived illegally. In July 1945, 24 elderly Mainz Jews were brought back from Theresienstadt and housed provisionally in a wing of the municipal hospital.[6]
All 20 surviving Jews in Mannheim had been married to Christians; and
in Hamburg in 1947, 70 percent of all married Jews were in mixed marriages.[7] In Karlsruhe, only 20 of the 90 persons persecuted as Jews considered themselves Jews. In Frankfurt, most of the surviving 600 prewar
Jews did not belong to any Jewish community.

This group of people, who at best had been on the margins of
Jewish society before the war, now had the difficult task of restoring
Jewish communities in Germany. Although most of them knew very
little about Judaism, and their identification with the Jewish religion was
extremely minimal, with few exceptions, they felt obligated by the years
of persecution to reconstruct Jewish life in some form. Their first tasks,
still marked by persecution, involved bringing German Jews who remained in concentration camps back to their hometowns, restoring the
physically ill and the mentally afflicted, and burying the dead. In addition,
those groups made the initial contacts with the American Jewish welfare
organizations, and arranged suitable places for prayer houses and offices
to replace the destroyed synagogues, at least temporarily.

In many places, these first steps toward the restoration of Jewish
life were taken in the first days and weeks after Liberation. The oldest

document for the reconstruction of a Jewish community is from Cologne, where the British military administration allowed the surviving German Jews to hold religious services on April 11. In the same month, a *Provisorischer Vorstand der Jüdischen Gemeinde Köln* (Temporary Board of the Jewish Community of Cologne) was mentioned, which demanded the appointment of a Jewish department to repair the Jewish cemetery and to build a prayer house. As in all reestablished communities except Berlin, the number of members was extremely modest, amounting to only eighty persons in February 1946.[8]

Other communities along the Rhine were also reestablished during 1945. In nearby Bonn, this took place in October 1945.[9] In Mainz, senior executive officer Michael Oppenheimer wrote the military administration of the intention of the local Jews to reestablish a Jewish community in that thousand-year-old center of Jewish life. The official founding assembly was held on November 9, 1945, just seven years after Kristallnacht, when the Mainz synagogue, like most other German synagogues, had been destroyed.[10] In northern Germany, the Jewish community in Hamburg was reestablished on September 18, 1945, after initial discussions of the surviving Jews in July.[11]

The restoration of Jewish communities generally followed the plan described by Nathan Rosenberger, who returned from Theresienstadt and was appointed the first chairman of the postwar community in Freiburg: "I began my work with a visit to all the Jewish cemeteries in my district and appealed to all responsible mayors to restore the cemeteries desecrated by the Nazi criminals. . . . The next important task was to gather all Jews in my region into a community. . . . My next task was to find a prayer room, and I was given adequate space by the responsible authorities." The prayer room was inaugurated on the Jewish holiday Shavuoth in June 1946. Religious services were held only on holidays, since the community could not produce the ten men required for prayer on every Sabbath. In 1947, about fifty Jews were living in Freiburg, about a hundred in all south Baden.[12]

A report of the veteran chairman of the Jewish community in Nuremberg, Paul Baruch, allows us to follow closely the process of restoring Jewish life in that city. Even before the war ended, three surviving Jewish men married to non-Jewish women had planned the reestablishment of the Nuremberg community. At the end of April 1945, when they were liberated by the Americans, they set up the office of the reestablished community in the former Jewish nurses' home, which had served as headquarters for the SS in the Main region during the war. After the Jews who survived in Nuremberg were traced and given apartments, the next task was to bring home the Nuremberg Jews who were still in Theresienstadt. In June 1945, two Nuremberg Jews came home from

Theresienstadt with a list of all former Nuremberg citizens in the camp. Fifty emaciated, sick people were finally brought from Theresienstadt to Nuremberg in two U.S. Army trucks. One of the board members of the reestablished community, Adolf Hamburger, was a butcher in the Nuremberg slaughterhouse and supplied free meat to the members of the community. Jewish émigrés from Nuremberg, including the wife of the former rabbi, appealed in the United States for aid to the Nuremberg survivors. In December 1945, the first assembly of members was convened for the approximately one hundred Jews living in Nuremberg at that time to elect a five-member board. The board's first task was to repair the partially destroyed Jewish cemetery at the expense of the city of Nuremberg. Meanwhile, Adolf Hamburger's son, Arno Hamburger, who had returned from Israel with the Jewish Brigade, took charge of the religious instruction of the school-age children.[13] (See interview with Arno Hamburger.)

By 1948, over 100 Jewish communities again existed in Germany, most of them numbering fewer than 50 members. Towns like Itzehoe with 6 Jews or Neumünster with 7 were listed as "communities" alongside Berlin with 8,000 and Munich with 3,300 members. The ratio of German to East European Jews in these communities varied considerably. While the overall proportion of former DPs of East European origin and German Jews was equal, in general, regional differences, which also reflected the division of Germany into the various zones of occupation, were clearly visible. In Bavaria, in 1949, the East European Jews constituted 93.7 percent of the total Jewish population, and they were also dominant in Württemberg with 81.6 percent. On the other hand, in Berlin, they were only 29.6 percent of the total Jewish population, in the northern state of Lower Saxony 24.4 percent, and in North Rhine-Westphalia 13.8 percent. The former French Occupation Zone of Rhineland-Palatinate also had a small minority of East European Jews of 13 percent in 1949.[14] Due to these regional differences, the leading German-Jewish institutions like the *Allgemeine Jüdische Wochenzeitung* [General Jewish weekly newspaper] and later the *Zentralrat der Juden in Deutschland* [Central Council of the Jews in Germany] were established in Düsseldorf, while postwar Jewish culture in Bavaria had an East European Jewish quality, and a Yiddish newspaper appeared in Munich until the 1970s.

The Struggle for the Communities

The composition of the Jewish communities led to conflict between groups of various origins, especially in southern Germany. The German Jews, who had reestablished Jewish communities in Munich,

Election to the representative assembly of the Jewish community of Berlin, 1948
(Bildarchiv Abraham Pisarek, Berlin)

Augsburg, Stuttgart, Frankfurt, and other south German cities shortly
after the war ended, were now pushed into the role of a minority. The
different religious traditions of the German Jews who were primarily
Liberal and the many East European Jews who had grown up in an Orthodox milieu, as well as language differences, made it hard to construct
common postwar communities. The fear that this situation could lead to
conflict was recognized in 1946 by the chairman of the Berlin Jewish
community, Hans Erich Fabian. In an article titled "Süddeutsche
Probleme" (South German problems), he wrote: "There is a danger that
the few people returning from the concentration camps are a minority,
and thus the continuation of the tradition of the community is in question. . . . Hence certain tensions arise, which do not exist in other areas."[15]

     Many Jewish communities that accepted the East European Jews
as members did not grant them equal rights. The Stuttgart board representing the interests of the Jewish community, founded in January 1946,
granted the DPs all rights, "with the exception of the right to vote for the
administration and status of the community. This is allowed them after
three years of membership."[16] In Munich, the Jewish community led by
German Jews tried to deny non-German citizens the right to vote in the
community elections of 1946.[17] This policy continued an inglorious tradition of many Jewish communities during the Weimar Republic, when
they were confronted with the same problem of a majority of East European community members. In the late 1940s and early 1950s, the struggle
of the East European Jews of the Weimar Republic for equality was re-

peated in the communities. A few German-Jewish communities stubbornly refused to accept non-German citizens into their ranks altogether. In Hanover, despite desperate efforts, Rabbi Zvi Helfgott-Asaria could not persuade the Jewish community to accept the East European DPs: "The appeal from Bergen-Belsen, that we all suffered in common and that the enemy made no distinction between Eastern and German Jew . . . apparently fell on barren ground in Hanover."[18] Here too, a certain historical continuity is striking: Hanover was the only large Jewish community that had refused to accept non-German Jews as members during the Weimar Republic.

In Augsburg, the Jewish community of the thirty-two local German Jews refused to accept the sixty East European Jews as members until the mid-1950s. As a maximum concession in the long conflict between the Jewish community and the Jewish Committee, the German-Jewish community was willing to grant the East European Jews two of nine board members and would allow half of them (!) voting rights. Only under pressure from the authorities could the German-Jewish leadership of the community be induced to grant the non-German citizens membership and equal rights.[19] (See interview with Julius Spokojny.) In Frankfurt, in the autumn of 1948, the Jewish community and the Jewish Committee agreed to the merger proposed by the board of the community and the rabbis, but they had to prevail over the resistance of a loud opposition group.[20]

Even when German and East European Jews were both represented and had equal rights in a community, differences often arose about the future organization of Jewish life, i.e., the issue of "staying or going." The official leaders of both groups responded to the future prospects of a Jewish society in postwar Germany in different ways. Jewish DP organizations generally regarded their presence in Germany as merely a brief and compulsory interlude on the path to the Jewish state they wanted to build in Palestine. No doubt, there were German-Jewish voices who also supported this position, such as Erich Nelhans, member of the board of the Berlin Jewish community, who wrote in the German-Jewish newspaper *Der Weg* in March 1946, "Our community should be a small homeland until the gates of our big homeland of Palestine are open and we enter the Promised Land."[21] In the same edition, however, and more representative of the official position of the German-Jewish organizations was the exhortation "to take a decisive part in the democratic education of the German people."[22] The founder of the *Jüdisches Gemeindeblatt* in the British Occupation Zone, Hans Frey, even expressed the opinion that "we German Jews have not only the right but also the duty to endure here in Germany."[23]

The Wiesbaden attorney Alfred Mayer was one of many German Jews who demanded the rapid emigration of East European Jews from Germany, those Jews who "were not tied to this country by any bonds of affection or any obligation of loyalty." Mayer contrasted the position of East European Jews with that of German Jews. Even after the end of Nazi rule, Mayer, whose family had lived in Germany since the seventeenth century, thought he had to convince the Germans that German Jews had a right to live in their native land: "Here we belong. Here we have a right to live and here we have to produce proof that the men and women of National Socialism lied when they wanted to deny us the same right as they had. Yes, we few, only a handful, have a mission to accomplish."[24]

One Jewish reader of *Der Weg* expressed his sense of being German most clearly. He opposed the demand to emigrate

> because we believe we are good and true Germans, Germans who received their cultural training in German schools, heard the word of God in German from the Jewish mouth of the rabbis, and hear it still and are not ashamed to announce that Germany is our fatherland and German is our mother tongue. I and people like me are staying in Germany because we do not want to leave, because no lunatic fool, no tempter should or could rob us of our German homeland, our Germany. . . .[25]

In 1946, in the German-Jewish press, advertisements appeared like that of a surviving Jewish physician, who announced in February 1946: "Have reopened my practice."[26] At the same time, belated obituaries were now published for friends and relatives who had perished in the concentration camps.

The warnings of the DP press could not prevent an increasing number of Jews from planning for a future in Germany. Opinion polls of 1949 show that the majority of Jews were no longer planning to emigrate. In Cologne and Düsseldorf, 70 percent of the Jews questioned at the time declared that they wanted to stay in Germany, and the real number must have been even higher since many people considered it a disgrace to admit such an intention publicly. In Berlin, 29 percent of 1,461 people questioned said they wanted to remain in Germany; another 19 percent felt they were too old to emigrate, and 13 percent wanted to emigrate but were tied to Germany by family or economic reasons. In 1949, emigration to Israel decreased steadily, falling from a monthly average of 150 persons to 50 at the end of the year.[27]

But the Jewish DPs who remained in Germany had different notions of integration into German society from those of German Jews. The contrasting positions of the two groups were manifested most clearly in the issue of mixed marriage. Most East European Jewish DPs found it inconceivable to marry non-Jewish Germans. Those who lived with German spouses were usually expelled from the community and were socially ostracized. In 1947, the editors of the Regensburg DP newspaper, *Undzer Moment*, felt it necessary to keep printing the following appeal in large block letters on its title page:

> The Germans murdered your father, your mother, your brothers and sisters. Eternal shame to those who marry German women! The Jewish public must expel those who have married Germans from the community.[28]

German Jews, on the other hand, often owed their survival solely to their non-Jewish spouse. If the German-Jewish communities excluded all members in mixed marriages, their membership rolls would have been cut by more than half. In Hanover, a resolution of the central rabbinate of the DP communities in the British Occupation Zone excluding Jews in mixed marriages from the boards of the communities provoked violent arguments between German and East European Jews.[29] Many large communities, like the one in Berlin, decided to disqualify for positions in the community only those with non-Jewish spouses who were bringing up their children as non-Jews.

Black market activities, in which many East European Jews were engaged, constituted an additional area of conflict. The Germans emphasized these activities, which were centered at Munich's Möhlstrasse, while they often overlooked non-Jewish black market activities. Many German Jews felt threatened by this identification of the black market with Jews, as indicated by the following statement: "If there is a God, why, after making us suffer so terribly in the past, has he punished us with the Moehlstrasse, which is a disgrace to us before the world and which must make every decent Jew blush with shame?"

Nor could the traditional differences between German-Jewish and Yiddish culture be completely eliminated by the years of common suffering. It was a thorn in the side of many German Jews that Yiddish, scorned as "Jargon," had now become the lingua franca in the reestablished Jewish communities. German Jews had absolutely no intention of identifying with a language they considered as "bad German." A contemporary witness made the following observation in the German-Jewish community: "Again and again, the majority of those who were born in the country in some way or another found the East European Jews unacceptable socially and rejected their religious customs, and sometimes gave as a reason for their lack of participation in communal life their aversion to having anything to do with the East European Jews."[30]

Yet sometimes circumstances were reversed, and German Jews felt discriminated against by East European Jews because of their language and culture. This was partly a matter of condescension among East European DPs with a strong sense of Jewish ethnicity toward the often assimilated Yekkes—German Jews who had severed their ties with Jewish ways and beliefs. For East European Jews, German had become the taboo language of the persecutors, and many of them reacted hypersensitively to those who used the German language, even when they were Jews. Thus a German Jew, who had survived Auschwitz and, after being liberated in Mauthausen, shared a room with six Polish Jews, reported: "They barely talked to me, even if I was supposed to get the soup. For them, I was the 'Yekke' they made fun of and otherwise only despised; but I was used to that from Auschwitz. While I was cursed in Germany as a Jew until my deportation, in the concentration camp, most of the Polish Jews despised us as 'Germans.'"[31]

More important for the German Jews than the contempt of their coreligionists were the material disadvantages they often encountered. In the British Occupation Zone, until Zone Policy Instruction No. 20 took effect in February 1946, the same stipulations that applied to the general German population also applied to the Jews. This attitude, based on a complete misunderstanding of the situation by the British authorities, was illustrated by the case of the English rabbi Moses Cohen. Cohen was to be sent to Berlin as an envoy but was rejected by the British authorities, since British citizens were not permitted to provide aid to the Germans (!).[32] A similar paradox occurred during the first months of UNRRA activity in Germany. While Jewish DPs were cared for by UNRRA, German Jews were initially prevented from receiving aid from them since this international welfare organization of the UN was to help the deportees and the refugees, but not citizens of the enemy state.[33] The same logic meant that only in exceptional cases did German Jews benefit from the support of international Jewish welfare organizations sent to the DPs.

But conflicts between German and East European Jews were not the only ones that arose in the postwar period. Within the German-Jewish communities, too, the first phases of restoration were often turbulent. In the Cologne community, the board was replaced three times during the first year after Liberation, when the current chairmen lost the confidence of the community members.[34] In Berlin, in the summer of 1945, the former opera singer and cantor Adolf Schwersenz established a rival community, *Berlin-Nordwest*, after weeks of quarrels in the Berlin Jewish community.[35] In Hamburg, in the summer of 1945, a group opposing the Jewish community emerged, the organization of the persecuted, *Wir aus Theresienstadt* [We from Theresienstadt], which admitted only "impeccable" German citizens of the Jewish faith who had been in Theresienstadt. This group accused the leadership of the community of representing only a small group of Hamburg Jews who had suffered relatively little. However, We from Theresienstadt could not achieve recognition and soon sank into insignificance.[36]

5. Victims and Defeated

What Jews called Liberation was "the collapse" in common German parlance. It was not only a state, a form of power, that collapsed in May 1945, but an entire system of values. Antisemitism was no longer "in vogue"—on the contrary, now it was desirable to have Jewish friends or relatives. Thus the headline of a Jewish newspaper of 1946 declared: "Jewish Grandmothers at Black Market Prices."[1]

The official political language quickly changed its tone from antisemitism to philosemitism. German politicians tried to express their sympathy toward the Jews, particularly in speeches and statements addressed to the outside world. Nevertheless, twelve years of antisemitic education could not be uprooted in a few months, and a systematic reeducation never took place in Germany. Neither a generally real disgust at Nazi crimes nor the fear of having to undergo a de-Nazification trial seemed to prevent many Germans from openly expressing antisemitic opinions once again.

Suddenly, Germans now confronted a situation they had not counted on: the discernible presence of Jews in Germany, which had been declared "judenrein." Moreover, the East European DPs were much more identifiable as Jews than the German Jews had been before the war. They had brought their own traditions, language, and often clothing from Eastern Europe. Many of them lived in Bavarian villages or towns that had never had any Jewish inhabitants, and the local population found it hard to understand that they were confronted with Jews now, for the first time, after most of European Jewry had been annihilated.

Antisemitism in the Postwar Years

It is no wonder that, for most DPs, relations with Germans were limited to necessary, primarily business contacts. Friendship and marriage were as exceptional as acts of revenge by surviving Jews against former Nazis. What usually prevailed was what a visitor to the Jewish DPs observed: "'I hate the Germans,' is the general expression. 'I can't bear to see them, I could kill them all in cold blood.' But when the conversation continues, it turns out that the subject is soon 'my friend Schmidt,' and 'our dear neighbors, the Müllers,' for even the greatest hatred cannot live in complete isolation when you have to go on living where the torment took place."[2]

For the younger generation, to go on living also meant to go on studying. Thus in the first postwar years, a considerable number of Jewish survivors attended German schools and universities. One of them was the sixteen-year-old Ruth Klüger, who had survived Theresienstadt and Auschwitz. Klüger, a future literary scholar, took her examinations in Bavarian Straubing and studied at the Philosophisch-Theologische Hochschule in Regensburg in 1947. "In these lecture halls," she later recalled, "we were tolerated, not welcomed, and I cannot get rid of the feeling that I had wormed my way in here. Nazism flourished and blossomed here. When the history professor mentioned that in Poland, Copernicus was considered a Pole, the whole lecture hall shuffled their feet to advocate the Germanness of Copernicus, who had become the German Nikolaus Kopernigk. Among the Jews, the tension was palpable at having to subordinate themselves again as students to the teachers, the exposed oppressors. A precarious mood with reciprocal aggression prevailed between them and the lecturers."[3]

This "precarious mood" could also be detected outside the lecture hall. There are several reports of verbal assaults against Jewish DPs and German Jews, and many sources even mention acts of violence. Although a pogrom like the one in Polish Kielce after the war was inconceivable—pogroms on the East European model had never really been popular in Germany—a few anti-Jewish acts should be cited. The only Jew who returned to Herford must have regretted his decision immediately: on November 9, 1946, his car was set on fire and his house was damaged.[4] Hardly a month went by without the desecration of some Jewish cemetery, and by 1949 more than a hundred such cases were officially registered.[5] In April 1946, several Jewish institutions in Frankfurt were defaced with swastikas and anti-Jewish slogans.[6]

East European Jews were more frequently the victims of antisemitic assaults than were German Jews. In some cases, identifiable Jewish survivors, who wanted to take vengeance on the Germans for the suffering they had experienced, provoked acts of violence. But many of these cases revealed the aftereffect of Nazi propaganda about "Jewish subhumans," which was now turned against East European Jews, while the few surviving German Jews suddenly became "good Jews."

Verbal and physical assaults in the early postwar years were aimed at East European Jews, who were accused of controlling black market activities, contaminating German cities, or causing all other possible problems of the restoration. In Oberammingen (Bavaria), two Jewish bicyclers were physically attacked by villagers in March 1946 and had to seek shelter in the village school, while stones were thrown at the door and shouts of "Heil Hitler" resounded.[7]

Official raids by German police in the DP camps were more serious than these local outrages. Pretexts for such raids were suspicion of black market activities or criminal incidents in the camps, and were approved by the Allied authorities. Yet the mere fact that German police, in uniform and accompanied by German shepherds, issued orders over loudspeakers in camps where Jews were living inevitably produced tremendous tension. The gravest of these incidents occurred in March 1946 in Stuttgart, when a German policeman shot and wounded a member of the Jewish camp police. In the ensuing exchange of gunfire, a Jewish survivor of the Holocaust was shot.[8]

Most Jewish DPs identified the Germans—especially the uniformed police—with the SS men in the concentration camps. To understand the description of the Stuttgart events in the Jewish press, it is necessary to keep this in mind. Thus one press report states: "These incidents recall the well-known scenes at the crematoria. Once again innocent Jewish blood is shed. Samuel Danziger, one of the few survivors of Auschwitz, was now a victim of the same murderers."[9]

In 1950, Rabbi Zvi Helfgott-Asaria reported a similar occurrence in Hanover: "On February 27, 1950, the customs office staged a raid on suspicion of a customs violation by the (Jewish) committee. . . . Some forty police officers were attached to the unit of customs officials. The officials of this unit lowered their chin straps and assaulted the Jews, swinging rubber truncheons, and flogged those they assumed were Jews. Fifteen Jews were wounded."[10] The identification of the German police with the SS guards was illustrated at a large demonstration organized by the Jewish DPs in Munich in response to an antisemitic letter to the editor published in the *Süddeutsche Zeitung* in August 1949. During the demonstration, in which several persons were wounded, the demonstrators painted swastikas on police cars, a symbolic assertion that the Third Reich was not yet over for them.[11] While in the late 1940s the Jewish community often reacted vehemently to antisemitic incidents, by the 1950s Jewish reaction to continuing antisemitism seems to have calmed down.[12]

There was often an amazing continuity of antisemitic tradition, as demonstrated most clearly in a trial in Memmingen in the Allgäu region, where a Jewish East European concentration camp survivor was accused in all seriousness of perpetrating a ritual crime against a Christian child. This charge clearly derived from the traditional blood libel accusation that has repeatedly surfaced all over Europe ever since the Middle Ages and was used with great relish by Julius Streicher in *Der Stürmer*.

The plaintiff in the Memmingen case was a landlady who accused her Jewish tenant of not paying his monthly rent. The following excerpt also appears in the indictment presented by her attorney:

> At a celebration held by the defendant on Easter 1947 in the contested apartment, the four-year-old son of the plaintiff, Harald, was taken to the defendant's apartment without the consent of the plaintiff. When he returned, he exhibited a completely abnormal boisterousness. The defendant and his guests had made the child drunk on red wine. On the same day, the plaintiff discovered that a vein in his left arm was punctured. Either the child was given an injection or blood was drawn from him. . . As far as the plaintiff is aware, there is a custom in the defendant's circles of making Easter biscuits (!) with a drop of Christian blood.[13]

There is nothing surprising about an old woman in a small Bavarian town believing the deep-rooted legend in the tradition of the Catholic Church; but it is amazing that an attorney could seriously present this statement to a German court in 1948! Apparently, it was not the only such accusation. At about the same time, three Jews in Bayreuth were rumored to have committed a ritual murder after a local citizen had disappeared.[14]

Cases of open antisemitism were hardly uncommon, but they were supported by only a minority of the Germans and were officially repudiated by the authorities. In addition, a number of non-Jewish Germans—primarily those who had suffered themselves under Nazi rule— publicly expressed their solidarity with the surviving Jews. Yet most Germans, along with the official authorities of the Jewish minority now living among them again, reacted to such incidents with indifference and total insensitivity, an attitude that can be read clearly in numerous official documents of the early postwar years.

Official correspondence with Jewish authorities conveys the distinct impression that 1945, the year of historical changes, had passed without a trace for many German bureaucrats. For example, there was a municipal official from Düsseldorf who stood at the gate of the recently reestablished local Jewish community, holding a writ of attachment, to collect "unpaid property taxes from 1938 to 1945," a figure calculated with Prussian thoroughness as: RM 3258.36 + late charges RM 65 + monitory charges RM 25.10. The fact that this writ of attachment went through several levels in the ranks of the bureaucracy and was finally delivered to the Jewish community indicates the blindness to immediate historic events remarked by the chairman of the State Federation of the Jewish Communities of the North Rhine: "I don't know whether to be more amazed at the ignorance or the shamelessness."[15]

Such insensitivity was not confined to the local level. The Committee for Social Policy of the Bavarian Parliament discussed Jewish DPs with a terminology usually reserved for criminals. For example, in debates on the DP camp of Kaltherberge, the settlements became "hideouts for unsavory elements not accessible to any German authorities." It was high time that "law and order be created here."[16] And in 1947, in a closed discussion of the ruling conservative party in Bavaria, the "Christian Social Union" (CSU), the following comment of the Bavarian agricultural minister Josef Baumgartner was warmly received:

> Without the Jews and particularly the Jewish businessmen in the U.S.A. and the rest of the world we will never manage: We need them for the resumption of our old trade relations! As regards the many Ostjuden here in Bavaria, I am of a different opinion: Gentlemen! I was unfortunately compelled to take part in the Jewish congress in Reichenhall: The one pleasing thing at the meeting for me was the resolution that was unanimously adopted: Out of Germany. (Laughter.)[17]

Summarizing the situation of the Jews in Bavaria during the early postwar years, historian Constantin Goschler concludes: "A dangerous brew had been created by the mixing of traditional prejudices against the Jews with resentment at privileged treatment as compensation for their sufferings under Nazism and their supposed massive participation in the black market."[18]

Locally, Jewish DPs frequently complained about their treatment at the hands of the German authorities, as exemplified in the following case. In 1946, the city of Bayreuth had difficulty providing milk to its citizens, a situation that was especially hard on the 320 Jewish DPs, who had no friends or relatives in the country. The city promised milk to those DPs who had spent the *full* six years in concentration camps, a stipulation that obviously excluded all DPs from the milk supply, since the earliest possible date for their deportation to a concentration camp was after the war began in late 1939. Five and a half years of concentration camps, however, was deemed insufficient by the Bayreuth municipal administration. The Yiddish newspaper *Undzer Hofenung* commented sarcastically on this decision: "If the crematoria had been in operation for another four months, the citizens of Bayreuth would not have needed to worry at all anymore."[19]

In light of frequent incidents like this, it is hardly surprising that public statements of Jewish survivors almost unanimously express skepticism about a possible normalization between Jews and Germans. In the second Congress of Liberated Jews in the British Zone in August 1947, they stated their opinion on this issue:

> In the last twenty-six months, not only have the great majority of Germans indicated that they have emerged from defeat without learning anything, but rather they prove every day that, on the Jewish question, they

still adhere to the same point of view that was taught by Nazi ideology. The Congress has demonstrated that this realization reinforced the decision of the overwhelming majority of the Jews in the British Zone to leave Germany.

The situation was especially problematic for German Jews who, because of their advanced age or their marriage with non-Jewish partners, often intended to remain in Germany and were personally struck by this indifferent or openly antisemitic behavior. A moving testimony for this group is the farewell letter of a retired Jewish senior official, who had survived Theresienstadt and had originally wanted to return to his hometown. In his letter to the Bavarian prime minister, he stated why this plan was impossible:

> One is amazed and shocked at the vulgarity of the mentality, the vileness, the stupidity, the lack of goodwill in the broadest circles of the population . . . the small daily stings that make one's life in Germany a martyrdom. . . . We are people who loved our homeland and believed in the better nature of the people. We suffered in our homeland with hope in our heart that reason would return. It was in vain.[20]

Leaders of the German-Jewish communities were also concerned about the continuing antisemitism. The comment of their leading spokesman in the first postwar year, Philipp Auerbach, was quoted in the magazine *Der Spiegel*: "it is not possible today for a Jew to go from Frankfurt to Hamburg and back without being cursed and spat on."[21] While this statement was obviously exaggerated, it does illustrate the deep disappointment of German Jews, which was constantly expressed in the Jewish press. Thus, one year after the Liberation, Philipp Auerbach reached the following conclusion: "One year in freedom draws to a close. A year of disappointment when we discovered with bitterness that, of the many promises granted us on the air, unfortunately, only very few were real."[22]

Another German Jew who contributed significantly to the restoration of the Jewish communities after the war, Norbert Wollheim, immigrated to the United States in 1951. In one of his last public appearances before his departure, he explained that his move was prompted by disappointment with the political development in Germany: "We are on the eve of a Nazi restoration in Germany. Good democrats cannot succeed here."[23]

Within the churches, there were serious attempts after 1945 to put Christian-Jewish relations on a new foundation. This was manifest in the societies for Christian-Jewish cooperation, which offered the beginnings of an honest dialogue with Jewish interlocutors, who were now hard to find. The first of these societies was formed in July 1948 in Munich and was followed in November 1949 by the establishment of a national coordinating council. A year later, the first "Brotherhood Week" took place in Stuttgart.[24]

Neither the establishment of societies for Christian-Jewish cooperation nor the many confessions of guilt of the churches for their own immediate past could obscure the fact that, in the early postwar years, the churches did not budge in principle from their traditional theological position toward the Jews. The "Stuttgart Confession of Guilt," issued in October 1945 by the Council of Protestant Churches in Germany, did indeed contain the self-accusation of not having mounted enough resistance against the Nazi regime but did not include a single word about the crimes against the Jews.[25] In the same month, the *Evangelisch-Lutherische Zentralverein für Mission unter Israel* [Lutheran-Evangelical Central Federation for the Mission to Israel] was reconstituted and admitted that after everything that had happened, a direct mission to the Jews was not possible at the moment; but at the same time, it did emphasize its adherence in principle to the Jewish mission as a future task.[26]

In 1948, the *Bruderrat der Evangelischen Kirche in Deutschland* [Brotherhood Council of the Evangelical Church in Germany] did concede that all nations bore a share of the guilt for the death of Jesus, but the same document emphasized the special guilt of the Jews: "Since Israel crucified the Messiah, it has rejected its election and destiny." Later, the document states: "That God cannot be mocked is the mute homily of the Jewish fate, a warning to us and an admonition to the Jews if they will not convert to the only one who offers them salvation too."[27] It is easy to imagine how such words were received by churchgoers after years of antisemitic indoctrination. Jews were still portrayed from the pulpit as deicides. After the Jewish persecution of the preceding years, many German Christians may have concluded that the Holocaust was merely a further confirmation of God's punishment of the nation of deicides.

Similar documents can also be found within the Catholic Church in the early postwar years. Thus, for example, the Committee for International Relations (*sic*!) of the Seventy-Second German Catholic Conference in Mainz condemned the most recent outbreaks of antisemitic violence in Germany only to state later on that "the future homecoming of the entire Jewish nation that is surely promised depends on whether we remain loving."[28] Thus the basic theological position of the conversion of the Jews is maintained even if it is emphasized that the means are to be nonviolent.

Returnees from Shanghai in Berlin, 1947 (Bildarchiv Abraham Pisarek, Berlin)

Return in Spite of Everything

In view of such fears, the number of those who returned to Germany from emigration was minuscule. By July 1947, only 62 Jews had come back to Berlin,[29] but a month later, this number increased considerably when 295 Jews who had survived the war in Shanghai—the last possibility of emigration during the war—came back to their hometown.[30] Altogether 732 persons returned from Shanghai: 429 of them settled in the Russian Occupation Zone, 234 in the British Occupation Zone, and 69 in the American Occupation Zone.[31] This wave of return from Shanghai resulted primarily from adverse conditions in China. Unlike America, the neighboring European states, and Palestine, China had never been a destination of Jewish immigration, a place where the DPs could imagine a long-term future for themselves. On the contrary, from countries where economic and political prospects were favorable, only a few returned to the home they had once been violently driven out of. Even the German-Jewish press, which encouraged the Jews living in Germany to remain there, had to advise against a systematic return: "We believe that the question of returning to Germany cannot be answered in the affirmative today; that those involved can only be advised to postpone the decision a while until conditions are clarified."[32]

Rare returnees from England, the United States, and Israel had often encountered political persecution before their emigration and now wanted to resume their political activity in their old homeland; or else they were actors, journalists, or attorneys who were tied to Germany linguistically and professionally. Politically active returnees included the future mayor of Hamburg, Herbert Weichmann; the future minister of justice of North Rhine-Westphalia, Josef Neuberger; the future chairman of the Association of German Labor Unions (DGB), Ludwig Rosenberg; the political scientists Richard Lowenthal and Ernst Fraenkel, as well as the sociologists Max Horkheimer and Theodor W. Adorno. Actors like Fritz Kortner, Ernst Deutsch, Ida Ehre, Therese Giese, and Curt Bois also looked forward to promising futures for their professional careers in Germany. Quite a few prominent returnees saw the fulfillment of their socialist ideals becoming tangible in the Soviet Occupation Zone, or rather East Germany, and decided to return to this part of the country. These included the writers Arnold Zweig, Anna Seghers, and Stefan Heym, as well as the literary historians Hans Mayer and Alfred Kantorowicz, the composer Hanns Eisler, and the philosopher Ernst Bloch. The future officials of the East German Communist Party (SED) Albert Norden and Gerhard Eisler also came back to East Germany shortly after the end of the war.[33]

Most of the prominent returnees had hardly any interest in the restoration of an organized Jewish life and took little or no part in the reconstruction of the Jewish communities. This task was taken up by those who were less famous; among them were the first secretary-general of the Central Council of Jews in Germany, Henrik van Dam, and the journalist Karl Marx, who played a decisive role in the formation of a Jewish press in postwar Germany.

Marx, who had returned to Düsseldorf from exile in England, had founded the *Jüdisches Gemeindeblatt für die Nord-Rheinprovinz und Westfalen* [Jewish community paper for North Rhine and Westphalia], in April 1946, with Hans Frey; in October of that year, the paper became the *Jüdisches Gemeindeblatt für die britische Zone* [Jewish community paper for the British Zone], and finally the *Allgemeine Jüdische Wochenzeitung* [General Jewish weekly]. Unlike the small German-language Jewish newspapers like *Der Weg* in Berlin, *Die Neue Welt* [The new world] in Munich, and the *Jüdische Rundschau* [Jewish review] in Marburg, the *Allgemeine* did not disappear from the German journalistic scene within a few years but rather secured a firm position there. Not only did it serve as the official information paper of the Jewish communities of the British Occupation Zone, and later of all West Germany, but it also formed a bridge between the Jewish communities of Germany and the Jews of the world.[34] The first edition was 500 copies, but circulation increased steadily to 2,500 by the end of the first year. One year later it was 7,000, in 1948 it reached 15,000, and by October 1950 it increased to 28,000. In 1951, the Berlin section of the *Allgemeine* was combined with the newspaper *Der Weg*, and the circulation once more increased, to 34,000.[35] (See interview with Lilli Marx.)

The leaders of the Jewish communities in the early postwar years included only a few who returned from emigration; but later on, in the 1960s and 1970s, some of the returnees who were younger in those days became leaders of their communities. This is true of the future president of the Munich Jewish community, Hans Lamm, who returned to Bavaria from exile in America as a translator in the Nuremberg Trials; or of the future chairman of the Nuremberg community, Arno Hamburger, who came to his hometown as a member of the Jewish Brigade and was initially employed as a religion teacher for the Jewish community. (See interview with Arno Hamburger.)

In terms of numbers, the returnees constituted only a minuscule percentage of the total Jewish population in the early postwar years. Thus in Berlin, in 1952, the 650 returnees formed 10.8 percent of the community members, and the same was true of Hamburg. However, on this point, too, regional differences have to be considered. While there were none or only very few returnees in the southern German DP communities, in Saarbrücken, they constituted 88 percent of the Jewish population. This special case was due to the fact that quite a few Saarbrücken Jews had survived the war in nearby France.[36]

Reparations

Linguistic and professional interests were the primary motives of the early returnees. They had been unable to adjust in the countries they had migrated to, and took the first opportunity to return to Germany. Although financial aspects usually played only a minor role for these first returnees, the conviction that they would be compensated for their material losses and receive at least a partial indemnity for their suffering in the previous decade may have been an additional motive for their return. They were supported in their struggle by the Jews liberated in Germany as well as by those German Jews who remained abroad. Their initial expectation suffered a bitter disappointment: instead of a quick response to their requests, they experienced the plodding construction of an administrative authority that considered "reparation matters."

The Bavarian government began in the early postwar years by appointing the concentration camp survivor and most prominent leader of the Jewish communities of Germany at that time, Philipp Auerbach, as state commissioner for those persecuted by the Nazis for their politics, religion, or race. In radio addresses and newspaper articles, he constantly exhorted the German public to assume responsibility for indemnifying the victims, and criticized their procrastination in paying compensation. The State Commission created in Bavaria in 1946 was the first such institution of a German government in which the Jews themselves were entrusted with the position of a state commissioner.

Despite the establishment of such offices and the ongoing discussions about a reparation law among the Germans, it took German postwar politicians a long time to decide on a concrete bill. The state governments were waiting for the national reestablishment of Germany, pleading that they would not take over the succession of the German Reich. Thus in the first postwar years, the Jews in the communities and the DP camps did not receive even a trace of at least partial compensation. Those who returned to their respective states received only a certain amount of welfare assistance. The state governments, however, failed to take a first step toward the rehabilitation of the German nation with a clear, common initiative. Finally, beginning in the American Occupation Zone on November 10, 1947, it was the occupation powers in all three Western zones who announced a law of restitution. Thus the first concrete initiative of reparation payments constituted an occupation law. In the American Occupation Zone, the first indemnity law regulating individual indemnity for liberated Jews went into effect on September 1, 1949, providing compensation for the denial of freedom, harm to body and health, claims for survivors' incomes, and payment for professional and economic property damage. It was valid not only for German citizens but also for the liberated Jews of Eastern Europe, whose inclusion in the law of restitution was resisted long and passionately by several German politicians.

The adoption of this law of restitution, however, did not mean that those in question received actual restitution. They had to undergo a tedious bureaucratic process. Since after liberation from the concentration camps they had no proof of identity or of their suffering, the door was wide open to corruption. Their restitution often depended on the goodwill of the responsible German official. During 1950, gangs of counterfeiters, who supplied the required papers, added even more confusion to the procedure. Only by producing all proof could one receive a payment of up to 3,000 DM while a final decision was pending "appeal," but it was not at all clear when this "appeal" would occur. This was especially hard for those who wanted to emigrate and needed cash as soon as possible, since they were left with nothing after the Liberation.

Uniform German laws followed only after a hesitant beginning. Most disappointing for the victims of persecution was the first official declaration of Konrad Adenauer's government on September 10, 1949, in which the West German chancellor made absolutely no mention of the obligation to pay reparations to the victims of Nazism but did say a great deal about the obligation to help war victims, refugees, and the homeless.[37] An agreement on reparation payments was signed by representatives of West Germany, the State of Israel, and international Jewish organizations in Luxemburg on September 10, 1952, as a prerequisite to diplomatic relations with the Jewish state. One year later, the first concrete result, the West German supplementary law of restitution for victims of Nazi persecution, went into effect, expanding the law of restitution that already existed in the American Occupation Zone to the other two Western occupation zones. Yet many years went by before the law passed in 1952 could be put into practice. Most survivors had to wait until the end of the 1950s for the actual disbursement of restitution payments to begin. By then they had had to take their fate into their own hands and build a life for themselves either in Germany or abroad.

Repayment for abandoned property turned out to be even more complicated than individual restitution. In this case, the primary question was who was entitled to inherit the estate of murdered people as well as of former institutions. The major Jewish organizations responded by uniting to establish successor organizations to take over unclaimed Jewish property, and using it for surviving Jews all over the world, especially in Israel. Thus, in June 1948, the JRSO (Jewish Restitution Successor Organization) was founded in the American Occupation Zone, while the JTC (Jewish Trust Corporation) performed the same function in the British Occupation Zone, and the Branche Française in the French Occupation Zone. Here, too, bureaucratic hurdles first had to be cleared. One major difficulty for the JRSO was that the law of indemnity had made December 31, 1948, the deadline for registering all property. This meant that the JRSO had three months to discover more than one hundred thousand unclaimed properties, and to comb through land registers, notaries' files, tax rolls, patent rosters, and several other records. They were able to do this job only because of an immediate emergency measure: the JRSO increased its staff to three hundred officials, who worked in three eight-hour shifts, processing about two thousand applicants a day.[38]

The tremendous efficiency of the JRSO did not produce unqualified approval in all Jewish circles. The JRSO's claim to be the legitimate successor of the prewar Jewish communities encountered the opposition of the organization of emigrated German Jews, the Council of Jews from Germany. Although this group was represented in the JRSO, it felt slighted in their decision-making process and seceded from the JRSO on

short notice. The Council of Jews from Germany, led by the former
Berlin rabbi Leo Baeck, considered its members, who were scattered all
over the world, as the major legitimate heirs to the property of the destroyed Jewish communities and demanded a larger share for them in the
distribution of the proceeds of this property.

This conflict was aggravated by the intervention of another
party: the newly established postwar Jewish communities in Germany.
Although they were only a pale copy of the prewar communities, they
nevertheless considered themselves their direct successors. According to
an agreement between the JRSO and the communities, possession of the
property of the former communities remained in the hands of the JRSO,
while the communities were granted the right to use it.[39] Yet many communities assumed they would be cheated in this solution and were afraid
they would be unable to manage independently the property they were
entitled to. Their fears were confirmed by hasty sales of formerly Jewish-
owned real estate by the JRSO, which considered the immediate support
of the beleaguered Jews in Israel an urgent priority. The chairman of the
Jewish community in Stuttgart, Benno Ostertag, spoke for many leaders
of communities when he warned in 1949 that the Jewish communities,
some of which had existed for over a thousand years, "do not wish to be
dependent upon the mercy of the JRSO."[40]

In most cases, the JRSO and the Jewish community were able to
reach an agreement that unambiguously apportioned the property of the
former community. The apportionment in individual communities varied quite a bit, depending on the amount of the property and the size and
needs of the postwar community. In Berlin, the JRSO got 60 percent of
the total property of the former community, while the community was
awarded 40 percent. In Stuttgart, the community received 65 percent of
the former community property; in Wiesbaden, on the other hand, it got
only 10 percent. In Kassel, whose Jewish population numbered only
twenty-eight, a piece of land that had once been owned by Jews was sold
to a Jew for a favorable price, on condition that two rooms of the house
be given to the Jewish community, rent free, as a prayer room and an
office.[41]

However, some disagreements between the Jewish communities
and the JRSO on the succession of the former Jewish communities extended to litigation. For example, in 1953, the Jewish community of
Augsburg took their claim to the property of the prewar Augsburg community to the District Court of Munich, which, like the Augsburg State
Court and the Reparations Chamber, declared the Jewish community of
Augsburg the de facto legitimate successor. This decision, however, was
overturned by the Restitution Appeals Court in the American Occupation Zone, which concluded "that the liquidation of the [former]

Augsburg Jewish Community did take place both de facto and de jure when it was integrated into the unification of the Reich," and that even though the reestablished community was "admittedly an organization with the same purpose as the original community which suffered religious persecution," it could not be its successor. Significantly, the JRSO's claim succeeded only because it regarded the liquidation of the Jewish communities by the Nazi state as legally valid.[42] (See interview with David Schuster.)

Similar decisions were issued in the quarrel over the succession of the Jewish communities in the French Occupation Zone, which were claimed by the local communities of Mainz, Coblenz, and Neustadt an der Weinstrasse. In those debates, the successor organization—in this case the Branche Française de la Jewish Trust Corporation for Germany—was awarded sole legitimate authority by the Restitution Appeals Court in the French Occupation Zone.[43]

The legal quarrel between Jewish communities and successor organizations was complicated by internal disagreement within the communities about the future of the former community property. Former DPs, who had in fact settled in Germany but continued to harbor theoretical misgivings about the future of Jewish life there, mainly agreed with the JRSO on the sale of former Jewish property. Even before the JRSO was established, the German-Jewish communities had tried to enforce their claim to succession—at that time, against the organizations founded by the Jewish DPs. Thus, in January 1946, the Jewish communities in southern Germany passed a resolution emphasizing their claim to succession against the Committee of Liberated Jews in the American Occupation Zone.[44]

When the issue of succession became relevant in the early 1950s, the opposing opinions about the legal status of the communities and the future of their members in Germany were clearly expressed. In the Augsburg case, the decision of the board of the Jewish community, composed of German Jews, to consider themselves the successor of the prewar Jewish community encountered the opposition of Jewish circles. In the Munich paper *Neue Jüdische Zeitung*, the journalist Ernest Landau announced himself as their spokesman and accused the "egotistical heads of the Augsburg Kehilla" of thinking only of their personal interest, "at the cost of Jewish society living in great hardship all over the world."[45]

Aside from the fate of individual and community property, the issue of succession ultimately concerned another aspect, i.e., the fate of abandoned synagogues and cultural artifacts. This problem was dealt with by a seven-member rabbinical senate, which carried on a two-year investigation of the case according to biblical and talmudic provisions, and concluded in 1949 that, wherever possible, synagogues and schools were to pursue their original purpose. Thus the sale of these buildings in places where there was still a Jewish population was forbidden, even if the structures were delapidated. Similarly, the restoration of destroyed synagogues was encouraged in places where Jewish communites still existed. However, the rabbinical court did display a sense of reality when it consented to the sale of synagogues in places without a Jewish population, adding the injunction that the proceeds were to be used only "for honorable and worthy purposes," primarily for building synagogues and religious schools. The rabbis maintained unequivocally that no cemetery of any kind could be sold, since Jewish religious law absolutely forbids disturbing the peace of the dead. Hence the JRSO sold several empty synagogues but kept all cemeteries in Jewish possession.[46]

Before 1933, Germany had been a center of Jewish culture. Rabbinical seminaries, Jewish schools, and Jewish libraries, as well as art collections and museums, existed in the larger communities. During the Nazi period, many of the countless Hebrew, Yiddish, and German books preserved in the Jewish communities and the public libraries were destroyed or sold. Yet at the same time, under the aegis of Alfred Rosenberg, two and a half million books were taken from libraries all over Europe and brought to the former Rothschild Library in Frankfurt, and were stored after the war in the Offenbach Archive. These included the holdings of the YIVO (Jewish Research Institute, founded in 1925 to explore the history and culture of East European Jewry) of Vilna, which were transferred to YIVO headquarters in New York. After the war, most books were returned to their original countries, while about 25,000 less valuable books stocked libraries for the Jewish DPs in the DP camps.[47] The Jewish Cultural Reconstruction Corporation (JCR) was set up jointly by the JRSO and the JTC to take charge of all other books and religious items. Its director was Columbia University's professor of Jewish history Salo Wittmayer Baron, and its staff included the philosopher Hannah Arendt. Working with the JOINT, the JCR undertook to trace any remaining Jewish cultural artifacts and to remove them from Germany in order to give them to Jewish communities throughout the world, on the assumption that Jewish life would never again be possible in Germany.

As ships laden with Jewish refugees, books from Jewish libraries, and Torah scrolls left German harbors, the remaining Jews prepared for their future in a new, democratic Germany. They founded organizations, opened new synagogues with old religious objects, and established their own libraries. They set out to show the Jewish world that even in Germany, a small branch of the tree of life of Jewish history was about to grow again and would soon show its first buds.

6. The Establishment of Jewish Life

Isolation in the Jewish World

In July 1948, at its first postwar assembly, the World Jewish Congress warned the Jews of the world never again to settle on the "blood-soaked German soil."[1] The Montreux resolution expressed the widespread opposition in the Jewish world to the presence of Jews in Germany. Even though a rabbinical ban against the resettlement of Jews in Germany was never issued, it was usually considered a moral stigma for Jews to settle in Germany, "since no life can flourish and no human being can live in a cemetery."[2] This attitude was shared by leading Jewish officials, like the first Israeli consul in Munich, Chaim Yahil (Hoffmann), who demanded in the American Jewish periodical *Jewish Frontier*: "All Jews must leave Germany." Such demands and accusations generally resonated with the suspicion that only material advantages kept them in the country of the murderers. For Yahil, the Jews who remained in Germany were "a source of danger for the entire Jewish people. . . . Those who are tempted by the fleshpots of Germany must not expect that Israel or the Jewish people should provide them with services for their convenience."[3]

Yahil's opinion was shared by most emigrating German Jews, who found it incomprehensible that Jews could feel comfortable in Germany after the horrors of the Nazi period. One well-known German Zionist who immigrated to Israel made this comment on their opting for a future in Germany: "Let them stay where they are. Let them wait in their beloved fatherland until their throats are slit too."[4] Many Jewish intellectuals, who considered Jewish emancipation in Europe failed, wondered whether Jews should not leave Europe altogether. The American Jewish writer Ludwig Lewisohn thought that Jews remaining in Europe were "outcasts, paupers, untouchables, in separate quarters of Europe, . . . [who could lead] a life without dignity, creativity, and hope."[5] The rejection of Europe was a welcome notion for some of the liberated Jews. The chairman of the Landsberg Camp Committee, Samuel Gringauz, delivered a programmatic speech on the future of the liberated Jews with the unequivocal title of "Adieu Europe."[6] And on another occasion, Gringauz underscored his doubt concerning the belief in progress in European history. For the surviving Jews, Western civilization could not be characterized by Westminster Abbey or Versailles, nor by Strasbourg Cathedral or the art treasures of Florence, but rather by the violence of the Crusades, the Spanish Inquisition, the pogroms in Russia, and the gas chambers of Auschwitz.[7]

The Jews who had decided to stay in Germany, on the other hand, became increasingly aware of their isolation in the Jewish world. Thus, as the German-Jewish periodical *Der Weg* put it: "But abroad, people are relatively unanimous in the perception that the time when German Jewry played a major role in Jewish life is finally past and will not return in the foreseeable future . . . Jewry abroad has lost interest in Germany; it is not willing to make considerable personal and material expenditures to stimulate Jewish life in Germany again."[8] German Jews criticized that Jewish mood abroad, which protested vehemently against a reestablishment of Jewish communities in Germany but had offered only little help in time of need. Thus the leading representative of Jewish postwar communities in Germany, Philipp Auerbach, lashed out:

> What did American Jewry do to prevent what happened to us, and how long did it take until the first help came to us from our brothers abroad? They can talk very well as bystanders. They can forget what we went through . . . You sat around the radio out there; you heard that six million Jews lost their lives, wiped away a tear, said, "I am sorry," and switched back to the music. And now we are the poor relatives one doesn't like to be seen with.[9]

After the establishment of the State of Israel, when pressure on the Jews remaining in Germany increased, Jewish society in Germany reacted with a clear and unequivocal statement of their desire to remain in Germany. In the summer of 1951, the *Landesverband der Jüdischen Gemeinden Nordwestdeutschlands* [State Federation of Jewish Communities in Northwest Germany] passed a resolution against the exclusion of German Jews by the World Jewish Congress and other Jewish organizations:

> The Congress of the Federation protests firmly against all attempts to defame Jews living in Germany. The Jewish communities, as always, consider it their duty to care for the preservation of the interests of their members and of Jewry in Germany, and therefore consider it their imperative mission to ensure the continuation of their work. The Jews in Germany and their communities consider themselves an inextricable component of all Jewry.[10]

Yet many years would pass before the international Jewish organizations, like the World Jewish Congress or the World Jewish Women's League, shared this opinion. In the 1950s, two different attitudes about Jews living in Germany emerged in the Jewish world. Most Jewish organizations thought that the remnant of Jews still in Germany could be motivated to emigrate by deliberate isolation. Thus, in 1951, the Zionist Jewish Agency closed all its offices in Germany and exhorted the

Jewish population to immigrate to Israel, since remaining in Germany contained the danger of "national and moral degeneration."[11] Within the World Union of Jewish Students (WUJS), during the 1960s, fierce arguments raged on the issue of the legitimation of Jewish life in Germany and the acceptance of the *Bundesverband Jüdischer Studenten in Deutschland*. The Thirteenth WUJS Congress of 1963 declared against accepting the Jewish student union from Germany and recommended the immediate emigration of all Jews living in Germany.[12] At a subsequent congress, in August 1967, resolutions were passed exhorting Jews living in Germany and Austria to "realise in the shortest possible period the incompatibility between being Jewish and living in Germany and Austria." The same resolution accused Jews residing in those countries of being "in search of personal advantage."[13]

Rabbis in Postwar Germany

A minority of Jewish leaders abroad were opposed to the isolation of German Jews, convinced that the existence of a small Jewish community in Germany was an irrevocable fact. Without absolutely welcoming this fact, they did call for the support of these Jewish communities to keep them from becoming increasingly alienated from Jewry. This view led the lawyer and journalist E. G. Lowenthal, who later returned to Germany, to remark:

> Isolation and insecurity have forced Germany's Jews to master their own fate. Nevertheless, as long as they continue to live there in small communities they will need spiritual and political guidance from an outside world whose doors are still not wide enough to open in both directions. And it appears that they will continue to need that help for a long time to come.[14]

Like Lowenthal, Rabbi Alexander Carlebach, who was born in Cologne and later served in Belfast, also advocated support for Jews living in Germany. From his new home in England, he wrote:

> Even if we had the choice, World Jewry could not disinterest itself in the fate of German Jewry, however much reduced in numbers and however poor spiritually and materially. But we have no choice, and, with so many problems and troubles in our hands already, this one must receive the loving and intelligent attention which the Jewish people owes its "lost sons" of Israel.[15]

Carlebach's concern for the "lost children" was thoroughly justified. Aside from a few Jewish chaplains who had come to Germany with the Allies and some East European rabbis in DP communities, the Jewish leadership in Germany remained practically without rabbis. In the annual report of the Berlin Jewish community of 1945/46, among the 540 employees of the community, one major position was unfilled: the community had not been able to find a rabbi willing to return to Germany. Not until June 1947 did the community hire a rabbi, Michael Munk, who had been trained at the Orthodox rabbinical seminary in Berlin and returned to his homeland from the United States for a year.[16] In 1948 a student of Leo Baeck (the spiritual leader of prewar German Jewry), Steven Schwarzschild, a Liberal rabbi, arrived in Berlin, and was succeeded in 1950 by another Baeck student, Rabbi Nathan Peter Levinson.[17]

Sadness was the characteristic mood among the returning rabbis, even when, as in Levinson's case, they were basically optimistic about the future of Jewish life in Germany. In his first sermon, Levinson, who was to serve in Germany longer than any other rabbi (in Berlin, Baden, and Hamburg), stated clearly that there could be no continuity of Jewish life with the Berlin he had left as a young rabbinical student: "A place is not a place, a place is with whom you are," he quoted an American writer, and added: "This is profoundly true. Berlin was not Berlin; Berlin was its people. I ask myself, where are these people? Where are the old and the young, the children and the women, the rabbis and the sages I once loved so much? They were ripped out of this city horribly, brutally and inhumanly, and they did not come back."[18] (See interview with Nathan Peter Levinson.)

It was even harder for smaller communities to find rabbis. In most cases, rabbis could be hired only on a short-term basis and would leave after several weeks or months. Thus, in the first postwar years, Rabbis Eli Munk, Paul Holzer, and Alexander Carlebach served in Hamburg, but the community had no permanent spiritual leadership.[19] In 1951, Siegbert Neufeld, a rabbi who had been active in the prewar German community of Elbing, was the first to return for a longer time. He was hired by the *Israelitische Religionsgesellschaft Württembergs*. Reflecting on his work in Stuttgart, Neufeld emphasized his initial isolation as a rabbi in Germany in the early 1950s: "In the long period when I was almost alone in Germany, I was often asked for religious information from the most diverse communities of Germany, sometimes by telegraph or telephone. I sometimes longed to discuss things with colleagues, but there weren't any there." Not until the early 1950s, when two more rabbis originally from Germany, Robert Rafael Geis and Zwi Harry Levy, returned to Baden and Hessen, did the Jewish communities in Germany once again enjoy systematic religious guidance. In 1952, Neufeld and his two colleagues established the *Landesrabbinerkonferenz* (later the Rabbinical Conference), which remained an active forum for the current problems of rabbinical service in Germany.[20]

Nevertheless, even in subsequent years, it was difficult for the Jewish communities in Germany to find rabbis. By 1960, only seven trained rabbis were serving in Germany, along with four or five nonacademic rabbis trained in Poland who served the smaller DP community organizations.[21]

The undisputed authority among the Orthodox rabbis in Germany, Rabbi David Kahana Spiro, served in the small community of Fürth. Spiro was the descendant of one of the most famous Polish rabbinical dynasties and was one of the youngest members of the prewar Warsaw rabbinate. After his liberation in Dachau, he went to Fürth, where he worked—despite numerous offers from large Jewish communities all over the world—until his death in 1971.[22] As an internationally acknowledged authority on *halakha* (Jewish religious law), Rav Spiro was a conspicuous exception among German rabbis, many of whom practiced the rabbinate as a second profession and had originally been bookbinders, pediatricians, veterinarians, journalists, or cantors.[23]

One of the major tasks of the rabbis in postwar Germany was not foreseen. The small Jewish community in Germany could have doubled within the first years after the war if it had responded positively to all applications for conversion presented by non-Jewish Germans. In June 1946, the Jewish community of Berlin, which numbered 7,000 members, received 2,500 applications for acceptance.[24] A separate community committee in Berlin dealt exclusively with the question of conversion but could decide on very few concrete issues, since there was as yet no rabbi to perform conversions. The future community rabbi Nathan Peter Levinson summarized his service in Berlin: "The task of interviewing and processing applications from candidates for conversion constituted one of the main concerns of the rabbi between 1948 and 1953."[25]

Initially, most of the requests came from Jews who had withdrawn from Judaism, and from non-Jewish spouses and their children. But later, the circle expanded considerably, encompassing both those who expected economic advantages as well as persons who preferred to identify with the persecuted rather than with the persecutors. Levinson estimates that only about 5 percent of the applicants were accepted: those who wanted to convert out of religious conviction or because of marriage to a Jewish spouse, and those who themselves or whose families were persecuted for religious reasons.

Another important function of the rabbis was the guarantee of religious unity in the respective communities. The prewar German tradition of unified communities was continued after 1945. The numerically insignificant Orthodox "secessionist communities," which refused to be controlled by a Liberal general community, did not reemerge after the war. There were not enough Jews for that, and, moreover, most Jewish communities after 1945 were oriented toward the Orthodox ritual in any case; in contrast, before the war, the Liberal tendency with organ music and a German-language sermon had prevailed. The Orthodox nature of the Bavarian DP communities was especially marked. Synagogues there were built with partitions between the men's and women's sections, a practice that had become outmoded in Germany by the nineteenth century, even in many Orthodox synagogues.

The Orthodox ritual could prevail in most communities since those who cared about religious matters came primarily from Eastern Europe, where there were only a few Liberal congregations. Despite the dominance of the Orthodox ritual in postwar German congregations, the overwhelming majority of their members hardly practiced personal religious observance. According to a 1949 estimate, fifteen Jewish families in Cologne, ten in Hamburg, and none in Düsseldorf observed the Jewish dietary laws (*kashrut*). Only in the south German communities with a high proportion of DPs was there a considerable observance of Kashrut. Thus, in Stuttgart, some seventy families lived in kosher homes; in Frankfurt and Munich the numbers were appreciably higher. Although there were many yeshivas among the Jewish DPs, in the German-Jewish communities, there were no institutions of higher Jewish learning. Only 4–5 percent of the membership in the large communities attended synagogue regularly on the Sabbath.[26]

These numbers also indicate that the religious element formed only a subsection of the Jewish communities. This had also been the case in prewar Germany, where synagogue attendance was equally low. Unlike the voluntary nature of Jewish communities in Anglo-Saxon countries, Jewish communities in Germany had always been administrative centers for several social and cultural establishments as well.

Social Problems

In the immediate postwar period, social aid was a primary function of the Jewish communities. In the first weeks after the war, the surviving German and East European Jews were completely dependent on help from outside. Emaciated by the strain of the concentration camp or the anxieties of hiding, most of them were unfit for work. In addition, they had been robbed of their property and often were incapable of acquiring even the basic necessities. Under the heading "Welfare," the 1945–46 report of the Jewish community of Berlin states:

> The issue of clothing is especially urgent for most members of the community because most of them were stripped of all property by the Nazi measures and because Jews were not issued a clothing ration card during the war, and so could not purchase any clothing replacements. There is a

particular lack of men's suits, shoes, and underwear. . . . Thus far, aid officials have been unable to acquire clothing. . . . 83.5 percent of the Jews of
Berlin lack adequate clothing.[27]

Housing presented a similar problem. After the war, 90 percent
of the Jews living in Berlin were homeless. Even a year later, the report
states that just under 60 percent of the community members had inade-
quate housing and that 72 percent lived in insufficiently furnished rooms
(lacking a table, chair, closet, and sometimes even a bed). Only a small
portion of the community members were fit to resume regular work,
particularly physicians and attorneys, who were able to start their practice again. The social problems of Jews living in Germany abated slowly.
Since most DPs who were physically restored to some extent emigrated
as soon as they could, those who remained in Germany were mainly the
weak and the sick. In 1949, most Jews living in Germany were still dependent on social aid, and often resisted integration into the German economy, because this would have represented a public confirmation of their
decision to remain in Germany.[28]

Nursing homes were created soon after the war in large communities. The Berlin Jewish community took over two transit homes, three
old people's homes, a children's home, a hospital, and a nursing home. In
1946, 540 persons were employed by the Berlin Jewish community, 272
of them in the hospital and 109 in homes and institutions. The construction of a social network within the Jewish community was primarily a
psychological need of the survivors, as Philipp Auerbach emphasized in
a 1949 speech: "It would be humiliating for Jews to ask for help from
German welfare institutions, even if this step would mean an improve-
ment of the desperate situation of the poor Jews. Welfare institutions for
Jews living in Germany must, as prior to 1933, be administered exclusively by Jews."[29] Hence the *Zentralwohlfahrtsstelle der Juden in Deutschland*
[Central Welfare Office of the Jews in Germany], which had existed between 1917 and 1943, was reestablished, providing an extensive autonomous welfare system for needy members of Jewish society in Germany.[30]

In the area of religion, the Berlin Jewish community had a staff
of ninety-one, including a preacher, a candidate for the rabbinate, five
cantors, three synagogue attendants, four teachers, and one kosher
butcher. Prayer service was held in three synagogues: on Rykestrasse,
Pestalozzistrasse, and at the Thielschufer (Fränkelufer); and four chapels
were also available. While most ritual objects still existed for the synagogue, prayer books, tallises, and tefillin were lacking. After negotiations
with the appropriate offices were completed, kosher slaughter and a
matza bakery were permitted.[31]

Matza from the United States for Berlin (with community chairman Fabian at left) (Bildarchiv Abraham Pisarek, Berlin)

The first report of the Jewish community of Berlin emphasized "a great need for cultural events" among the community members. Initially, however, lectures were not feasible, "because of a lack of suitable manpower." Thus cultural presentations were limited mainly to the traditional Jewish holiday celebrations of Hanukah and Purim. Religious instruction also presented difficulties, since there were only four Jewish religion teachers in all Berlin. Moreover, since the various schools attended by individual Jewish students were at a considerable distance from one another, religious instruction had to be centralized, and many students could not participate because they lacked transportation.[32] In small communities, like Hanover, Kiel, Heidelberg, and Wiesbaden, there was no Jewish religious instruction at all in 1949. Even in larger communities, adults hardly had the opportunity to enrich their Jewish knowledge. In Berlin, Stuttgart, Cologne, and Hamburg, a few courses—predominantly instruction in the Hebrew language—were offered within the framework of adult education; but in Frankfurt, Mannheim, Düsseldorf, and other communities, even this language instruction ceased after most DPs emigrated.[33]

Reorganization on the Regional Level

The development of the social and cultural institutions of the Jewish communities would hardly have been possible without their increasing mutual cooperation. The expansion of community activities was accompanied by the development of a regional superstructure of individual communities. Within one year after the Liberation, most reestablished Jewish communities were combined into state associations. The first of these state associations emerged in the North Rhine province, in Westphalia, Rhineland-Palatinate, Baden, and Württemberg, as well as in the Soviet Occupation Zone. Individual state associations differed considerably from one another, both in their conception of themselves and in their structure. Many state associations, like the Supreme Council of the Israelites of Baden, considered themselves successor organizations to prewar associations. Other state associations represented brand-new creations, based on the new political borders, a phenomenon particularly conspicuous in the Soviet Occupation Zone. A few state associations were identical with the large communities in their jurisdiction. Thus Stuttgart became the only community within the realm of the Israelite Religious Society of Württemberg. In other state associations, only the smaller communities are combined. Cologne, for example, is not a member of the North Rhine State Association, and after initial membership the Frankfurt community left the Hessian state association. The *Landesverband der Israelitischen Kultusgemeinden Bayerns* [State Association of Jewish Communities of Bavaria], founded in 1947, comprised twelve small communities, along with the large community of Munich (which seceded in 1996). In Berlin, Bremen, and Hamburg, so-called stateless communities emerged.

In the French Occupation Zone, the difficulty of organizing Jewish life was aggravated by the negligible number of Jews living there. The great distances made it almost impossible for the widely scattered members to hold regular religious services. Members organized into the three communities of Coblenz (130), Mainz (80), and Trier (40) lived mostly in smaller towns of Rhineland-Palatinate and were only nominally attached to the nearby city. To ensure more effective activity, the communities of Coblenz and Trier merged in May 1946 under the name of *Jüdische Kultusgemeinde der Regierungsbezirke Koblenz und Trier* [Jewish Religious Congregations of the Districts of Coblenz and Trier], with their main offices in Coblenz.[34] A similar development also took place in the Bavarian administrative district of Swabia, where the widely scattered members of the state communities were all included in the *Israelitische Kultusgemeinde Schwaben-Augsburg*.

The chairpersons of the state associations as well as of most large communities were almost exclusively German Jews. The future Bavarian commissioner of state Phillip Auerbach was particularly outstanding: in March 1946, he was the first chairman of the *Landesverband Nord-Rhein-provinz und Westfalen* [State Federation of North Rhine Province and Westphalia]; then he moved to Bavaria, where, within a few months, he became the first chairman of the Bavarian Association of Jewish Communities. Although the overwhelming majority of Bavarian Jews were East European DPs, German Jews headed both the state associations and the two big communities of Munich and Nuremberg. Even in a few smaller communities consisting almost exclusively of East European Jews, the chairman of the community was a German Jew. In Fürth, for instance, a typical DP community organization, Jean Mandel, a concentration camp survivor born in Fürth, led the postwar community for more than a quarter of a century.[35]

The restoration of the Jewish communities in Germany, considered provisional in many quarters, was clearly consolidated in the early postwar years. The "liquidation communities" had struck roots in German soil and acquired an organizational superstructure with the state associations. With the founding of West Germany in 1949, the transition phase of the Jewish communities also came to an end. They now had to plan for the future: were they to lead the Jews out of Germany or were they to be a solid component of a new democratic German state?

This was the question that preoccupied the sixty-three participants in a July 1949 conference in Heidelberg on the future of Jews in Germany, which was attended by representatives of major Jewish organizations like the American Jewish Committee, the World Jewish Congress, the JOINT, and delegates from HIAS, ORT, and B'nai Brith, as well as deputies of the German-Jewish communities and state associations. Representatives of the Jewish Agency were also present, along with the Israeli consul in Munich, Eliahu Livneh, and the former victim of persecution and editor of the *Frankfurter Hefte* Eugen Kogon. Invitations had been issued by Harry Greenstein, adviser of the American military administration on Jewish issues. In his introductory remarks, Greenstein emphasized that the existence of Jewish life in Germany could not simply be denied, even for the future. Therefore, it was an urgent goal of this conference to find a way leading to the future and to improve the organization of the Jews in Germany. As Greenstein emphasized in his opening remarks:

In the past few years the Central Committee of Liberated Jews has been primarily concerned with the Jewish Displaced Persons in the camps and the Kultusgemeinden have confined their attention to the Jews living in the communities. The time has come when we should deal with the problem of the Jews in Germany, not from a separatist point of view, but united in our aims and purposes. I hope that at some point of our discussion we can consider and, I trust, agree on the desirability of setting up an over-all Jewish organization which will make it possible for us to plan together for *all* of the Jews in Germany.[36]

The main premise of the conference, according to Greenstein, was the exclusion of any discussion of whether or not Jewish communities should exist in Germany. However, proscribing debate on this pivotal issue at an assembly with such varied participants was a hopeless proposition from the start, and many delegates emphasized their attitude toward the question of "stay or go." The representatives of international Jewish organizations who spoke against staying in Germany received loud opposition from the ranks of non-Jewish delegates. The main speaker of the conference, the high commissioner of the American Occupation Zone, John J. McCloy, called for an invigoration of Jewish life in Germany and was optimistic that it could be realized:

> The Jew in Germany will be restored to a position which he occupied in the past in this community and will reach even higher levels. . . . What this community will be, how it forms itself, how it becomes a part and how it merges with the new Germany, will, I believe, be watched very closely and very carefully by the entire world. It will, in my judgment, be one of the real touchstones and the test of Germany's progress toward the light.[37]

And Eugen Kogon publicly criticized those who advocated the withdrawal of Jews from Germany: "Permit me to say with deep sadness that your entirely understandable decision means the final triumph of Hitler. What Hitler desired to achieve has now been accomplished."[38]

Even though Kogon encountered harsh resistance from several Jewish representatives, there were also calls for a new beginning in Germany from Jews. The American rabbi Isaac Klein recounted a Jewish tale about a man with a profoundly pessimistic view of life, because, as was finally discovered, all the windows in his house overlooked a cemetery. The rabbis advised him to open the windows onto the world of the living in order to change his view of life. "The time has now come to open our windows to the future and do some planning for the morrow which will surely come."[39]

In the spirit of this parable, the concrete result of the conference was the creation of a committee chaired by the Israeli consul Eliahu Livneh, to put together an umbrella organization of all Jewish communities and organizations in Germany. An organization of this sort had not been created in the early postwar years, first, because of the political division of Germany, but also because of the reluctant attitude of the

Jewish communities themselves. Historical factors also played a role. Even during the Weimar Republic, a national organization of Jewish communities was never established, despite repeated attempts. It was only under the pressure of Nazi rule that a Reich Association of German Jews came into being in 1933. As in the Weimar Republic, so after 1945 a few communities and state associations were not willing to yield authority to a central organization. Moreover, an umbrella organization would also have to surmount the tension between the German-Jewish and the DP communities. Hence the communities and state associations of the three Western occupation zones originally formed only a loose representation of interests of Jewish communities and religious associations, which was first mentioned in March 1946 and initiated by Hans Lamm, the future president of the Jewish community of Munich.[40]

A year later, in June 1947, the *Arbeitsgemeinschaft Jüdischer Gemeinden in Deutschland* [Working Alliance of Jewish Communities in Germany] developed out of the representation of interests as a loose union of communities and state associations with headquarters in Frankfurt. Its board of directors consisted of five mediators in the four occupation zones and Berlin. Additional meetings of the *Arbeitsgemeinschaft* took place in October 1947 in Berlin and in January 1948 in Bremen. The committee formed at the Heidelberg meeting accelerated efforts for the creation of a general organization for Jews living in Germany, resulting in the establishment of the *Zentralrat der Juden in Deutschland* [Central Council of Jews in Germany] in Frankfurt am Main, in July 1950. The council included representatives of the Jewish communities in all four occupation zones, and of the central committee of the DPs, comprising seven state associations, four communities not affiliated with a state association, and the Jewish Committee of the British Zone. The founding meeting of the council took place in January 1951, when the attorney Hendrik van Dam was elected secretary-general of the organization. The support of Israeli consul Livneh was very significant for the founding assembly; Livneh underscored the necessity of this union and emphasized that "Israel doesn't forget its children wherever they live."[41] With the establishment of the council, the Jews remaining in Germany sent an unequivocal signal: against all internal and external opposition, they were laying the cornerstone for a long-lasting Jewish infrastructure in Germany.

II.

Witness Accounts

In the DP Camps

1. ERNEST LANDAU
THE FIRST DAYS OF FREEDOM

Ernest Landau was born in Vienna in 1916 and, until 1938, was a member of the editorial staff of various Austrian newspapers, like the Neue Freie Presse *and the* Telegraf. *Until 1941, he was active in the Belgian resistance movement, was then arrested, and survived several concentration camps.*

I was liberated in Bavaria, between Tutzing and Feldafing. We were then in a transport that was supposed to go somewhere in the Tyrol, I think, in any case, in the mountains, to some so-called Werewolf post.[1] But it didn't get that far. It was May 1, the evening of May 1, 1945; we were between Tutzing and Seeshaupt, on the railroad track, in a train consisting of plain freight cars. About a hundred people were crammed into these cars. This train also had one flatcar with guns on it, a cannon or a small howitzer, something like that. The Allies mistook us for a Wehrmacht transport and bombed us. We lost about sixty people. The train came to a halt. We were accompanied by SS men, but by then they were pretty subdued because they had found out that the Allied troops were quite close. They did still try to "fulfill their duty," as they called it—that is, to keep guarding us—but they were visibly milder. So the train stood still, near Lake Starnberg, and it was evening. We had fastened our blue-green striped inmates' jackets, the concentration camp uniform, on the roofs of the freight cars in case another plane appeared. If it intended to attack us, the pilot should be able to recognize that these weren't soldiers here but concentration camp inmates.

Late at night, it was already dawn, a car came with a flag: a white cross on a red background, Switzerland! Not the Red Cross! Their head-lights were dimmed, so they could just barely see where they were going. Then they got out, two men, and asked to speak to somebody in charge. So the SS master sergeant went up to them and asked what they wanted. Well, this was the Swiss consul and he wanted to talk to whoever was in charge of this transport. "Yes, that's me," he answered. "Yes, but you're SS. I don't want to talk to you, I want to talk to one of the inmates." Naturally, that humiliated the SS man a little. He realized that he had lost his authority. So he went back to the group. There was a short chat between him and his men, and then he sent the senior camp prisoner over. That was an old Jew named Alfons Bär, actually a decent guy. So he told him to go to the Swiss man, which he did. He was used to obeying orders. The Swiss man asked, "Who are you?" He said, "I'm the senior camp prisoner." "Who made you that? Was it the SS?" "Yes." "No, I don't want to talk to you. We want to talk to an inmate, an average inmate."

Naturally, in the meantime, a whole circle formed to hear what was going on there. We were all curious. Such a thing had never hap-pened before. Civilians ordering SS men around! Then the following hap-pened: Alfons Bär came back completely miserable and told us his story. They didn't want to talk to him! So who did they want to talk to? I was pushed forward: "Go, you talk to them." So I went. Very skeptically. I didn't know who the people were. Anybody could say he was Swiss, and therefore I first asked him, "Si vous êtes Suisse, vous parlez certainement français." He gave me a look; I said, "Je préfère de parler français avec vous." Thereupon he answered immediately in French. I thought that if it was one of those German spies, he certainly wouldn't know perfect French, French with a Swiss accent.

That was my first encounter with anyone from the outside world after almost five years. So the Swiss man said to me, "Tell your people that the Americans are about eighteen to twenty kilometers from here, tomorrow morning at the latest you will be free. What can we do for you?" I say, "What can you do? We have had no food for four days. We haven't gotten anything, everything seems to have collapsed for the Ger-mans." "Yes," he says, "look, down there is a field hospital, the Wehr-macht is down there, now I'll make sure they send something up to you. What do you want?" "Everything, bread, hot soup, whatever there is."

The Swiss went off; I went back to the group and informed them that the Americans would be here the next day, and that we would prob-ably get food from the Wehrmacht camp in Possenhofen. Meanwhile, however, interest had shifted to another group on the other side of the train. They were Lithuanian boys, and a few Greeks, who were still pretty strong. They wanted something quite different. They had pushed one of the SS men down, taken his weapon, and killed him. Not with a bullet, but with a bayonet. His own bayonet. This SS man was a horrible guy. I said before that, at this point in time, the SS were mild, but he was the exception. So he didn't live to see our liberation. And this single weapon was enough to disarm the whole SS. A Lithuanian held it in his hand and everyone could see he wasn't joking. He called to the SS men, "I'll shoot you, even if I get killed, if one of you takes out his weapon." And that helped. Suddenly, these Lithuanian boys were holding all the SS weapons. The SS men were rounded up and locked in a car. All of us were now below, next to the tracks, in the meadow.

That night, trucks did come with Wehrmacht soldiers and brought kettles of soup and bread. The starving people—the inmates—pounced on the food. The result was unfortunately very bad. Almost all the soup was spilled; hardly anybody was lucky enough to get a spoon and eat it. Things went better with the bread. They brought army bread that was already cut into portions because they knew it had to be distributed. They had brought a lot, whole baskets of bread. They were quite decent.

We hardly slept that night. The next morning the Americans were in fact there. The first thing we saw was an airplane, then on the horizon a column of soldiers. At first we were scared they were SS. But the closer they came, the clearer we saw that it wasn't SS. A jeep pulled out of the column and came directly to us. They had obviously seen us from a reconnaissance plane. A lieutenant jumps out of the jeep: "Is there somebody who talks English?" There were three of us who spoke English; I was one of them.

The lieutenant: "Who are you?" "We are concentration camp inmates, mostly Jewish." There were a few non-Jews with us. They were *Kapos*, but mostly decent, most of them red triangles, that is, political [prisoners]. There was also a single green triangle [with which the Nazis designated "criminal prisoners"], but also a really decent guy, not a "professional criminal," as the Nazis often indicated. Then the American asked, "What can we do?" I say, "First of all, take care of those who are really weak and sick and wounded." That is, a few of us were wounded in this air raid. The corpses he had seen immediately, because we had taken them out of the cars and lined them up in a row. They dug a grave right on the spot, which still exists today, near the railroad embankment in Seeshaupt.

The American went back to his jeep, broadcast a radio message, and maybe ten minutes later, two or three ambulances with Red Cross staff showed up, and another jeep with two clergymen—one of them wore a cross, the other the Tablets of the Law. It was a Jewish chaplain, Major Max Braude, who stayed in very close touch with us.[2] He would later be director-general of ORT and played an outstanding role in the rehabilitation of people. The Red Cross staff, including women, to my surprise, provided great help. Then a delousing campaign began. I must say that we were literally stiff with filth. We had had little opportunity to clean ourselves, and in those last days there was no chance at all.

I explained to the American rabbi (at that time, I didn't know the word "chaplain") that this was a Jewish transport: at least 95 percent of us were Jews. The chaplain, Major Braude, asked me if any of us were rabbis. There were in fact some distinguished rabbis among us, like Rabbi Yekutiel Yehuda Halberstam,[3] who later served as rabbi in the Föhrenwald camp. We gathered a few rabbis and held the first religious service in the open field. No one had a hat, no one had a cap, handkerchiefs (to cover your head) were rare. We tried to take something to cover our head; we put the jacket of the concentration camp uniform on or just put our hand on our head. A jeep came with a portable altar. On one side it was a Jewish altar, with the Tablets of the Law and the Ten Commandments; and on the other side, it was a Christian altar with the Cross. I had never seen such a thing, and the others hadn't either, naturally. We knew that a lot of our families had perished, so we first recited the *El male rakhamim* (a memorial prayer for the dead); many recited the *Kaddish*; others still hoped that their parents were alive. Among us Jews, if you hope that your parents are still alive, you're not supposed to recite the *Kaddish*. In any case, it was the most moving religious service I have ever experienced. I don't know anymore how many people were there; there must have been about fifteen hundred or maybe even two thousand.

Soon after this first encounter, all the American soldiers came. They were shocked when they saw us. They walked around and talked with us. When they noticed that someone spoke English, they immediately stood around him and gave everything they had on them: cigarettes, cookies, or a chocolate bar. Then they took us to Feldafing. In Feldafing, there had been a so-called Nazi national political school. Here the young leaders were trained; these were the party cadres. And in this Feldafing was our DP camp. It consisted to some extent of apartment buildings, also villas, where the party big shots had lived. Most of the inhabitants of the area had fled; those who remained were taken to a prison camp in their party uniform. I was in a bedroom, a medium-sized room with several cots. There were four of us in a room. On the floor below us were offices, which had quickly been set up.

The Americans gave us a camp commander, First Lieutenant Irving J. Smith. After about a week, we found out that he was also a Jew. There was nothing Jewish about him, I must say. How did we find out that Mr. Smith was a Jew? It was Friday evening, and we were holding a religious service out in the open. It was May, a warm night; the people sang "Lekha Dodi" ("Come my beloved," a song to greet the Sabbath). Smith was making his rounds, then he stood still and listened. I looked at him, he looked at me, and I said to him, "Why don't you admit that you are Jewish yourself?" He did admit it and said he didn't want to be guilty of favoritism.

One day, Smith asked all English-speakers to report to him. So we met with him, and he wanted to know what we could do to keep order in the camp so that everything would function smoothly. I made two suggestions, which he immediately accepted: first, to set up an index of the survivors so we would know how many there were and who was here; and second, to have democratic elections in the camp. Someone else suggested establishing a camp police force, and he accepted that immediately too.

As for the elections, I suggested that every regional group of refugees should elect one or two or three people they trusted to deal, so to speak, with the American officers. Otherwise some officious character—and they were everywhere—would try to play a role. My suggestion was accepted. There were the following regional groups: the biggest was the Hungarians (the Romanians counted themselves as Hungarians), then came the Poles, then the Lithuanians, then the Greeks, finally the Austrians, Germans, Czechs, Italians, French, Belgians, Dutch, and Luxemburgers as one common group. This last group agreed to choose me as their representative. All together, we were the biggest group, but each separate group was smaller than the others. There were maybe a dozen Belgians, two dozen Dutch, maybe thirty Germans, and the same number of Austrians—all together, there were about 250 persons in our group. Though it's very hard to reconstruct.

Soon after the Liberation, we published a book titled *She'erit ha-pleyta*, with all the names of the people who lived in Feldafing at that time. We published it after the Central Committee of Liberated Jews in the American Occupation Zone was established. The Central Committee originated in the Feldafing camp. The first meeting took place here, and the second one, the founding meeting was in the Landsberg camp. A Lithuanian Jew, Dr. Zalman Grinberg, a physician, was elected chairman. The second one was Dr. Samuel Gringauz, a judge from Memel, I think. The elections took place the Sunday after we came to Feldafing. That was arranged purely by the regional organizations, and there were no parties. We mainly wanted to keep the Americans from unwittingly sending some *Kapo* as their representative; that was why the elections were so urgent.

UNRRA took over our rations, the distribution of aid from America. There were packages, whole cars full of packages. The first food, I still remember precisely, consisted of hard rusks and hard chocolate, and you couldn't bite them—you scraped them with your teeth. That was good, because when people had the chance to "stuff themselves," they didn't stay alive. They weren't used either to fat or to rich food. So for us, who were on this strict diet, the overwhelming majority remained alive. Naturally, there were nevertheless a great many who were so weak that they did live to see the Liberation but couldn't survive anymore. Thus one of the first internal Jewish institutions was the *hevra kaddisha* (burial society).

There was a field hospital in what is now Hotel Elisabeth, which had been requisitioned by the Americans for that purpose. American military physicians and Red Cross physicians served in this hospital to begin with. But there were also German physicians because there weren't enough Americans to fill our demand for physicians, and they also called on all physicians among the liberated people. There were five or six doctors among us who had survived and could take care of other people. Everybody would have been willing.

In Staltach-Iffeldorf, not far from Feldafing, was a group of liberated Poles, with a few Jews among them. Camp Commander Smith allowed an exchange: the Jews came to Feldafing, and the few (non-Jewish) Poles or Russians among us went to Staltach-Iffeldorf. From this time on, Feldafing was a purely Jewish camp.

Meanwhile, we set up offices and requisitioned typewriters. We had some idea about German firms because they had used us as forced labor for a long time. We were familiar with German construction companies. They had offices where you could get what you needed. The army issued us a confiscation order, and we led the American soldiers to the places we knew about. This was how we got hold of about twenty typewriters. Naturally, we made the Germans give us what we needed. For example, we needed fresh milk for women and sick people. All this went through the military administration of the camp, but we gave them the ideas. We argued that, up to now, the Germans had fed us, even if they did it badly; so why shouldn't they keep on doing it now? It was very important for us to stop the indiscriminate distribution on the principle of "something for everyone." We told the Americans they were ruining the people, turning them into beggars. Instead, everyone who worked was to get a ration. Obviously, sick people would also get food; but those who didn't want to do anything, not even clean up their room, would get nothing, no chocolate bars, no cigarettes. And it worked right away. So we avoided making the concentration camp, where people threw paper or garbage away wherever they wanted, the standard of hygienic conditions in Feldafing. It can't go on like this, we told them.

On May 27, 1945, I got married in the DP camp. That was the first wedding there, a real event. A bunch of journalists were there; the

American newsreel filmed it. I had met my wife in the concentration camp. She was in the Hungarian transport that came to the Mühldorf concentration camp at that time. At the wedding, every single inmate got a bottle of wine because we had managed to find the hidden cellar of the Dallmayr Gourmet Store and confiscated everything in it. How did we get there? A lot of Germans are informers. One informs on the other: this one was a big Nazi who did this, that, and the other. So this German guy comes to us and says that here and there are the greatest delicacies you can imagine; they were supplied to the Führer's bunker in Berchtesgaden . . . This guy must have really hated Randlkofer, the owner of Dallmayr at that time. We listen and ask, is that so? "Yes, I'll show you." So we take a jeep and go. He shows us the entrance to the cellar. A full cellar with white wine, red wine, cognac, champagne, sardines, caviar, smoked salmon. I posted a guard and said, "Nobody touch anything." I returned and went immediately to the commander, no, first to Chaplain Braude, and said, "Listen, we have to get all that for our camp. We don't need to drink it all, but we can exchange it with the army for bread and other things that we do need urgently." Braude came with me and took along a sergeant. As a result, a few trucks with crews came and cleared out the whole cellar. The job took a day and a half.

The joke is that, soon after the currency reform [which replaced the Reichsmark with the Deutsche Mark], I got a bill from the Dallmayr Gourmet Store for 70,000 DM—I, as the responsible spokesman of the Feldafing camp. I was pretty upset, since I was already working professionally in those days and was making money. Fortunately, Max Braude was then in Heidelberg in the headquarters of the Seventh Army, which had moved from Bavaria to Baden. He laughed and said, "Don't worry, we'll take care of that." The JOINT had a legal adviser, who asked only, "When was it delivered?" "In 1945." "If it was delivered in 1945, the bill has to be in Reichsmarks and not DM." The 70,000 DM became only 7,000, and the JOINT immediately paid it.

How did I get out of Feldafing? One Sunday, a jeep comes to the camp with American officers. One of them asks where the office is, and comes in to me. He wants to see the list of survivors. I ask him why. "I'd like to see, maybe there's somebody from my family. We come from Vienna." "Oh," I say, "then we're from the same place." You have to imagine what we looked like then: I had no hair on my head, no eyeglasses (that is, I had two lenses that were temporarily tied together, since I am very nearsighted). Then he said to me, "You're from Vienna too. Where did you live? What did you do?" I say that I was an editor at the Karl Franz Bondy Publishers, on the *Telegraf*. He looks at me, goes to the window, opens it—two other officers are standing outside—and shouts, "Jules, Jules, come in." Jules, another lieutenant, comes into the office,

and the first one says to him in English (up to then, we had been convers-
ing in German), "This gentleman claims to have been an editor of the
Telegraf in Vienna. Do you know him?" He looks at me and shakes his
head, "No." I thought, "If he knows me, I should also know him." I say
to him, "Please take off your helmet." He obediently takes off his helmet,
and I say, "My God, Djussy Bondy!" The publisher's son. He looks at me
in amazement: "He knows me!" Djussy was his nickname in Vienna—in
America they called him Jules; his real name was Julius—the family had
come from Hungary. He was surprised to hear someone call him by his
nickname. We sat down in the armchairs the Nazis had left behind in
their hasty collapse, and tried to go over the years since 1938 at lightning
speed, he now an American officer, I a concentration camp survivor who
had just come back to life. We had a lot to tell each other. Lieutenant
Schreiber, who had first asked me for a list of survivors, had gone back to
the window. Outside in the jeep, there were two more officers who were
talking with a group of liberated prisoners. He shouted, "Hans, come in!
We have an old acquaintance here." Hans was an unmistakable personality, dapper, a real beau; he had had all the women in Vienna at his feet.
"Hans Békassy," I say and hold my hand out to him. As he gripped mine,
he corrected me. "It was once, my friend, but now it's Hans Habe."[4] This
name was originally his pseudonym; he first used it in 1936 for his novel
Drei über die Grenze. Habe was not a Jew but was of Jewish origin; so he
was searching for his relatives with us.

It was only when I met these people I had known before, because they were from the same city and traveled in the same circles or
practiced the same profession, that I felt as if I really came back to life. So
now I was once again with people I had something in common with.
Now I could think of the future, make plans. Hans Habe must have been
reading my mind when he said, "You have nothing more to lose in this
camp. We're starting a newspaper in Munich. That's where you belong.
We need people like you." He took out a card and wrote an address.
"Call on Max Kraus at Schellingstrasse 39. We'll hire you on the spot." So
I was hired under the news office of the U.S. military administration.

> *Ernest Landau, one of the founders of the Central Committee of
> Liberated Jews in the American Occupation Zone in 1945, was editor-
> in-chief of the German-Jewish newspaper,* Neue Welt *[New world]
> from 1948. He worked as an editor at Kindler Publishers and at the
> Bayerische Rundfunk [Bavarian Radio]. Landau was a veteran board
> member of the Munich Jewish community.*

2. JULIUS SPOKOJNY
ZIONIST ACTIVIST IN THE DP CAMP

Julius Spokojny was born in 1923 in Miechow (Poland), into
a distinguished religious Zionist family. After being imprisoned in
sixteen different concentration camps, he was liberated in April 1945
in Buchenwald.

I remember, soon after the Liberation, the Germans were terribly scared of us. Back then, the Americans took a lot of Germans from
Weimar and Erfurt to see the Buchenwald concentration camp. I thought
that now they would stay in the camp and we would go to their houses—
since the Germans had produced everything here and were responsible
for the war and the murder. Now our liberation has come—so how could
it be any different? I looked at every German and said to myself, Now I
get his house and he goes to my camp bed. But it turned out that they
were sent back home in the evening, as if it didn't matter what crime had
taken place, and we had to stay in the camp beds. And for years, we were
kept in locked camps.

Once, Eisenhower came to the camp. I showed him around,
even though, at twenty-two, I was one of the youngest ones there. He
told me that if I needed anything, I should tell the commander. I took
advantage of that and went with an American soldier to the English Zone
to bring my sister and my friends, who had also survived, to Buchenwald.
We stayed in Buchenwald until the Americans turned this area over to
the Russians. That was the exchange with West Berlin.[5] Then we left

Buchenwald immediately and went to Wildflecken in Lower Franconia. There we were locked in. We weren't allowed out of the camp because former inmates had gotten food from the villages. The Jewish Brigade even came to visit us, but they didn't let them in. The American administration really sealed off the camp.

Conditions in Wildflecken weren't much better than under the Nazis. Housing conditions were indescribable: ten to fifteen persons in a room. We had to ask for everything. If there was an apple tree on the camp grounds, we first had to ask if we could pick the apples—that was how freedom looked, after everything we had gone through. In fact, after the concentration camp, there was still a concentration camp, only without annihilation, without gas chambers, but the same closed camp. With armed guards.

When JOINT vice-president Schwartz came as an envoy, I was a member of a delegation to High Commissioner McCloy.[6] We complained about the situation in the Wildflecken DP camp, and the Wildflecken camp was liquidated and we were transferred to Landsberg. Back in Wildflecken, we once went to Nuremberg, where we sewed a piece of blue cloth on a white sheet for an Israeli flag. With this flag, we marched over Adolf-Hitler Square and sang "Hatikvah" (later the Israeli national anthem), a real demonstration—that was in late May 1945.

The Landsberg DP camp was where the army barracks are today. In Landsberg, several people lived in one room, no families, all single people. Things slowly started getting back to normal; the major indication of that was that people began getting married. Even after they were married, several couples lived in one barracks room: four families, separated by blankets in the middle of the room, army blankets. Those were our homes. Sanitary conditions were very bad. But Landsberg was an open camp; that is, you could always leave the camp.

In Landsberg, I founded the Zionist youth organization. At first it was a unified Zionist organization, not yet split into individual parties. The overwhelming majority of the camp was Zionist oriented, but there were also religious groups like Agudat Israel or socialist ones like the Bund (*Algemener Yidisher Arbeter Bund*, established in Vilna in 1897). Then, in about 1947, the Zionists split into individual groups. After this split, I was chairman of the National-Religious Party. At the time of the UN decision to partition Palestine, in November 1947, David Ben-Gurion came to visit the camp. He delivered a fiery speech to an audience of fifteen thousand. Then the right-wing Zionists—the opposition to Ben-Gurion—walked around with loudspeakers and, alluding to Solomon's judgment, said, Ben-Gurion is the false mother, he wants to divide the State of Israel. Ben-Gurion replied that the borders were not final, that they could be changed, and he referred to the Polish borders. I greeted

Ben-Gurion on behalf of the Zionist youth. That was my first official greeting speech; my knees were shaking. Then he took me aside and said, "In the future, you won't have stage fright anymore."

Landsberg was one of the biggest DP camps. It was also one of the most culturally active camps. Back in Wildflecken, we created the first theater, as well as a Jewish cultural group and, of course, a chapel. The people were starved for culture. Besides, they had no regular work. We began building a library and writing down our experiences. In Landsberg, not a day went by that there weren't several cultural events.

Relations with the Americans were generally good. Once, however, I remember, there was an incident in Landsberg. Two DPs had disappeared, and people in the camp accused the Germans of kidnapping them. The camp inmates demonstrated by burning two buses. It later turned out that there were other reasons for the disappearance of the two. In any case, the camp police surrounded the camp after this event. There was a lot of resistance. Women with newborn babies sat down on the streets and didn't let the Americans pass. Some fifteen young people who protested were arrested and spent about half a year in jail.

Contacts with the Germans were very rare. Jews and Germans did not live together but maintained a tense relation. The Landsbergers were scared because there were more inhabitants in the DP camp than in the whole city. Some liberated people preferred to live in the city itself, outside the DP camp. But there were only a few of them, because, first, the Germans didn't want to rent apartments to us, and also because there was no money around to rent apartments. You had to live on the food that was distributed and you traded it. That was the only way you could save a little money.

Life in camp was regarded, mainly, as preparation for emigration. How was it for me, personally, to live in Germany? At first I couldn't leave because I was busy taking care of sick people and leading the Zionist youth. But I didn't think I would stay for long. My mother went to Israel; then my sister followed, along with my brother-in-law, whom she had married in the meantime. I had set two goals for myself: to help the sick, especially those who had come from the other side of the Iron Curtain; and I also wanted to help those who were trying to build their lives in Germany. Meanwhile, I also started my family here.

I was one of the founders in the Landsberg camp and remained until the liquidation of the camp, from the first to the last hour. When the camp was dissolved, we protested to the American military authorities. All remaining inmates were to go to the last DP camp in Föhrenwald, which most did. From Föhrenwald I went to Augsburg.

In Augsburg at that time, there was one community of German Jews and one of East European Jews. Most of the East European Jews soon emigrated, but the German Jews didn't want to accept those who remained as equal members. At that time, there were about 150 German Jews and 350 East European Jews. The community of Augsburg included the whole Bavarian district of Swabia. To attain full rights, you had to be born as a German citizen. When I protested that rule at a members' assembly, I was immediately thrown out of the hall. So I filed a complaint with the administrative court. The court suggested we reach a compromise. Finally, the two sides united. A German Jew, Ludwig Müller, became the first chairman of the community; I became the second. Ever since, there have been equal rights for all members.

Julius Skopojny was chairman of the Augsburg Jewish community from 1963 until his death in 1996. The textile manufacturer represented the Jewish community in the Bavarian Senate, and was vice president of the State Association of Jewish Communities in Bavaria and a board member of the Central Committee of the Jews in Germany.

3. ARNO LUSTIGER
KEEPING THE MEMORY ALIVE

Arno Lustiger was born in 1924 in Bendzin (Poland). He was imprisoned in various concentration camps and went on the death march from Auschwitz to Gross-Rosen, ultimately ending up in the Buchenwald concentration camp. In late March 1945, he escaped a death march from Buchenwald and fled to the Harz Mountains.

We were sent on a march from Langenstein, an outside camp of Buchenwald, some four thousand people. For most of them—some thirty-five hundred—it was to be their death march. Anybody who couldn't march or who fell down for any reason was killed immediately. I escaped from this march. The whole time, we didn't get any food, and that was the real reason I decided to escape. To put it brutally, when I escaped, I was maybe one day away from my death. I already knew what I could expect if the *Volkssturm* people brought me back to the camp.[7] You were shot for attempting to escape. I didn't escape alone, but in a group of eight people. We escaped at night and moved only at night so we wouldn't be seen. Nevertheless, I was nabbed, but on the way back to camp, where I would have been shot, I escaped again—that was in the Harz Mountains.

After escaping from the death march, and after many adventures, I reached the American army. That was my liberation, in early April 1945. I was fortunate to receive good care in an American field hospital, so that I gained weight in a relatively short time. Then I stayed for a while as a translator with the army; that was still in the area of what became East Germany. Then I retreated with the American army to what became West Germany. When I recovered a little, I went looking for members of my family. In every city, every town in Germany where there were Jews, a so-called ad hoc Jewish Committee was formed, organizations of non-German Jews. In the summer and fall of 1945, the German Jews quickly joined together in Jewish communities.

One of the major functions of these committees was to prepare search lists. In fact, everybody was on the road, looking for family. In every committee, there were lists on carbon paper, and many copies of these lists of the Jews in a city were made. When anybody went to another city, he took these lists along and showed them. You needed a lot of time to go through these lists because you hoped to find members of your family. Transportation wasn't yet functioning, railroad lines were destroyed; you had to get around by hitchhiking, and that was risky. And there weren't any identification papers either. In my opinion, it was a disgrace that the few concentration camp survivors actually had to sneak across borders illegally to look for members of their family. Like thieves in the night! And the borders of the occupation zones were real borders, guarded by military police.

Naturally, a lot of people looked for their family in their hometown, where they had grown up. But in most cases nobody was there. I found the surviving members of my family in a village in Lower Silesia, where they had been in a concentration camp. I decided not to stay in Poland or any place under Soviet control. In the concentration camps, I had talked with a lot of Soviet prisoners and had learned about the real nature of the regime there. I didn't want to spend my life there. So I took my surviving family members—my mother and three sisters survived; my father and my brother perished—I took them illegally over many borders. I had to do that in two stages, because five of us couldn't have made such a big trip. The group would have been too big for such a "smuggling tour."

In September 1945, I came to Frankfurt am Main. I hadn't been in Frankfurt before; it was pure chance, pure chance. I had heard that a DP camp, the Zeilsheim camp, had been founded here for Jews and former concentration camp inmates. So I registered here and set out again for Poland to pick up the rest of my family. This operation took several months. So that was the autumn of 1945.

The Zeilsheim camp had about four thousand inhabitants. At first they wanted to lodge all DPs—Jewish and non-Jewish—together. It unleashed a storm of rage among the Jewish DPs. That was justified because most non-Jewish DPs came from Eastern Europe where they had often collaborated with the Nazis. So former Ukrainian or Lithuanian or Latvian SS helpers took off their Nazi uniforms and pretended to be persecuted DPs. In the camp, we were supposed to sleep under the same roof with these murderers—sometimes they were even worse than the Germans. That wasn't possible. Therefore, a directive was immediately issued that Jewish DPs had to be taken to special camps.

The Zeilsheim camp wasn't really typical of the other DP camps. In Bavaria, former barracks or even former concentration camps were used as camps. In Zeilsheim, the situation was different. It was an industrial suburb, where thousands of workers of the chemical plant IG Farben had lived; later it was the Hoechst Factory. The poor workers were ordered out of their homes within a very short time and had to leave their furniture. So at least we had homes, not barracks. Nevertheless, we lived in horribly cramped conditions.

Initially, everything was cooked in a central kitchen in the camp, because nothing was available, no dishes, no cutlery, etc. Little by little, the food was handed out, and everybody could make their own meals in their own little kitchen. We got our supplies from UNRRA, and more rations came from the American Jewish aid organizations. Field workers of the JOINT were also in many camps and helped with the administration and distribution of aid. Later, an almost self-sufficient life developed, an autonomous society with elementary schools, a high school, vocational schools, religious institutions, political parties, youth organizations, sport clubs, and newspapers.

In Zeilsheim there was the Yiddish newspaper *Untervegs*, which was the paper for all the Jewish DPs in Hesse. For a time I was also a member of the editorial staff. The paper was edited in Zeilsheim and printed in Hoechst. In early 1946, there wasn't enough Hebrew type, so only the first and last pages were set in Hebrew letters; the rest were in Latin letters transliterated phonetically according to the rules of Polish grammar and spelling. We got the Hebrew letters from America. The JOINT got them for us.

We had outstanding journalists. The editor-in-chief was a former professional journalist from Vilna. The amazing thing was that all these people worked without any facilities, no reference library. I was the youngest one on the editorial staff, without any journalistic experience; the others were all experienced journalists. We were connected with the Jewish Telegraph Agency and other news organizations. Our newspaper was very informative—we reported all world events, as well as what was going on in our DP camp and in other DP camps.

A very important institution was the *Zentrale Historische Kommission* [Central Historical Committee], which collected thousands of documents, photos, and songs from the concentration camps, and published its own journal, *Fun letztn khurbn* [From the last destruction], which was printed in Munich. The material from Germany in fact formed the cornerstone of the collections of Yad Vashem. They got the American military government to instruct all mayors and magistrates not to destroy any material relating to the persecution of the Jews. Then the staff of the local historical committees recorded thousands of witness accounts, some of which were printed in *Fun letztn khurbn*. There was a special section of the collection with statements from children. There was also instruction for those interviewing children so the children wouldn't be emotionally damaged.

We were deeply moved by the performances of Jewish actors from America. That was the first living message from there. I can remember these performances very very well. They were very good for our morale because we saw that we had not been completely forgotten. The feeling of being deserted, that was there. For a long time there was absolutely no medical care, and maintenance was bad too. The first artist who came, back in the summer of 1945, was Yehudi Menuhin. He gave a concert in Bergen-Belsen that I helped organize, since I was helping out a little in the administration of Bergen-Belsen in those days. Menuhin proved to be a glorious exception in those days. We saw nothing, nothing of all the others!

Another point was our clothing. I escaped from the concentration camp in the striped suit. If we hadn't been able to filch something, we might have gotten nothing all year, and we would have had to walk around in our prisoners' uniforms. Then there was used clothing from the JOINT. So this was what the big Jewish world had left for us: used clothing. There really weren't so many of us: unlike the six million killed, a few surviving concentration camp inmates were infinitely small.

The American military government had a special DP department in Frankfurt headed by an American general, at the headquarters of the American army in Europe. They thought the DPs shouldn't loaf around without work but should participate in the construction of the German economy. That was an abstruse idea that we should help the Germans build their economy, when they themselves had destroyed it with their own guilt and their own crimes. They had to drop that idea immediately. It didn't work.

Germany, DP camp—for us, that was in fact a temporary shelter. Nobody would even have dreamed of staying here, not a single person, not one. The routes to Palestine were blocked, so you couldn't leave and you had to stay. I couldn't go to Palestine illegally. My mother and my sister were very sick and my leaving them was out of the question. So my bad conscience made me actively support the *berihah*—the illegal immigration to Palestine.

We passed the time by studying. There were vocational schools and language schools and similar institutions. And the DP camps were also centers of black marketeering. For one thing, they were extraterritorial institutions, not under the jurisdiction of the German police. The American military police were solely in charge here. Furthermore, you have to know that we got necessary foodstuffs for the survivors, but nothing else. Everything else you needed, from combs to shoes, you had to get by trading. The black market developed out of trading. I don't think a moral judgment is appropriate in this matter. The Jews had nothing to trade, while the Germans could at least trade their property.

In Frankfurt itself, there were also Jewish DPs who didn't live in the camp but had somehow gotten a place in the city. They were organized in the Jewish Committee on Sandweg. Its first task was to search for survivors; second was the distribution of JOINT shipments. These auxiliary rations really allowed people to survive, since that was the only way you could trade something. In 1945, the Westend Synagogue was only temporarily furnished;[8] we went to the synagogue on Baumweg—where the community offices were—for prayer, together with the German Jews. In general, there was only sporadic contact at first with the German Jews and the communities they founded. Then, in 1948, there was a fusion between the Jewish Committee and the Jewish community. Some of the foreign Jews then assumed positions on the board of the unified community.

The Zeilsheim camp was disbanded in 1948. About eighty people were left. There was then a quarrel because the Frankfurt municipal administration refused to accept these people, who couldn't or wouldn't emigrate for some reason. In those days, there was very little housing in the city, and those who wanted to move to the city had to have a residence permit. But that they acted so restrictively against the few Jewish DPs in a city where there had once been thirty thousand Jews! The adviser for Jewish affairs in the headquarters of the U.S. army, a Jewish officer, in my opinion didn't behave very well either, since he gave his word that these Jewish survivors wouldn't stay in Frankfurt. Where should they have stayed? Should they have dissolved into thin air? I had to use all sorts of tricks in the housing office, where I had a friend, a German who was persecuted by the Nazis and had also been in the concentration camp. The few of us who remained alive had to arrange everything through the back door; officially it wouldn't have worked.

The lord mayor of Frankfurt, Walter Kolb, made a big speech on Radio Frankfurt on New Year's 1947, calling on the Frankfurt Jews to return to their hometown. As a result, there was a flood of letters to the editor of the *Frankfurter Rundschau*, from Frankfurt Jews who had come back telling of the bad experiences they had had after they returned— with the authorities and with their fellow citizens.

> *After the war, Arno Lustiger remained as a textile manufacturer in Frankfurt am Main, where, for years, he has been a member of the council and the board of the Jewish community. He was also chairman of the Zionist Organization of Germany. After his initial cooperation with the Historical Committee of the DP camp, he worked decades later as a historian and published works about the Jews in the Spanish Civil War, as well as about Jewish resistance in the Third Reich. He is the editor of Vassily Grossman and Ilya Ehrenburg's* Black Book: The Genocide of Soviet Jews.

4. NORBERT WOLLHEIM

JEWISH AUTONOMY IN THE BRITISH ZONE

Norbert Wollheim was born in Berlin in 1913 and grew up there. Both grandfathers served in the Prussian army, and his father, who came from a traditional religious family in Posen, was also a frontline soldier and received several medals. Norbert Wollheim studied law and economics, and after 1938 he helped organize the Jewish community children's transports to England. Until 1941 he was responsible for the vocational training schools of the Reich Association of Jews in Germany. On March 12, 1943, he was deported to Auschwitz with his wife and child, and was the only one of them to survive the death camp. When Auschwitz was evacuated on January 18, 1945, he was part of a so-called death march that led him through Gleiwitz and Mauthausen to Sachsenhausen.

We stayed in Sachsenhausen until April 1945. When the Allies approached, we were driven out of the concentration camp again and went north. On the night of May 2, I ran away from our murderers along with three or four friends. I reached a unit of the Eighth Division of the American army and spent my first day after the Liberation near the city of Schwerin.

I was lucky to meet someone from American reconnaissance who was a friend of a friend in New York. He helped me get out of Schwerin in late May, because this area didn't stay under American control; and I went to Lübeck. Originally, I wanted to go back to Berlin, but I was afraid of losing contact with the West if I set out for the Russian Zone. It was more or less accidental that I went to Lübeck; one reason was that Lübeck was one of the cities that wasn't so destroyed. When I arrived, there was a group of about eight hundred Jewish DPs in Lübeck. I immediately took up again what I had done before I was deported: I became active in Jewish community life. Our first task was to bury the dead in the old Jewish cemetery. We buried them in a special section of the cemetery; I think there were sixty to a hundred who had died soon after the Liberation.

At the same time, we tried to make contact with the outside world, which wasn't easy given the catastrophic state of communications. Our question was: where can we get help? The British army wasn't prepared for this situation, and the German administration had totally collapsed. To produce some contact with the outside world, we got hold of a radio; and on this radio, we heard that there was a group of Jews in Belsen. We had never heard the name Belsen. Neither in Auschwitz nor in Sachsenhausen had I ever heard of Bergen-Belsen. Now all of a sudden we find out that Bergen-Belsen was a big concentration camp with thousands of Jews. Every day, there was a report on their deplorable condition, and on the aid of the British army that was organized by Jewish chaplains. After I heard about that, I decided to get to Belsen somehow; it was about a three-hour drive from Lübeck. But that was easier said than done.

I undertook the first trip to Belsen, I believe, in June, with the help of the International Red Cross, which had an agency in Lübeck. In other words, I sneaked in with a truck transporting aid packages the Allied soldiers didn't need anymore, from Lübeck to Belsen. When I arrived, the original camp had been burned down and the survivors were housed in barracks in nearby Hohne. There for the first time, I met Yossele Rosensaft, who was then chairman of the ad hoc camp committee. That was the beginning of a long cooperation and friendship. I told him I had come seeking help for Jews stranded in Lübeck without any assistance, and had no one to turn to. Rosensaft said immediately, "We're in exactly the same situation." Almost 90 percent of the Belsen camp was a hospital at this time, but people were still dying in the camp every day.

That was my first impression in Belsen. Then Rosensaft told me that an ad hoc committee already existed and a meeting was to take place the following week with representatives of the aid organizations. "Try to come back next week." Meanwhile, as I was preparing to return to Belsen—that is, trying to get hold of a car, etc.—I came upon a delegation of representatives of the JOINT and its English counterpart, in Lübeck. They helped me get back to Belsen for this meeting, where we began building a clearly structured organization. At this time, UNRRA was completely overwhelmed by the enormous demands, and we saw that we had to establish an organization by ourselves.

We were convinced that we had to find a democratic basis for our operations and worked to organize a conference of survivors from the entire British Zone. We established the Central Committee of Liberated Jews in the British Occupation Zone. We had our problems with the organization of this conference. Rosensaft took the position that he was now liberated and not subject to any restrictions of the British authorities; the British, on the other hand, were somewhat annoyed, since he hadn't asked them for permission.

The fact that the trial of the criminals of Bergen-Belsen was taking place in Lüneburg at the same time helped us, since there were a lot of journalists from all over the world in that nearby town. We also told our story to the journalists, who publicized our fate abroad—especially in England. Another factor that contributed immeasurably to our morale was the visit of a delegation of the Jewish Brigade in the camp, a special event for the survivors. On this occasion, there was also a captain who served as official reporter for the British commander-in-chief, Bernard L. Montgomery. The captain was Chaim Herzog, who later became president of the State of Israel.

In the election for the Central Committee, Rosensaft was elected chairman and I was elected vice-chairman. We also passed resolutions. There were several hundred delegates not only from Belsen but from the entire British Occupation Zone. One delegation came from Neustadt on the Baltic Sea, where there was a DP camp, others from Lübeck, the Rhineland, etc. Our origin—German Jews or East European Jews—played no role, not even in my election; we were all Jews and considered ourselves only as Jews. In the American Occupation Zone, the situation was completely different. There were certain conflicts there that we didn't have. The only case in the British Zone where German Jews and

DPs established separate organizations was Hanover, where both a Jew-ish community and a Jewish committee emerged.

In the American Zone, there was no attempt to achieve coopera-tion. I think that the atmosphere in the British Zone was different. Natu-rally, we also had our differences, but we discussed everything; this was especially the case after the Bad Harzburg conference in 1946, when we created the central committee for the entire British Zone, where DPs, and the German-Jewish communities were represented. It was obviously not easy to bring all these under one roof, and it took us several hours of discussion to reach that point. But what prevailed was the will to act together. Another difference between us and the American Zone was that we had more tensions with the occupation authorities, since the British were acting against our interests in Palestine. I need only mention the *Exodus* affair. So we needed a very special unanimity in our own ranks, and I must say that it worked splendidly.

A few times we tried to make contact with the central committee in the American Zone, but it never worked out. As many as 250,000 DPs were living temporarily in the American Zone, while only 15,000 were in our zone. This gave the central committee in the American Zone a great superiority even politically, which we didn't accept. I regret to say that we worked side by side with one another instead of with one another, a situation that may also have had to do with various personal problems. The chairman of the central committee in the American Zone, Dr. Grin-berg, was a very intelligent man, a physician, who had studied in Ger-many, but cooperation was hardly possible. Rosensaft, his wife, and I once visited Dr. Grinberg in St. Ottilien, where he ran the Jewish hospi-tal, and discussed a possible cooperation; but there was no spark that could have been ignited.

The British soldiers were excellent soldiers, but they weren't so-cial workers. They were absolutely unprepared for the tasks that arose after the liberation of the concentration camps. In this respect they should have been prepared for the most urgent necessities. In Belsen, for example, this caused enormous problems; Colonel Jones, who was in charge of the camp—I think he had previously been active in the secret service in Palestine—was a typical product of the British nobility. People of this class regarded the DPs as scum; they didn't understand that among these people who had just been liberated from the concentration camp, there were also physicians and lawyers and professors, and such. This created real problems, aggravated by the fact that few of our people spoke English. I myself still knew my schoolbook English, which was just adequate for communication.

Once a Jewish Labour Party member of Parliament from En-gland, Sidney Silverman, came to visit the camp and demanded to speak with Colonel Jones. Admittedly, he looked pretty sloppy, and from his external appearance you couldn't tell that he was a member of Parliament. Colonel Jones treated him quite arrogantly and Silverman noted how the camp was run. "I am indeed not strong enough to change Bevins's policy toward Palestine, but I can get you out of here," said Silverman. And in fact it wasn't long before Jones was removed. Belsen was then commanded by an outstanding man, Colonel Murphy, who had a profound understanding of our situation. Our relation to the British administration thus improved considerably; and naturally it was also because we slowly came to understand how to deal with each other. For instance, I learned that in negotiations with the English you had to talk a lot about "cooperation"—they liked that very much. I used this word as often as possible. We had serious problems at the time of the *Exodus* affair, that's clear. Our notions of the future of Palestine were naturally different.

Nevertheless, I was glad to be active in the British Zone and not in the American Zone; for, whatever their political opinion or their conviction was, fairness was one of their great virtues. You could rely on that. With all due respect to my current American fellow citizens: The British administered Belsen better than the Americans could have. In this respect, the Americans were even less prepared and trained than the English.

In Lübeck, the situation was completely different from that in Belsen. First we had to separate the Jewish DPs from the non-Jewish ones. Many of them could be housed in the intact former community center; others lived in former barracks, thus in a DP camp. In the former community headquarters, we set up a kind of kibbutz. We had the support of the British authorities for that, even though they couldn't understand what we were up to. For them, Judaism was a religion and not a nationality. I stayed in Lübeck and often traveled back and forth between Belsen and Lübeck.

I never thought of staying in Germany to live. I had lost my first wife and child in Auschwitz. I had the good fortune to meet my second wife in Belsen, where she was also liberated, and we got married there too. None of us wanted to stay in Germany. I left Germany when I thought the work was done. This didn't mean only the dissolution of the camp but also the clarification of important questions concerning reparations and the restoration of Jewish life.

In 1951, Norbert Wollheim immigrated to the United States and has been living in New York. He has been a spokesman for former concentration camp inmates, and in the 1950s he publicly led to a successful conclusion the tensely awaited test case against IG Farben for individual reparations payments.

Berlin

(Bildarchiv Abraham Pisarek, Berlin)

5. HEINZ GALINSKI
NEW BEGINNING OF JEWISH LIFE IN BERLIN

Heinz Galinski, born in 1912 in West Prussian Marienburg, lived in Berlin after his training as a textile salesman. His father was disabled in World War I and died shortly after being imprisoned by the Nazis. His mother and his first wife were murdered in concentration camps. Bearing the tattooed inmate number 104412, Galinski survived Auschwitz and reached Berlin after his liberation.

From Auschwitz, I came to the Dora camp, and then from Dora to Bergen-Belsen. On April 15, I was liberated in Bergen-Belsen and set out for Berlin; that was very risky, because at that time the demarcation line had just been shifted, and I got caught up in that whole whirlwind. Even though I had a document, they wouldn't believe that I had been released from Bergen-Belsen, and that I was a Jew; so my trip to Berlin was very risky. I arrived in Berlin in July. There was not yet a community here in any sense of the word. I and a few others restored this community. It consisted only of rubble. So we started building district offices by sectors to complete the Jewish work in the individual sectors.

In the concentration camp, I had resolved to devote my life to serving the community. That was naturally an illusion, but it gave me courage to get through the difficulties. Then when I saw all that had happened, the misery of the few survivors, I considered it my duty. So I stayed here, even though it really wasn't predictable. I got married in 1947, and we had already sworn to emigrate, but our daughter was born prematurely and our move to the United States fell through.

I have always represented the point of view that the Wannsee Conference [at which the extermination of the Jews was planned] cannot be the last word in the life of the Jewish community in Germany. Therefore, I participated with a few others to restore the Jewish community in Berlin. I have never been one of those who considered the community here as a liquidation community, but rather I have endeavored to give back to the survivors the belief in a restored, new life. So first we started acting morally and socially here. That was the first concern, and then we started building the institutions to restore Jewish life here.

Perspectives developed only in the course of time. In the beginning, it was practical things, making the synagogues functional again: the synagogues in Pestalozzistrasse, Joachimsthaler Strasse, Fränkelufer, the structure of the community, the first election of the assembly of representatives, the old people's home on Iranische Strasse. The Jewish Hospital simply could not be maintained anymore, so we had to give that up.

Until 1953, we were one unified community in the Western and Eastern parts of the city; I was a member of the board of the Association of the Victims of the Nazi Regime (VVN). But the situation became increasingly intolerable. We were observed in every meeting, and a Jewish life, as I had imagined it, simply could not be carried out anymore under the authority of the East German Party of Socialist Unity (SED). So, at that time, I prepared everything to direct a real Jewish community on Joachimsthaler Strasse (the seat of the West Berlin Jewish community), which was no longer possible on Oranienburger Strasse (seat of the East Berlin Jewish community). Thus Jewish life was again possible without interruption.

Jews in the various zones came together in the *Arbeitsgemeinschaft Jüdischer Gemeinden* [Association of Jewish Communities] in Germany. After staff members of the association, like Norbert Wollheim, emigrated, I was really one of the original spirits behind the founding of the Central Council. We had enormous difficulties because the Jewish world wouldn't understand that Jews were staying here, and even less that they were also rebuilding communities; this discussion will never really cease, even if it has abated somewhat today. In the early days, we were relatively cut off here. We weren't invited to meetings of international Jewish organiza-

tions, but we did prevail. I don't think there is any other Jewish community
after the Shoah that has been so politically active and has fought so actively
against forgetting and repressing as the Jews in Germany.

> *After the war, Galinski devoted himself to caring for Nazi victims. He
> was deputy director of the "Main Department of the Nuremberg
> Trials" in the Berlin City Council. He was a founding member of the
> board of the Central Council of Jews in Germany, and after Werner
> Nachmann died, he became its chairman in 1987. From 1949 until his
> own death in 1992, Galinski was chairman of the Jewish community
> in Berlin, served on the boards of several international Jewish
> organizations, and received many national and international awards.*

6. ESTRONGO NACHAMA
THE SINGER OF AUSCHWITZ

*Estrongo Nachama was born in 1918 in Salonika. In 1943, he was
deported to Auschwitz. He was the only one of his large family to
survive the war.*

In 1943, I was deported from Greece to Auschwitz. After three
weeks in quarantine, I went to Goleschow, where I worked in a quarry.
In early 1945, we were taken to Oranienburg, to the Sachsenhausen
camp—on foot, naturally. By then there was no longer any real food in

Oranienburg. We survived because there were dogs in the camp who were still fed, naturally, by the SS. At nine in the morning and at two in the afternoon, the dogs got their dog biscuits. There was no guard for the dogs—the dogs themselves were the guard. A friend and I got through to the dogs and succeeded in taking their dog food away from them. One of us diverted the dogs and the other went quickly to the dog food. It was very dangerous because, doing this, we came right up to the dogs. In any case, we could feed three or four people like that. We wouldn't have survived on the watery soup and the little bit of bread. That's how we stayed alive during the last months of the war.

In early April, all of a sudden, there was a big racket, shots, and sirens: "Roll call! Get up!" We saw that something was wrong. The Russians were coming! We were quickly evacuated toward Hamburg. We were in one of the "death marches" from Berlin through Nauen and Neuruppin. Twelve thousand five hundred prisoners left Sachsenhausen at the Liberation; maybe two thousand of them remained alive. One evening, on May 3, 1945, we suddenly see air battles above us. Shots, shouts, a whole mess—and in addition, it started raining. We were a group of three Greeks. We lay down under a tree, protected from the rain with blankets, and fell asleep. At four the next morning, we wake up and see that nobody's there anymore; the whole camp has disappeared. What do we do now?

In the distance, we saw a little light and went toward it. All of a sudden, we hear behind us, "Heil Hitler!" There were soldiers who saw us in our inmate clothes. They smashed their weapons and threw them away. We stood there terrified. They just shouted, "Out, out, out, out!" So we ran farther away to the fields, wet up to our knees, toward the light. When we come to a road, we see a figure who called to us, "Halt!" Again we were scared. "Back!" shouted the figure, and we went back to the road. Then the farmer came holding a light: "Here, come here! You want to sleep?!" He gave us a place in his shed; we climbed up a ladder, a very steep, narrow ladder. That was near Kyritz. We stayed with the farmer for fourteen days, until the war was over. Then we marched on foot through Nauen to Berlin.

In Berlin, we came to the Lichtenberg railroad station. We stood there not knowing anybody. We stood at the railroad station until the station manager closed the station. He asked if we didn't want to go home. We answered that we didn't have a home to go to. When we registered with the police, we were given a flat. That is, I was given a flat, the other two Greeks went somewhere else; I lost them and never saw them again. Soon afterward, I contracted a bad case of typhus and had to be taken to the hospital. Until February 1946, I stayed in Lichtenberg, in the hospital. Then I went back to the police, with my suitcase in my hand,

and asked, "Where shall I sleep tonight?" They gave me another room. In those days, I was still wearing my blue and white inmate suit. On the way, I met a woman who took me into her flat and gave me linen, shoes, and everything.

One day, I was at the weekly market in Lichtenberg—it was more a kind of black market—when I see a man with a Star of David. In the hospital, I had learned a few words of German, so I called to him, "Hey, you, I'm also a Jew, shalom, shalom!" He wrote down the address of the Jewish community for me; in those days it was still on Oranienburger Strasse. The next day, I took the subway, which was altogether broken down. You had to go two stations and then walk. So I went to Alexanderplatz and walked the rest of the way. At the community, I immediately met a friend from the camp. He just said, "Are you the singer from Auschwitz?" "Yes," I answered, and asked him, "Where is the synagogue?" I was soon introduced to the head of the community, and he was told, "A Greek with a marvelous voice." The head of the East Berlin community in those days was Julius Meyer, who asked me, "Did you get JOINT packages?" "No," I said. "I have no idea of what they are. What am I supposed to get?" We immediately drove in his car to where the JOINT packages were distributed. God almighty—seven months of packages I got retroactively! From summer 1945 to February 1946. I said, "I live in Lichtenberg, how am I supposed to take the packages there: two rides and three walks!" Then I got a big carton and a backpack and set off on the way every day for a whole week. My house was like a black market. Since I didn't smoke, I could trade the cigarettes for other things. That was like money.

In those days, the synagogue was on Rykestrasse, and there you were always invited on Saturday and Sunday. Once, after the meal, a young man says to me, "Nachama, I have an engagement party in Schönhauser Allee, you have to come." Fine, I go there. All of a sudden, the bridegroom says I should sing a song. So I sing a Hebrew song; then he asks for a religious song. So I sing "Ve'shomru" (Sabbath prayer). Mr. Rotholz, a member of the synagogue board, from the West Berlin organization, from Pestalozzistrasse, was invited to that party too. He came to me: "What are you making here?" "A good impression," I answered him. "In other words, nothing. I'm looking for work." "You don't have to look anymore," he said. "You're getting everything from us. But you have to come to our synagogue." I didn't even know there was another synagogue in Berlin. I asked him where it was. The next Friday, I came to Pestalozzistrasse and was introduced to everyone. The head cantor, Leo Gollanin, who had been the cantor on Oranienburger Strasse before the war, was an old man by then. One week later, he let me sing the lead at the service. So I sang a solo. The organist, Zeppke, had already been there before the war. After the service, Gollanin came to me and asked, "Herr Nachama, I am old. Don't you want to take my place and help build the community?" I replied, "Cantor, I can sing *hazanut* [Jewish liturgical chants], I was trained to do that in Greece, but I would like to go back to Greece." Every week he tried to persuade me: "Help us, please." So I studied with Gollanin for half a year. Then he died.

Every time it took two hours to come from Lichtenberg to Pestalozzistrasse. And to do that every day: walk—ride—walk. But the community soon got me a piano, so I could practice at home a little. On Shavuot 1947, I came for rehearsal to Pestalozzistrasse. Many members of the East Berlin congregation came; the pious ones even came on foot. At the end, there was a big *Kiddush,* and head cantor Gollanin said, "Keep your eye on the boy—he's got a future!" My beginning was July 2, 1947. In October 1948, I was invited by the radio station RIAS to prepare a twenty-minute Sabbath service for the radio, and I still do it today, with a choir.

I never thought I would stay so long in Berlin. At first it was only for a short time. In 1951 I got a letter: none of my family remained alive. My parents and my two sisters were killed. I came to my singing teacher with the letter and said, "Maestro, I'll remain a cantor!" He looked at me and answered, "What is that? You could be an opera singer. Just because of the letter?" Even as an opera singer, I could say *Kaddish* [the prayer in memory of the dead] for my parents. Two weeks later, I went to rehearsal at the State Opera. But I preferred to remain a cantor, and I have never regretted that decision. In Greece, no one from my family remained alive. Out of eighty thousand Jews, a few hundred are left.

The community in Berlin was still strong in those days. There were two rabbis: Schwarzschild for the Liberals,[9] and Munk for the Orthodox[10]—and there was also a Polish rabbi whose name I don't remember. Community life was more active than later. When everybody's got money, they keep to themselves; in those days there was a real community. The old people have all died in the meantime. I've buried them all. In the East and in the West. After the community split in 1953, we could no longer bury our dead in Weissensee [the largest Jewish cemetery, located in the East]. The community in the West then acquired its own plot of land for a cemetery.

Soon, religious services on Pestalozzistrasse were very well attended. When I began in 1947, there were hardly any people there. Maybe fifteen came. They told me, "Mr. Nachama, the people don't come. They don't believe in God anymore." I answered, "Give me their addresses and I will visit the people." Then, every week, I visited ten to

fifteen families. It went like this: "Please come, I'm the cantor here now."
"No, no," was the answer at first. After their families were killed, a lot of
people lost their faith in God. "But, I'm asking you, come." And I did it.
At first two came, then four, then ten, then twenty. One Friday evening,
we suddenly had four hundred people at the service. I was glad that so
many people came, but we didn't have enough space in the small room,
which was big enough for only two hundred persons. We asked to hold
the service in the big synagogue, and it was inaugurated in 1947. But
there wasn't enough wood to heat it. I said, "So we have to get some
wood." "Fine, Nachama, you get wood or coal." I went to the district
mayor, with the little bit of German I had learned in the meantime, and
explained to him, "Mr. Mayor—synagogue small—two hundred seats—
four hundred people come—big synagogue cold—not wood, not coal."
He said, "Mr. Nachama, we don't have any either." I answered insolently
about the heating in his room, "Heating warm!" Back and forth like that:
"Good, Mr. Nachama, I'll give you ten crates of wood every week."
"Thank you very much, I'll come get it." Three times a week, I came
with a wheelbarrow to get the wood from the Schöneberg town hall, and
we heated [the synagogue] every time. The people were happy. Later,
coal was distributed to us. The Pestalozzistrasse was always well attended, better than the (Orthodox) synagogue on Joachimsthaler Strasse.
Many of the Polish Jews also came to Pestalozzistrasse.

> For almost five decades, Estrongo Nachama has accompanied the
> members of the Jewish community of Berlin—first as cantor and then
> as head cantor—in all their religious ceremonies: from the Brit Mila,
> the circumcision, through Bar Mitzvah and wedding, to the prayer for
> the dead at the grave. On Friday evening, his voice rings out in the
> Liberal synagogue on Pestalozzistrasse, as well as in various German
> radio broadcasts. Nachama, who has appeared in several film and
> television roles (including the film Cabaret), has a worldwide
> reputation as one of the best Jewish cantors.

7. NATHAN PETER LEVINSON
THE FUNCTIONS OF A RABBI IN POSTWAR GERMANY

Rabbi Nathan Peter Levinson was born in Berlin in 1921. He grew up in the religious-liberal tradition of German Jewry and, after graduating high school in 1940, began training for the rabbinate at the Hochschule für die Wissenschaft des Judentums [Liberal rabbinical seminary in Berlin] under Leo Baeck. In March 1941, he immigrated to the United States with his parents, going through Russia and Japan, concluded his studies at Hebrew Union College (the Reform rabbinical seminary) in Cincinnati, and accepted a position as rabbi in Selma, Alabama, in 1948.

In 1940, when I started studying at the rabbinical seminary, I really didn't want to emigrate. I was nineteen years old, and even though all the horror was going on around us, we at the seminary were on a kind of island. If you can attend lectures by personalities like Rabbi Leo Baeck or the historian Eugen Täubler, you necessarily abstract yourself from everything going on all around.[11] Those were such important, fantastic things, those lectures, so you really did dismiss the other things. Then, when I could emigrate—I was fortunate enough to still get a visa in 1941—I went to Baeck and asked him, "Should I really go? The nightmare has to end soon." And Baeck said very seriously, "You have to get out of here." He knew a lot. You have to go, he said urgently.

My feelings about Germany in America were really more feelings of fear for my friends, and I was furious that relatively little was done in America when the whole story became known. I really didn't deal very much in those days with my attitude toward Germany, and there was no need to. In 1945, I didn't want to hear anything about going back to Germany; I was still in the rabbinical seminary in Cincinnati. I would never have come back to Germany, if a few years later, in 1950, Dr. Baeck hadn't asked me to go there. Rabbi Wolfgang Hamburger (another of Baeck's former students at the Center) and I each went to New York separately in those days to welcome Baeck there. Then I flew back to Berlin the first time in 1950, under the auspices of the World Union for Progressive Judaism; Baeck was its president at that time. My colleague Rabbi Steven Schwarzschild had been in Berlin from 1948 to 1950 and didn't want to stay there any longer, so Baeck asked me to replace him. Baeck didn't think of going back himself. But he thought someone should be there. It was important to him; he also visited Berlin himself. I still remember how I walked around Berlin with him. We went to the Jewish cemetery in Weissensee, to his wife's grave. And I took him to other old places he remembered.

At that time, I planned to stay only two or three years—until my wife finished studying medicine. She had started medicine in Germany and wanted to finish there. When I came to Berlin, there was also an Orthodox community rabbi, Dr. Freier, who had once been known as a Revisionist Zionist. Dr. Freier left after about two and a half years, and for over a year I was the only rabbi in Berlin. I must add, however, that in the first two years, I was paid by the World Union for Progressive Judaism, so I was only "on loan" to Berlin, as it were. Only after two years could the community itself pay my salary. The last year, I was an employee of the community. By that time, Heinz Galinski was the chairman, and I served initially in East Berlin, too, on Rykestrasse, in the so-called Friedenstempel. I even had my office in East Berlin. That was a strange thing. The community put a car at my disposal with East Berlin license plates, which was extremely difficult, since as an American I couldn't get a driver's license for it. I worked mostly in the Western part, on Pestalozzistrasse, but also in the other synagogues, except the Orthodox one on Joachimsthaler Strasse. In the West, there were still synagogues on Fränkelufer and in the old people's home on Iranische Strasse. So there were five synagogues altogether in Berlin.

Naturally, it was hard for me to be accepted by the community, for, when I came, I was just twenty-nine years old—very young for a rabbi. And without a beard, to boot! Most of them had never seen such a rabbi. And I used to wear a tweed jacket. To get accepted wasn't easy at first. I still remember how I gave a sermon against the black market when I first came. In those days, this trade was flourishing between Waitzstrasse in Berlin and Möhlstrasse in Munich. The big cigarette warehouse was in East Berlin. East Germany even welcomed the black market, to disgrace the West. I did say that antisemitism didn't depend on the black market, but that we shouldn't make it so easy for the anti-semites either. Naturally, they didn't like to hear that. A few Jews gathered outside and wanted to attack the synagogue. It ended mildly.

We also had good things, like the protest march against Veit Harlan (the director of the antisemitic film *Jüd Süss*). We all protested. There is a picture with my late first wife and Hänschen Rosenthal and the only (later) Jewish colonel in the West German army, Wolfgang Konrad.[12] We protested and we got beaten up. I marched in my American uniform to bring a bit of peace. I had really never been on active duty but was in the reserves. It was not an official demonstration of the community, but something like the later Frankfurt demonstration against the Fassbinder play.[13] Galinski was against it at first, but then he joined us.

In the first postwar years, a lot of people wanted to convert to Judaism. For a wide variety of reasons. There were six thousand Jews in Berlin—and there were six thousand applications for conversion. A large part of my work consisted of screening these things. But I got them only after the community itself had made its decision. Once a week, a community committee met, and if anyone had been in the German army or was the child of Nazis, the file was immediately thrown out; that is, the first selection was purely political. Only then did the cases come to me. I dealt with these things once a week. Most cases were rejected—obviously, in six thousand applications! At that time, there was still no doubt that conversion with Reform Rabbi Levinson would also be recognized in Israel. Some converted out of conviction; for others it was *the* protest against the Nazis to identify with the victims; for others, on the contrary, it was opportunism, to get CARE packages—there were those too. And then there were the nuts, who changed from one religion to another. There was one case of someone who circumcised himself and almost bled to death. Other reasons were theological or had to do with marriage. It was obvious to Jewish DPs who married German women that they had to have Jewish children, so the women had to convert.

In those days, I never thought of getting involved in the Christian-Jewish dialogue, in those days that was a pretty absurd idea. The Shoah was just behind us, all the DPs were there, so you really didn't have any . . . any relation to the non-Jewish environment. It wasn't like later, when you had friends among Christian theologians—well, maybe one or two, but in general . . .

I still remember how I left the hall when I was invited to establish the Society for Christian-Jewish Cooperation. The director at that time, Church Director Jacoby, said that naturally one should treat all people as brothers, but that one could treat only the people of one's own religion as real brothers. I was so furious that I got up and left. I was sitting in the first row. Then I saw a journalist friend of mine and told him, You are free to write that I left. And the next day it was in the *New York Times*. Observers said the speech wasn't antisemitic, but it wasn't very tactful. In any case, it was a scandal. So at that time, I was against such dialogues. There weren't yet any theologians who were in it with all their soul and weren't trying to convert Jews. This single experience was enough to make me not want to have anything to do with these things for a long time.

The separation of the Berlin community started with the Slánský Trial in Czechoslovakia, then came the Doctors' Trial under Stalin, and then it also began in East Germany. Jews came and said they were persecuted. I told them all, "You should disappear. I've already gone through that." So I urged them to leave East Germany, and then I held a press conference with my friend the historian Josef Wulff and an attorney. Galinski and the rest of the community board immediately tried to prevent that press conference and came to my home. In one room was the press, in the other the board. He told me, "If you go through with this press conference, you will be fired on the spot." The next day, Galinski said the same thing I said. In fact, I forced him to do it. He couldn't say, No, I'm against it. Internally, he naturally said I was playing American politics, and I was in fact fired on the spot.

When I think back on it today, the time in Berlin was a kind of interim for me, the sort of thing you have to do. To help the remnant, the *she'erit ha-pleyta*. First you have to try to restore, reestablish confidence in Judaism. It was the attempt in spite of everything to participate in a reconstruction, to advance it somehow. A rabbi can't leave the Jews alone.

> *Rabbi Levinson returned to the United States in 1953 and served in the following years as a rabbi in Mississippi, as well as at an American military base in Japan. In 1958, he came to Germany again, where he first worked as an American Jewish chaplain in Ramstein (Pfalz), from 1961 as a congregational rabbi in Mannheim, and between 1964 and 1986 as state rabbi of Baden and Hamburg. For decades he was a leader of the Christian-Jewish dialogue, first as the Jewish chairman of the German Coordinating Council for Christian-Jewish cooperation, and from 1976 on, as president of the International Council of Christians and Jews.*

The Reconstruction of Smaller Communities

8. JOSEF WARSCHER

FROM BUCHENWALD TO STUTTGART

Josef Warscher was born in 1908 in what was then Austro-Hungarian Krosno, and grew up in Stuttgart. After his arrest in 1939, he spent five and a half years in the Buchenwald concentration camp. He returned to Stuttgart in May 1945.

A few of the prisoners in Buchenwald managed to put together a radio near the end of the war. So in April 1945, we heard that the Americans weren't far away. We no longer believed we'd live to see the Liberation. We thought the SS would kill us before the Liberation, but at least they would also catch hell . . . But then we started thinking: what will we do if we survive. I still remember how we said, when we came home, we would help other survivors and make sure they could get accustomed to being normal people again. That's not just talk; we really meant it.

The Liberation was on April 11, 1945. You kept hearing shots, you even saw airplane battles over the camp. Then the SS took a transport of prisoners every day, on foot, and those who couldn't run were shot on the way. I was assigned to such a march, and as we marched out, I saw a friend with a prisoner number like mine and I said to him, "Come on, we came here at the same time, let me through here." He left me behind. I don't know if I would have held out on the march. On April 11, at noon, the political prisoners staged an armed attack with weapons they had hidden. The American tanks came and the first thing they did was to roll over the electrified fence around the camp. Well, and then we were liberated, so to speak. And if you ask me if we danced or shouted for joy—neither! That was a long time: five years and ten months in Buchenwald!

On April 11, the war wasn't yet over. First of all, you couldn't go wherever you wanted. We had a Jewish chaplain named Eskin, and you could send letters through him. I had a brother in Palestine who had somehow found out that I was liberated. Whether he even knew I was in a concentration camp, I don't know. Until May 25, I stayed in Buchenwald, over a month in the same barracks. There were inmates who then went down to Weimar, to the German women. I found that coarse; I couldn't figure it out. I'm no clergyman and not especially religious, but I thought, This isn't why you survived, to use your freedom like this. I found it undignified. The inmates from Buchenwald came from all possible countries, and they then formed their own ad hoc committees. I worked with the committee of German inmates and wrote reports on events during the period of the camp and so forth. That was all to be written down immediately. Then two or three inmates from the local area went to Stuttgart on a military pass, brought back a bus and relatives, and took us—inmates from Stuttgart—to Stuttgart.

There were no welcoming committees and such—nothing. In some cities the lord mayor himself came to take his inmates. The bus dropped us off in the eastern part of the city—and there I was. It's funny, you get out in some part of the city, stand in the middle of the street, and ask yourself, What now? I came home and there was no more home. I spent my first nights in Stuttgart in a school, slept in a classroom. Then we went to the housing office. Finally they gave us a confiscated Nazi flat, which was completely furnished. Three of us lived there. In the concentration camp, I thought I was in a block with only Jews. But now it turned out that there were a few baptized Christians here, whom the Nazis had simply made into Jews. In our apartment there was also somebody who was no longer a Jew by religion. I didn't know anyone anymore when I came back to Stuttgart. I can still remember, once some Jews came from Palestine—today we would say Israelis—and asked me whom they could talk to. I couldn't even help them. I had to tell them, "I'm sorry, I don't know these people anymore."

On Reinsburgstrasse, the Americans requisitioned a house for the Jewish community. The old synagogue was destroyed. All that was preserved were the Tablets of the Law and a big wall plaque with the names of those who had fallen in World War I. So, at Reinsburgstrasse 26, we had a whole building, which, moreover, had formerly belonged to Jews, for the Jewish community. On the ground floor was the office of the JOINT, on the second floor, the community offices. On the third floor lived the caretaker, who had lived there previously. We set up the chapel in a big apartment. I myself lived on the same street, but much farther up. In the early days, only those who lived in private houses were members of the community. Those from the DP camp were separate. We had a regular Sabbath service, a few more than a minyan (ten grown men) gathered together. In the beginning, the majority were Stuttgart Jews. In the first year, we had about seven hundred members in the Jewish community in all Württemberg, about five hundred in Stuttgart; at most 5 percent of them were from old established families or were born in Germany.

In the concentration camp, I had thought, first you go to Stuttgart and you see what's going on. Once, in 1947, I think, I seriously considered immigrating to America. It wouldn't have been a problem to get a visa to America. But I still considered it my duty to rebuild the Jewish community in Stuttgart, and this work was so interesting, fascinated me so much, that I stayed here. I was on the board of the Jewish community of Württemberg, and for a time even its chairman. The people on the board were all German Jews at first. You needed people with a certain education, who could also express themselves verbally.

It took me about two years until I could go into a café or restaurant again. There was an invisible wall. It was a long time before I could have anything to do again with non-Jews. That wasn't deliberate, no, I simply couldn't. And naturally there weren't many Jews to be in touch with either. Therefore, you had a lot of time for work. First of all, the reparations cases demanded much time. And we had a lot to do in the cemeteries too—the Nazis had even robbed the bronze plaques from the tombstones.

Josef Warscher contributed significantly to the rebuilding of the Jewish community of Württemberg and was a member of its board from 1945 to 1960. He was one of the founders of the Stuttgart Society for Christian-Jewish Cooperation, and since 1981 has been its Jewish chairman. For twenty-three years, Warscher was a member of the radio council of South German Broadcasting.

9. WOLF WEIL

A "SCHINDLER JEW" IN THE BAVARIAN PROVINCE

Wolf Weil was born in Kraków in 1912. He survived the ghetto in Kraków and the Plaszow concentration camp by working as an agent in Oskar Schindler's enamel factory. Weil was liberated in May 1945 in Schindler's Brünnlitz camp in Moravia.

Before the war, I had been an official in the "Rekord" enamel factory, which Oskar Schindler took over at the beginning of the war. When he came to me at home to get the key to the factory, I told him, "Mr. Schindler, please bring me an official document." "Fine," he said, and came the next day at the same time to my parents' flat with the appropriate document. "I'm no professional," he said. "Would you please help me in the factory?" I objected: didn't he know he couldn't employ any Jews. "Let me take care of that, I'm taking the responsibility," he answered. So I started working for him. Four weeks later, the Gestapo came and arrested me. Schindler tried to release me, and seven weeks later he did. So I was with him in Kraków, in the Plaszow camp, then in Gross-Rosen, and finally in Brünnlitz in Moravia.

I was liberated at Oskar Schindler's factory in Brünnlitz in May 1945 and immediately set out for Kraków on foot. There I searched for my parents and siblings. I was in Kraków for fourteen days without finding anyone. When I went back to the old enamel factory, where I had been an official, the Polish workers greeted me effusively, sat me in a chair, carried me around, and sang, "Our Mr. Weil is alive!" I was very popular among them because I always had intervened on their behalf. I could do that because the owners of the company were my cousins.

One day in the street, I met an acquaintance from the camp who told me, "You know, Frida is here." That was the woman who is now my wife; she was a good friend of my first wife, who, along with our little daughter, was murdered by the Nazis. We decided to leave Poland together, even though the Poles in the company where I worked insisted I stay. Afterward, when an acquaintance told me that my brother had survived and was now in Hof, I decided to go there.

How did I get to Hof? I never heard of Hof. In any case, I rushed home and said to my wife, "I'm going to Hof." "What do you want in Hof?" she asks me. I show her the map and explain why I want to go there. I didn't have much to take with me, one small suitcase. And I went to the railroad station. In June 1945, in the middle of the night, I arrived in Hof, crossed the border illegally from Czechoslovakia, with a fever of 103 degrees. Then I found Marienstrasse 31; a woman came out: "Who do you want?" "My brother Heinrich." "He went back to Poland yesterday."

I couldn't go right back to Poland because I was sick. At first, the woman didn't want to let me in; she didn't know me. She sent me to a man who came out in his underwear. I said to him, "You have to go with me so the woman will let me in." Finally I came in; the next day she brought the doctor. I had to stay another week until the fever went down. Then I went back to Kraków, where I finally met my brother, who said to us immediately, "You're not staying here! You're coming to Hof with me." So we finally wound up in Hof, all that still in June 1945.

I didn't want to stay in Poland in any case. The memories in Poland, no ... Friends of mine had been hidden in Kraków for forty months during the war, until the war was over. And when they came out of hiding, the husband—it was a family with children—was shot by Poles. What can you say? Even though I personally had not had any comparable experiences with antisemitism, I said to myself, never again in Poland. And I never again went to Poland even for a visit.

When I arrived in Hof, there was a small Jewish Committee. The people who knew me from Kraków said immediately, "Mr. Weil, you establish the community here." In fact, I did this at once. The first thing I found out here was that over a hundred dead Jews who had been shot on the death marches were strewn in the forests around Hof. My first task was to bury them in the Jewish cemetery.

The American commander here in those days was a real antisemite. I went to him and told him that there are so many corpses lying around in the forests. They have to be buried in a mass grave. He replied, "Out of the question!" He sat there with his feet on the desk. I mustered up my courage and said, "First of all, take your feet off the desk. That's not how you talk to me." He had put a riding crop on the desk and started swatting it. I said, "If you swat that once more, I'll turn your desk upside down." "No," he went on, "I won't allow the dead to be buried." I then went to his secretary and said, "Tell him I will do it without his permission." He looked at me in amazement and repeated that he wouldn't allow it. I went out and slammed the glass door so hard all the glass broke. I finally carried out everything, and he himself was even present. Today, the memorial stone, with the inscription that 142 concentration camp inmates are buried here, is still standing.

In those days, there were about six hundred Jews in Hof, that is, in the city. In addition, there were another two thousand in the DP camp in the barracks. They had all come over illegally from Czechoslovakia, since the border is only a few kilometers away. I was regularly called out at one or two o'clock in the morning: "Another transport with thirty, forty, fifty Jews has arrived." For a while, that went on almost every night. I would get up at once. I had already arranged everything with the owner of a trucking company—in those days, there weren't any buses here—and we went to the border. Then we brought the people here to Hof, first to the barracks. The community and the DP camp had nothing to do with one another, in terms of organization. The DP camp in the barracks was dissolved in 1949.

The Jews who lived in the city had apartments in German homes. Relations between them weren't so bad. Right after the Liberation and under the impact of events, most Germans behaved like human beings; later that wasn't always the case. Naturally there were often quarrels, with the courts of the city of Hof, etc.

Our synagogue was burned down on Kristallnacht. After the war, the city wanted to build a new synagogue here. I thought, "For whom?" All the people—including me—were planning to move out of here. But about seventy Jews did remain in Hof. I thought, we don't need a new building. So the city provided us with a room in an existing building. When this was torn down, we got another one. But I did arrange for a memorial plaque to be erected on the site of the former synagogue.

My brother was one of the first to leave Hof, back in April 1947. He hated the Germans. But in America he didn't do very well. He didn't know the language, and everything he started went bad. He then wrote to me, "Stay where you are." In those days I really wanted to leave too. But my wife was very sick. And my friends—two attorneys and a physician—went to America and also wrote, "Stay where you are." Stay where you are, stay where you are, stay where you are . . . So I stayed where I was. First I opened a grocery store, then a china business, and then textiles. Then the children were born . . .

I get along with the authorities here just fine. I know a lot of people, but we don't get together, let's say, for an evening, not that. If you meet somebody in a restaurant, fine—but I don't go to their homes and they don't come to mine. But my children, they've got good friends here.

> *From its reestablishment in 1945 until his death in 1988, Wolf Weil was the chairman of the Jewish community of Hof. He was also deputy chairman of the Association of Jewish Communities in Bavaria and a delegate to the Central Council of Jews in Germany.*

10. ARNO HAMBURGER

COMING HOME IN THE UNIFORM OF THE JEWISH BRIGADE

Arno Hamburger was born in Nuremberg, the son of a wholesale butcher and later chairman of the Jewish community, Adolf Hamburger. In 1939, he immigrated to what was then Palestine with the Youth Aliyah movement. In 1941 he volunteered for service in the British army. When the war was over, he came back to Germany as a member of the Jewish Brigade.

When the war was over, I was stationed with the Jewish Brigade in Italy, near Bologna. I immediately tried to get leave to make it to Germany. From the day I left Germany until May 1945, I had heard nothing from my parents. I didn't know anything that had happened to them. Naturally they didn't know anything about me either.

So I overcame a lot of obstacles and got back to Nuremberg—hitchhiking from Bologna through Munich. In those days, that wasn't so easy. I was in uniform. On March 27, 1945, on a Sunday, I got out of an American jeep in the center of Nuremberg. I saw the city, which I didn't recognize anymore, walked around in Nuremberg, and finally made my way through to the Jewish cemetery, where I arrived at about two in the afternoon. I rang the bell there and Mr. Baruch came out; I had known him since childhood. He had been very active in the Jewish sport group where I was also a member. So he saw an English soldier and asked how he could help me. I answered that I was Arno Hamburger, and asked if he recognized me. He became as pale as a ghost. I asked him if he had any idea what had happened to my parents. Yes, they were living in one room, back in the morgue. Then I asked him to tell my father to come out, because I was almost afraid to go in. They were all in very bad health.

Mr. Baruch fetched my father, who had been building train tracks since 1939. He came to me and, naturally, he didn't recognize me. It was only when I took off my cap that he recognized me. He shrieked and embraced me. Then my mother came, saw us embracing, and immediately fainted. We sat together all Sunday afternoon. They told me that my grandparents had gone to Sobibor, my aunt to Izbica, my uncle had been shot in Mauthausen, and everything else that had happened. I was in Nuremberg about four weeks until I went back to my unit. We were stationed in Holland then, until we were transferred to the Austrian-Italian border, and finally to Belgium. Meanwhile, I kept going to Nuremberg. In the middle of 1946, we were transferred back to Port Said in Egypt and then to Palestine. In September 1946, I was discharged from the army and immediately went back to Nuremberg. I had previously tried to get a job as a translator at the Nuremberg War Crimes Trials, and I finally did get hired.

Even earlier, in 1945, I had intervened actively to acquire the first building for the postwar Jewish community. This building had originally been a house for Jewish nurses and had been Aryanized in 1935. At my initiative, it was given back to the Jewish community in May 1945 by the military administration. As a soldier, it was naturally easier for me to pull strings in the American military administration. It was certainly a great advantage for the Nuremberg community that there was someone here who (a) was familiar with local conditions, and (b) had immediate access to every military post both in terms of language and in terms of appearance.

So, in late 1945, we held the first election here in the Nuremberg Jewish community. In 1945, we held the first Rosh Hashana service with the help of the Americans, in the former town hall on Bieling-Platz. These were the first steps toward the restoration of a community.

Right after I came back in September 1945, I began to be active in the Jewish community. Naturally, through my father, I was also very involved in community events. I was the only son and Papa said, "Arno, you do it!" We always had a close relationship. And precisely because of the separation and the suffering we had all undergone, our relationship was much much closer than usual.

In 1949, I resigned my job as translator and went to work for Father in the business, since I had previously studied to be a butcher. My father had a wholesale butcher shop in Nuremberg and thought that if I wanted to go into the business, I had to understand it from the ground up. So, at the age of twenty-seven, I started an apprenticeship as a butcher.

From the first day, our community was a mixed one. We had a big DP camp here in Fürth, and there were a lot of people who were lodged in our old-age home on Wielandstrasse, as a first stop. Many of them emigrated, but a lot stayed here in Nuremberg. I would like to emphasize that the difficulties between the so-called East European Jews and the German Jews were relatively—I deliberately say, relatively—minuscule. I imagine that I served as an intermediary between the two groups because of my experiences in the army. In the Jewish Brigade, we weren't a pure German-Jewish army or a Polish-Jewish unit, but a real unit with Jewish soldiers from various backgrounds. In any case, there were relatively few quarrels in the Nuremberg community. People worked together and tried to rebuild a Jewish life together.

Only a few Nuremberg Jews came back from the camps: from Theresienstadt, about sixty; from Riga, sixteen; and four or five from Auschwitz. No one who went to Izbica on the last big transport returned. The community building on Wielandstrasse served these eighty Nuremberg Jews as a first gathering place. In Nuremberg itself, some ten Jews survived the war, including my father.

My father and I had a very violent discussion about whether we should stay here. After everything that had happened, I couldn't imagine settling down here again under any circumstances. But he told me that after everything he had gone through, he was neither physically nor emotionally able to start all over again somewhere else, to learn a new language and adjust to another place. He wanted his business back; he was relatively young, only forty-five. In terms of social life, as I said, I couldn't imagine settling down here. But I was his only son and I considered it my duty to support my parents, who were physically and emotionally low.

So I came back, even though it was very very hard for me. In the first years, I had no social relations. Contact with Germans in the early postwar time was nonexistent. In the Jewish community, there were only a few young people my age; three youths came back from Auschwitz. There was only one Jewish girl from a mixed marriage who was my age. All in all, there was really no Jewish social life here.

Arno Hamburger stayed in Nuremberg. In 1966, he was elected vice president of the Jewish community of Nuremberg, and in 1972 became president. At the same time, he served as a deputy chairman of the Association of Jewish Communities in Bavaria. Hamburger was also the chairman of the Social Democratic Party in the Nuremberg City Council.

11. DAVID SCHUSTER
RESTORATION OF A SMALL JEWISH COMMUNITY

David Schuster was born in 1910 in Franconian Bad Brückenau. After imprisonment in the Dachau concentration camp in 1937–38, he emigrated to what was then Palestine, where he worked for eighteen years in a construction company in Haifa. In 1956, he returned to Würzburg and soon brought his wife and small son to join him.

My father had already returned from Palestine before me, to have a look at our property. That was in 1954/55. He maintained that those who had seized our property should not keep possession of it. I came in 1956. My father didn't want to sell anything. Right away I saw that it couldn't be managed from a distance, and I sent for my wife and son. This wasn't easy for me. Once you were in a concentration camp and got away with a feeling of "Thank God," you didn't think of coming back. This idea came only later, after my father registered for the law of restitution, and the family had to be present on the spot. He was an old man when he came back. The first ten years after the war, we hadn't thought of coming back at all.

We came straight to Würzburg. From here, it's not far to Bad Brückenau, so we could go there whenever we had to. I had gone to school in Würzburg in 1920; at that time there was no *Gymnasium* in Bad Brückenau. My feelings on returning were quite mixed. I had recently taken leave from my company, a construction company, because I wasn't clear, or, more precisely, because at first I intended to go back to Israel.

But it turned out that you had to be on the spot. My father did arrange for a manager, but that didn't work. Either sell or stay here—those were the alternatives.

One of my first experiences after returning was the following: When I came to Brückenau, I saw an old acquaintance, who hadn't exactly been friendly to the Jews. "David," he said, "I have something for you. If you're interested, keep it. I saved a photo because I told myself I'd see you again." And he showed me a photo of my father and me with two policemen on the way from the jail in Brückenau to the transport to Dachau. That's what he showed me. As he said, he had to keep it for me. That was in fact a gem in his photo album.

Before 1933, there was a considerable Jewish community with some thirty-five families in Brückenau. No one came back after the war. I took up residence in Würzburg. There was already a Jewish community there in those days. Most of the members were refugees, DPs or even returning emigrants. I didn't run into many familiar faces. The first chairman of the community after the war was Mr. David Rosenbaum, who was also from this area, and his colleagues on the board were also from Würzburg, so that here the customs of the previous Würzburg community were continued—naturally, to a very modest extent. In Würzburg, the community was concentrated more or less on the old people's home. There was a small, disgraceful room for prayer there. One of the first things I did after I returned was to insist that a synagogue be built. Later, it wasn't only a synagogue that was built, but in fact a whole community center, which was opened in 1970. Not all the community members thought a synagogue should be built. Some people said, "For whom? For what?" I argued that if a Jew who goes through what we did is back in Germany, he has to feel an obligation to do something for Jewish public works.

The Würzburg community, as everywhere else in Germany, didn't get back its previous property. The JRSO got it. That created problems. Even the old people's home, which was fully occupied in those days, wasn't owned freely by the Jewish community. There was a notation in the land register stating that it would be transferred to the JRSO as soon as it was no longer needed as an old people's home. I tried to get this notation deleted and finally succeeded. Würzburg had been a community with a lot of real estate, and we didn't get any of it back. In the 1950s, in a test case, the Augsburg Jewish community sued the JRSO and lost. The highest American restitution court judged that the new Jewish communities were not successors of the original ones. That was an absolutely wrong decision in my opinion. Because the student Jewish associations, for example, which were also dissolved, which also had real estate, did get it back. We could have built the synagogue on the property of the former hospital, but we didn't get this lot back. So we had to choose a smaller place.

Since 1958, David Schuster has been chairman of the Jewish community in Würzburg. For many years he has been the vice president of the Association of Jewish Communities in Bavaria, and represented the Jewish community in the Bavarian Senate from 1976 to 1981.

Jewish Organizations and Institutions

12. SIMON SNOPKOWSKI
THE JEWISH STUDENT ASSOCIATION

Simon Snopkowski was born in Myszkow (Poland) in 1923. After his liberation from the concentration camp, he reached Munich where he became chairman of the Jewish Student Association of the Survivors.

On May 8, 1945, I was liberated by the Red Army at Langenbie-lau in Lower Silesia, which was under the command of the Gross-Rosen concentration camp. A few months after liberation, I came to Bavaria with a lot of Jewish survivors. This was after I found hardly any Jews in and around my hometown or any survivors of my large family. The stream of liberated people from the concentration camps went toward the American Zone—toward Bavaria. I came to the DP camp of Landsberg am Lech. I stayed in Landsberg until 1948/49; then I moved to Munich. In spring 1947, after I passed an examination, a verification committee appointed by the ministry of education confirmed that I filled the high school requirements, and I was admitted to the Ludwig-Maximillian University to study dentistry and, ultimately, medicine.

At about the same time, in 1946/47, a Jewish student organization was founded in Munich. Its function was to enable the students to fulfill high school requirements by directing them to the verification committee, helping them find housing, getting them support from the JOINT, and assisting them when they went to look for a job. The student organization numbered about five hundred members altogether, practically all the Jews who were studying in the Munich high schools. We should note that almost all the Jewish students were orphans. There was a lot of motivation in those days to come together: the alien environment, our common poverty, help in studies, in subsistence, and in getting housing. The organization was called *Ihud ha-studentim ha-yehudim shel she'erit ha-pleyta*, or the Association of Jewish Students of the Survivors.

In those areas that required employment, like an internship in medicine, for example, the student association tried to get a job for the victims in the few places of employment, thus guaranteeing that they wouldn't have to study longer because there was no internship. In the first postwar years, the humanities weren't much in demand, not because people weren't interested, but because they needed to study something they could use wherever they could immigrate. Hardly anyone at that time could allow himself to study philosophy.

Since almost all Jewish students were orphans and had no family, our entire social life was concentrated in the circle of the student association. We also organized performances for the general Jewish population, particularly on the Jewish holidays of Purim and Hanukah. These performances were an urgently needed source of income, which allowed us to provide help in especially needy cases.

In the American Zone, aside from Munich, there were other Jewish student organizations in Marburg and Frankfurt. There were also a few Jewish students near Stuttgart, where there was a school of veterinary medicine. An umbrella organization was established later. The British Zone had very few Jewish students, and I can't say anything about the French Zone. And there was also a significant number of Jewish students in Berlin.

As a student organization, we were completely separate from the German students—there were individual contacts here and there, but all in all they were very rare, on both sides. For example, when I studied dentistry, I worked at the same table with a non-Jewish classmate and there were unavoidable contacts. The same was true in the preparatory course. After studying, you often went to some coffeehouse. But these contacts weren't usual.

In the first years after the war, Zionism was widespread among the Jewish students. You came upon disillusioned Communists and Bundists rarely, usually among the older students. In the late 1940s, the great immigration, mainly to America or Israel, began. From 1949 to its dissolution in 1954, I was president of the student association. After its dissolution, I was also the one who sent all the files and documents to the YIVO Institute in New York. Thus the *Ihud ha-studentim ha-yehudim shel she'erit ha-pleyta* concluded its activity. What was later established as a Jewish student alliance was a phenomenon of the second generation, or rather of the émigrés who returned from Israel.

The Jewish community of Munich was established in 1945, and I have been a member since the late 1940s. After the wave of immigration and the dissolution of the DP camps, other Jewish communities began to be established in Bavaria. Some of their constitutions incorporated the clause that half the board had to be composed of Jews with German citizenship. In time, this constitutional clause became invalid, since the Jews who remained here established themselves, became naturalized, and enhanced the building of the community.

> *After completing his studies, Dr. Snopkowski worked in various hospitals, first as a resident, then as a specialist in surgery and as a senior surgeon; finally, since 1966, he has been head of the surgical department of a municipal hospital in Munich. Since 1970, he has been president of the Association of Jewish Communities in Bavaria.*

13. LILLI MARX
RENEWAL OF THE GERMAN-JEWISH PRESS

Karl Marx was born in 1897 in Saarlouis to a Jewish family that had lived in the region for over six hundred years; he grew up in Strasbourg. In August 1914, after a special matriculation exam, he volunteered for wartime service as a soldier. During the Weimar Republic, he made a name for himself as a journalist and was active in the youth movement as well as in the German Democratic Party. In March 1933, he emigrated through the Saar, Paris, Italy, and Tangier, to England. Remitting his passport to the Prussian interior ministry in 1942, he explicitly renounced his German citizenship. Lilli Marx, who had immigrated to England from Germany in 1939, met her future husband in London, and went back to Germany with him in 1946.

After the war, Karl Marx expressed the conviction that he had to go to Germany, because there were too few surviving Jews and he felt obligated to help the remnant of the Jewish community in Germany. So, in late 1945, he wrote a letter to the authorities in England requesting repatriation. When he went to Germany soon after, that was, however, not yet a final determination. The decision to stay in Germany was made only after we learned the full extent of the tragedy.

He didn't think of starting a newspaper. Before the war, he was neither a publisher nor an editor, but a freelance journalist. By accident, he got stuck in Düsseldorf, where the British licensing officer—a former Austrian Jew—asked him to take over the license for the Jewish newspaper here, a very small information paper for the Jewish communities in the British Zone. But even before he had the license, the first thing he did was to go to the city of Düsseldorf and say, "You have to put up a memorial plaque for the murdered Jews. That is an obligation of honor for the city." That was—in 1946—the first memorial plaque in Germany, I believe. It was the first act that gave us a little satisfaction, a tiny consolation.

I had the pleasure of working with my husband for twenty-two years, and an opportunity to learn a great deal from him. Along with the weekly paper, he established the Humanitas Publishers in Coblenz, but that passed away peacefully after two or three years. My husband was no businessman; he was a man of the community. We also founded an intellectual monthly journal on a higher level, *Zwischen den Zeiten* [Between times], which perished both for lack of money and for lack of an intellectual audience. As a matter of fact, in those days, the Jewish communities were horribly poor intellectually. Naturally we felt this poverty. A lot of people had to climb down off pretty high pedestals, adjust somehow, make the best of it.

The editorial office of our paper, the *Allgemeine*, which was then called *Mitteilungsblatt* [Information paper], was in Benrath, a suburb of Düsseldorf, where a local newspaper, the *Benrather Tageblatt* [Benrath daily paper], a family enterprise, existed with an antiquated rotary press. So we rented a room there, and Karl Marx composed the first newspaper of his life. He knew nothing of layout and made a big impression on the printers because he did everything just right. We also had a young staff member, Heinz Kaufmann, the son of a Jewish father from Düsseldorf, and a secretary. I ran the business. And in our home, we cut and pasted, wrote news items and established the archive. So it was a regular family business.

In the spring of 1947, we changed the name of the *Mitteilungsblatt* to *Allgemeine Wochenzeitung der Juden in Deutschland* [General weekly newspaper of the Jews in Germany]. We refused to say "German Jews"; that was taboo. We had outstanding contributors, even abroad. They were still suffering from the need to express themselves in their mother tongue. And here was a Jewish newspaper in German! For example, our first freelance contributor was E. G. Lowenthal; or PEM, that is, Paul Ernst Marcus, whom we had met in London. He had been a well-known feature writer on the *B.Z. am Mittag* before the war. After the war, he made—hectographed—a circular letter with news about German-speaking actors scattered all over the world. A lot of famous journalists, Jews as well as non-Jews, were glad to contribute their skills to us, even though we could pay only small fees.

We tried to advertise the *Allgemeine* abroad and made contact with the general Jewish press. We visited newspapers and began building a modest sales system. The reaction abroad? Understandably very difficult. We felt the rejection very strongly. In later years, we became friendly with people who had previously rejected us. In 1948, Karl Marx took part in the first postwar meeting of the World Jewish Congress, in Switzerland. He had a particularly hard time there and suffered a lot.

This situation lasted a long time. At some point, around 1960, there was a meeting of the Jewish press at a Zionist congress in Israel. The atmosphere was cool for it was also linguistically difficult. Not all journalists spoke English, my husband spoke no Hebrew or Yiddish, and his French was bad—and I was the translator, as it were. But there were a lot of people who didn't talk with us at all. And what I experienced later at assemblies of the International Council of Jewish Women as the representative of the *Jüdische Frauenbund* [League of Jewish Women]! The way they talked to me there! Or they spoke English so I wouldn't understand: "Did you hear that Jewish women from Germany are to be represented here? You can't talk to them." I turned around and said, "Oh, yes, you can!"

Right after we came back to Germany, we heard that there was a big DP camp in Belsen. We had very close contacts and also tried to get contributors from there. The difficulty, however, was that most of them didn't speak German; and Karl Marx and I didn't speak any Yiddish or Hebrew. Only those who spoke German could contribute to our paper. Nevertheless, there was a close, friendly cooperation. We also tried to coordinate the newspaper with the needs and wishes of the DPs. We communicated with each other, visited back and forth, and wherever possible cooperated closely, as in the *Exodus* affair. We had much less contact with southern Germany; I knew the camps there only from the descriptions and news we got from journalists there.

In those days, there was another small newspaper in Berlin, *Der Weg*, which we bought, and published as *Berliner Allgemeine Wochenzeitung*, after negotiations with Galinski and the owner of the *Weg*. The proviso was that we would allow the Berlin Jewish community to publish two pages in it for free. There was also the *Münchner Jüdische Nachrichten* [Munich Jewish news] as a German-language Jewish weekly.

My husband always claimed he was managing an independent newspaper, independent even from the Central Council. Whether that was correct, I won't go into, because there were violent arguments with the Central Council during his last years. Maybe it would have been better if the newspaper had become a publication of the Central Council at an earlier stage; my husband would certainly have lived longer. At first, cooperation with the Central Council was no problem. In fact, we published everything the Central Council wanted, since it didn't have its own publication. There was a close, friendly cooperation with Hendrik van Dam, the secretary-general of the Central Council. He also wrote outstanding editorials. Together they put out the first book about the German restitution law; his wife and I read the proofs, a Sisyphean labor.

In the years before and right after the founding of West Germany, people stood in line to meet Karl Marx and buy his name for their businesses. International businesses offered him seats on their boards of trustees and shares of stock just to be able to go on producing. We could have been millionaires. But we were too dumb, or, let's say, too moral. He never considered it. In the 1950s, all the parties asked my husband to be a candidate for the Bundestag. He was still friendly with Ernst Lemmer of the CDU [Christian Democratic Union], Theodor Heuss [of the Free Democratic Party], and many SPD [Social Democratic Party] people from their work together in the youth movement.[14] But he refused every party affiliation. He didn't want to and said, "I'm not a court Jew."

My husband belonged to a generation that was absolutely rooted in Germany, one reason why he could feel good here again so easily. And he had charisma; he was a strong personality whom people respected and liked a great deal. I, who had left Germany when I was very young, in fact remained a foreigner for a long time. I admit that I like to live here; it's comfortable. I'm no hypocrite.

Aside from us, there were only a few who came back right after the war and were active in the Jewish community. First, there was Hendrik van Dam, a very close friend of my husband's. They were basically different and complemented each other marvelously. One was a lawyer, an outstanding editorial writer; the other—Karl Marx—was a practical man, an outstanding organizer. And naturally there was E. G. Lowenthal, director of the Jewish Relief Unit here. The name "Humanitas Press" came from him. He also came up with the title *Allgemeine Wochenzeitung der Juden in Deutschland* and the title of the supplement I later published, *Die Frau in der Gemeinschaft* [The woman in society]. A lot of good ideas came from him.

In the Jewish community, people of all trends came together. One wanted an organ in the synagogue, another wanted a choir. There were horrible debates about trivialities. They finally decided on the principle of homogeneous communities to be fair to everyone. It was even more complicated when the DP camps were dissolved and the people were integrated into the communities. The city of Düsseldorf declared that it was willing to accept a certain number of Jewish DPs, only weak and sick families; the others had long ago migrated to Israel or other countries. In fact that was hard. I myself immediately volunteered to help the Jewish community. That was simply a matter of honor. In the 1950s, there was the wave of German Jews who came back from Israel, then emigrants from Czechoslovakia, Romania, Poland, and the USSR.

In 1948, my husband, who had never been a Zionist before, discovered his great love for Israel. The establishment of the State of Israel, the influence of the DPs, the friendship with Robert Weltsch [the German Zionist]—it was a wonderful challenge, so he immediately said, "If you want to elect me president of the Zionist organization in Germany, I am available. I will establish my position." He then remained its chairman until he became very ill in 1966. That was important because he wasn't a veteran Zionist, and so he could be the ideal intermediary. However, there were hardly any more debates between Zionists and anti-Zionists. Aside from Professor Hans-Joachim Schoeps in Erlangen, I don't think there were any more outspoken anti-Zionists among German Jews.[15] Common sense prevailed with a lot of them, even if they didn't think that way deep down.

> As the first postwar chairman of the Zionist Organization for Germany, Karl Marx vehemently supported the recognition of the Jewish communities of Germany on an international stage. He was also active as a leader and served on the board of the Jewish community of Düsseldorf, and published the Allgemeine Jüdische Wochenzeitung until his death in December 1966. Lilli Marx founded the Jewish Women's Association of Düsseldorf in 1949 and was the executive chairman of the reestablished Jüdische Frauenbund in Deutschland [League of Jewish Women in Germany] from 1954 to 1972. She was and still is active in various work for the Jewish community of Düsseldorf. From 1969 until his death in 1986, she was the companion of the Israeli writer Alexander Czerski.

Leo Baeck (left)
and
E.G. Lowenthal
(1948)

14. E. G. LOWENTHAL
ON BEHALF OF THE JEWISH AID ORGANIZATION

*Ernst G. Lowenthal was born in Cologne in 1904. After obtaining a
doctorate in sociology, he performed various functions for the Central
Association of German Citizens of the Jewish Faith between 1929
and 1938, including editing the* Journal for the History of the Jews
in Germany. *In 1939, he immigrated to England. On behalf of
international Jewish aid organizations, he returned to Germany in
1946, where, among other functions, he was director of the Jewish
Relief Unit in the British Occupation Zone in 1947/48.*

Within the Board of Deputies of British Jews, a committee was
formed during the war to deal with "postwar relief on the Continent." I
immediately volunteered. At that time, I wasn't yet a British citizen,
which I became only in late 1946. As the only non-Britisher, the only one
from Germany, I was on the "selection board," which evaluated volun-
teers. In late 1946, I came to Germany myself, after working for seven
years with the Jewish Refugees Committee in London. I am a returnee
sui generis, since I didn't really return until 1969, maintaining my residence in England all that time. However, since late 1946, I have worked
almost constantly in Germany on behalf of British or international Jewish
organizations.

First I lived in Cologne and had my office in the building of the
military administration. There I was active essentially in social work. My
area extended from helping with emigration to getting medicine for sick

people; my district was the entire British Zone. So I went from Bonn to Flensburg, from the island of Amrum, where a few Jewish refugees from Danzig had wound up, to Bergen-Belsen. I was often in Bergen-Belsen, but it was really a separate entity, where the Jewish Relief Unit maintained its own unit with physicians, nurses, and several staff members.

I worked primarily for members of Jewish communities. But you couldn't separate that sharply from the DP camps, even though relations between the DPs and the members of the Jewish communities weren't very close. For a time, in 1947/48, I was director of the Jewish Relief Unit in Germany, and therefore I was often in Berlin. But I couldn't do that for long because it was too much for me. I didn't want to sit in the car continually and drive through the country; I wanted instead to help people. So I said I wouldn't do it anymore.

Our cooperation with the JOINT was outstanding. That was important because people got their rations from the JOINT. Once there was a small incident with the German authorities. A truck-transport was reported stopped at the border of the French and British zones, between Bonn and Coblenz. So I went there and dealt with the Ministry of Agriculture to let the transport with food donated by the JOINT go through. It took half a day, but I got it. The transport went to Belsen because the distribution of the food was controlled from there. Then it was redistributed by the cities. Every Jew got a package; if he was a representative of the community, he got two; if he was chairman of the community, he got three; and if he was president of the regional association, he got four. These packages were very important, not because people consumed them, but because most of the contents could be used as currency.

After a few months, I left Cologne and moved to Düsseldorf. When I came, the Jewish community there consisted of about twenty-five people, mostly those in mixed marriages and a few returnees from Holland and Belgium. Later it was mostly people from Bukovina and the northern part of Romania who came. Why? An attorney from Czernowitz had settled in Düsseldorf and brought others. That wasn't exceptional at all. The same thing happened in other communities; in Hamburg, a bit later, there were Persian Jews. In Hanover, there were two Jewish groups: the Jewish community with an overwhelming majority of German Jews, and the Jewish Committee, consisting of DPs, mostly from nearby Bergen-Belsen. They had their centers in different parts of the city, were of different origin and social composition.

That was not the case in Düsseldorf. However, the few children were instructed by a DP, a man named Abraham Fischel. He wasn't a trained teacher but a man who knew Hebrew and could lead a religious service. He got along splendidly with the children. Most of the children had one Jewish and one non-Jewish parent. There were also children of members of the British military administration. The whole children's group numbered only ten. The religious service took place in a room of the regional courthouse, a big room, where I visited the community for the first time during a Hanukah service. Afterward they moved to a prayer room—not yet a synagogue—on Arnoldstrasse. That was fine; it was small, dignified, simple. It wasn't until the 1950s that a synagogue was inaugurated.

In late summer of 1948, I made a tour through Germany with Leo Baeck. That was his first reencounter with Germany. In London, he had asked me to travel through Germany with him as an escort for two weeks, and naturally I was glad to do it, because I had known him well earlier in Berlin. The tour began in Hamburg, where Baeck spoke at the university. Then we went to Belsen, where at first they didn't want to receive him, because to the people there, who came from an Orthodox religious background, he was a Liberal. And what happened? There was a lunch for him in the former SS club, with all the representatives of the thirty different Jewish organizations, from the Orthodox Aguda to the socialist Zionist groups. They weren't just reserved toward Baeck, they were almost afraid. Baeck always spoke freely, and what he said was so overwhelming that the people were pretty flabbergasted. They were sincerely grateful and almost lionized him. He then went on to Hamburg, where he delivered a public lecture about Leibniz.

In Hamburg someone came up to him, a person whose marriage Baeck had performed before the war in Berlin. In Düsseldorf, Baeck spoke to the community. Then we went to Cologne, where he spoke at the university—my alma mater. I asked Baeck to stay in Bonn for a while, where a survivor of Theresienstadt was living, the geographer Alfred Philippson. Then on to Frankfurt. We made another stop in Mainz at the old Jewish cemetery, where a memorial stone had recently been put up, thus reviving the place in the public consciousness. In Darmstadt, we attended an event of the *Deutsche Evangelische Dienst* [German Protestant Service] for Israel. There Baeck spoke of "Judaism on Old and New Paths"—the titles of his lectures were always imaginative. He also made an enormous impression on this exalted group—much more exalted than at all previous performances. Finally, I made an excursion with Baeck to the Black Forest. That didn't have anything to do with the official tour. He had a few non-Jews there who had helped him a great deal in Berlin between 1939 and 1943. He didn't tell me any details either about that or about Theresienstadt. As far as I know, he didn't tell anyone else those details either.

In England there were attempts to let help for the Jewish communities in Germany peter out because a few shortsighted people here had little appreciation for the restoration of Jewish life. Baeck always argued otherwise: "Wherever Jews live, communities arise, and these communities are not to be despised"—that was his motto. In Germany in the early postwar years, there was the unfortunate expression "liquidation communities," and later they talked of "Jews who are sitting on their suitcases." Both expressions were wrong. Naturally, there was uncertainty, but as reparations became more apparent and more intensive, that subsided. This single, great issue has had an enormous effect to this day. Jews in Germany certainly couldn't have gone on without reparations.

After his activity in the Jewish Relief Unit, Lowenthal worked two years for the Jewish Cultural Reconstruction Corporation in Wiesbaden where Hannah Arendt was his colleague. Subsequently, he was appointed to the Jewish Trust Corporation in Hamburg, and finally worked for the Conference of Jewish Material Claims against Germany in Bonn and Frankfurt. Here he devoted himself primarily to applications for indemnification of Jewish community employees and the implementation of accords for Jewish concentration camp inmates who had performed slave labor. Until his death in 1994, he lived as a freelance journalist in Berlin, published several articles and books on German-Jewish history, and was distinguished by the Senate of Berlin in 1985 with the title of "Honorary Professor." In 1986, he received the Leopold-Lucas Prize of the Protestant Theological Department of the University of Tübingen.

III.

Five Decades of Jewish Life
in Postwar Germany

1. From Auerbach to Nachmann

With the establishment of the Central Council of Jews in Germany, an era of consolidation began for the approximately fifteen thousand Jews who had decided to stay in Germany. However, those who expected an end to the turbulence of the preceding years were soon disappointed. The second phase of Jewish life began with a real drumbeat: the trial of the two most prominent leader of the postwar Jewish communities in Bavaria: the chairman of the Association of Jewish Communities in Bavaria and state commissioner of the Bavarian administration, Philipp Auerbach; and the Bavarian state rabbi, Aaron Ohrenstein.

The case of Philipp Auerbach, the best-known leader of German Jewry in the early postwar years, clearly demonstrated the fragility of the cornerstone of Jewish life in postwar Germany. The stages of this tragic case were marked by shock waves through the new structure of Jewish organizational life, new outbreaks of antisemitism among the Germans, the temporary suspension of reparations payments, and the suicide of the accused. Auschwitz survivor Auerbach had achieved a solid place in German public life, along with representatives of political parties and major business interests, through newspaper articles, radio talks, and numerous interviews. More than any other leader of postwar German Jewry, he combined loud warnings against a Nazi resurgence with the firm conviction that Jewish communities must also take their place in the new Germany. His political ambition and his penchant for demagoguery had brought him attention but had also created enemies.

In January 1951, Philipp Auerbach became a member of the board of the newly founded Central Council of Jews in Germany. His exit from the political stage began one month later. Irregularities in reparations cases led to the suspicion that, as state commissioner for victims of racial, religious, and political persecution, Auerbach had been guilty of forging documents. The "Caesar of Reparations," as *Der Spiegel* called him, had to resign from his position, as the charges were corroborated.[1] Other accusations were added: his title of doctor was obtained under false pretenses; Auerbach had contacts with the KPD; he had misappropriated public money.[2] When Auerbach was arrested, a certain malignant glee was fairly widespread among the Germans. Only a few years after the war, the Jews seemed to have emerged from their role of victim and had to stand trial in a German court! This was the tone of several newspapers, from the sensational press to *Der Spiegel*. And this time, the issue was not the banal black market offenses of anonymous DPs but the misappropriation of reparations money by a Jewish undersecretary of state.[3]

Jews living in Germany reacted in various ways. Some of them regarded Auerbach as a Jewish Robin Hood, who took not for personal gain and gave to the victims. That he did not do this in an absolutely correct way did not bother his supporters, given the extent of the Nazi crimes and the delayed inception of reparations payments. Others, however, were deeply embarrassed by reports of irregularities in the reparations payments and supported the public outcry for prosecution of Auerbach. As for the newborn Central Council, it could hardly have been in a more awkward situation. One of its board members had to stand trial in a German court, the achievements of the reparations negotiations were jeopardized, and those who wouldn't listen to reason could openly express their antisemitic feelings again. During the first week of the scandal, the Central Council preferred not to take a public position. On February 25, 1951, the board finally issued a statement, directed primarily against a new rise of antisemitism. The board protested "the invidious attack that would be aimed against the Jews at this opportunity." The Central Council called for a "thorough and objective investigation of all events" yet demanded "that this investigation not be used as a pretext to cripple the work of the reparations officials."[4]

The fears of the Central Council were realized when, as if in connection with the Auerbach case, the Bavarian Regional Indemnity Office was closed until further notice, bringing work on reparations to a standstill in the West German state with the most rightful claimants.[5] The Auerbach case ended as dramatically as it had begun. On August 14, 1952, Auerbach was sentenced to two and a half years in prison and a fine of 2,700 DM by five judges, at least three of whom had had some connection with the Nazi Party. On August 16, Philipp Auerbach, who had proclaimed his innocence to the end, took his own life.[6]

Auerbach's tragic death marked the end of the charismatic Jewish leaders who shaped the political interests of the Jews in the first postwar years. The sociologist Michal Bodemann defined the subsequent phase of Jewish leadership as characterized by "bureaucratic patronage."[7]

Culturally, many of the leading figures of Jewish community life in West Germany had only a cursory awareness of German-Jewish traditions prior to 1933, while the heritage of East European Jewry could not be transferred. Of course there were exceptions. Among the returning German Jews, as among East European Jews, some linked the management of the intellectual heritage with the community administration. Thus Hans Lamm in Munich and Stefan Schwarz in Straubing, as later Arno Lustiger in Frankfurt, contributed important historical and cultural studies to the intellectual revival.[8] In terms of community politics too, the heritage of Weimar was generally unknown. Prior to 1933, there had indeed been unified communities, *Einheitsgemeinden* (of which, with the exception of a few secessionist Orthodox communities, all the Jews of one locality were members); but this external unity was accompanied by internal diversity in worldview and religion. In general Jewish communities, election campaigns had clearly demarcated fronts and substantive contrasts between individual parties—Zionists, Orthodox, Liberal. The numerically small postwar communities professed neither ideological nor religious diversification, and community elections generally became personal, not substantive, quarrels.

Within the communities and the community organizations, the first generation of leaders often ruled with wide-ranging authority but were usually reelected to their positions in democratic elections—out of honest respect and recognition of their administrative achievements, as well as for lack of any alternative. Their positive activities for the stabilization of the Jewish community were hardly noted by non-Jews, so that the scandal of the best-known leader of German-Jewish society, Werner Nachmann, had to be especially glaring. Shortly after his death in 1987, it came out that Nachmann—whose "German" correctness was never doubted, especially by the majority of East European Jews—had made over thirty million marks on the side from reparations money during his tenure as chairman of the board of the Central Council. Like the court Jews a few centuries earlier, he had been in favor with the politicians; and reminiscent of the case of Philipp Auerbach a few decades earlier, he was guilty of embezzlement. But unlike the court Jews (who managed money for the absolutist state) and Auerbach (whose embezzlement was never proved, and who acted for Jewish victims), Nachmann worked for his own pocket. So it is understandable that after the embezzlement became known, there were no Jewish spokesmen for Nachmann, quite unlike Auerbach's case.

The explanation for Nachmann's rise, however, cannot be considered apart from the special situation of postwar German Jewry and its momentous dilemma, i.e., the slim potential for leading personalities. The journalist Henryk M. Broder formulated this situation of the postwar

German-Jewish elite, pointing out bitterly as he summed up the Nachmann case:

> If history hadn't taken that turn it has, he would have been a deputy
> recording clerk with a Jewish skittles team or glee club. But because a
> large number of Jews were driven out of Germany, were murdered in
> Germany, people like Nachmann got the chance of their life: to move up,
> to take positions for which they needed only two prerequisites: brutality
> and servility. The Nachmanns made Germany kosher again because they
> served as living proof of how well the Jews were treated. Therefore, they
> were wooed, courted, festooned with Distinguished Service Crosses, in-
> vited to the chancellor's parties, and taken on trips abroad by ministers.[9]

With Nachmann's death and the decease of his successor Heinz Galinski
a few years later, the time of the founding generation's leading the Jewish
communities came to an end. Although Ignatz Bubis, who was elected
chairman of the Central Council at the beginning of the 1990s, was a
concentration camp survivor, like Galinski, his policy, which is characterized by cautious pluralism internally and greater transparency externally, introduced a new phase in postwar German-Jewish history. Neither
Broder's characterization of Nachmann nor Galinski's strict, often embit-
tered behavior typifies the leaders of the Jewish communities in the
1990s. As a popular guest on talk shows and as a speaker at countless
public events, within a few years Bubis became better known and more
popular among the Germans than his predecessors. His popularity
reached its apex in the discussion of the presidential election in 1994,
when he was mentioned as a possible candidate by one of the weekly
journals—a suggestion he quickly dismissed.

2. DEMOGRAPHIC DEVELOPMENT

Approximately 5,000 emigrants returned to Germany during the
first seven years after the war; between 1952 and 1954, only about 1,000
more came back. However, their number doubled by the end of the
1950s and in 1959 totaled roughly 12,500. The percentage of returnees in
the total number of emigrants fifteen years after the war was barely 5
percent.[10] While most of those who returned early were impelled by
ideological reasons, like political commitment, in the late 1950s material
considerations assumed a more important role. Naturally this generaliza-
tion does not apply to all returnees, and in individual cases family, health,
language, and profession were also often decisive factors.

Whereas immigration, or rather return, to Germany in the 1950s constituted a considerable share of the total Jewish population (25 percent), emigration from Germany in the late 1950s was lower than 10 percent. Despite the relatively high average age of community members, there was a significant increase in the Jewish population in Germany in this phase. The nadir of 1952, with a population of 17,427 persons, was quickly surpassed, and at the end of that decade Jewish communities once again numbered more than 23,000 members.[11] This development of an unnatural increase—that is, an increase caused by immigration and not births—of the Jewish population in Germany continued over the next decades, although less intensely. Waves of immigration from Poland, the Soviet Union, Iran, and Israel produced a slow but steady increase of Jewish community members in Germany to 30,000 in the 1980s. In addition to this figure, there were also an unspecified number of Jews who did not become members of the Jewish community because of either taxes or ideology. This group includes an especially large percentage of immigrants from Israel born after the war, who define themselves primarily as "Israelis," not as "Jews." Their social lives often revolve around Israeli clubs or loose groups of friends, but they usually stay away from the synagogue and the community center, unless they happen to be employed there as security guards, Hebrew teachers, or directors of Israeli dance groups. Naturally, however, there are also many exceptions; and mainly in smaller Jewish communities, immigrant Israelis occasionally assume important functions in community life.

Another reason many Israelis stay away from the community is their bad conscience about leaving the Jewish state and coming to the country of Jewish persecution. This applies to the returnees of the 1950s and 1960s, as well as to the immigrants of the 1970s and 1980s, who often had no German family background and represent only a small fraction of emigration from the Jewish state, which has gone mainly to the United States but also to other West European states. In Israel, emigrants are generally considered renegades, fleeing from the economic and political problems of their country to the fleshpots of America and Western Europe.

This attitude was also partially shared by the Jewish communities of Germany. Many of the communities, particularly in the first couple of decades after the Liberation, were completely oriented to Israel and tried to prepare their young members for migration to the Jewish state. Among the DPs who remained in Germany, the older generation justified their staying with the excuse that they were tied to Germany because of business, but they would send their children to Israel. Understandably, these circles found it paradoxical when young Israelis now chose Germany of all places as their new destination. In religious instruction, Hebrew was taught along with information about Israel, but nothing of German-Jewish history was conveyed. The community halls were adorned with portaits of the current Israeli prime minister and military heroes, but hardly any documents about local Jewish history. The members of the communities often knew about the development of the newest kibbutzim in Israel but were thoroughly ignorant of the history of their own communities.

The immigration movement of the 1950s and the concomitant consolidation of the Jewish communities also led to the building of new synagogues and community centers. In only a few cities had synagogues weathered the pogrom of November 9, 1938, intact or only slightly damaged. Where this was the case, the old synagogue could be used again after minor renovation, as was done in Berlin (Pestalozzistrasse, Fränkelufer), Munich (Reichenbachstrasse), Frankfurt (Westend), but also in smaller DP communities in Bavaria, like Amberg, Straubing, and Weiden. Elsewhere, the construction of new synagogues coincided with the start of the return movement and the optimistic outlook for the future entailed in that development. In West Germany, between 1950 and 1967, altogether forty synagogues and chapels were either built or reconstructed.[12]

Further demographic development was indicated by the stagnation of new synagogue construction until the mid-1980s. Increased immigration of Jews from the Soviet Union and its successor states as well as a new self-conception of the Jews living in Germany then produced a new wave of synagogue construction, which replaced those prayer and assembly rooms that were temporary or outgrown. From the mid-1980s on, new synagogues and community centers emerged in such places as Nuremberg, Mannheim, Heidelberg, Freiburg, Darmstadt, Frankfurt am Main, and Essen.

3. ON THE OTHER SIDE OF THE WALL

The fate of the Jews on the other side of the Wall was a special chapter in postwar German-Jewish history. As described above, many emigrants, including prominent Jewish writers and politicians, found the Communist and anti-Fascist East Germany more attractive than the bourgeois republic in West Germany. While there were considerably more Jewish intellectuals and party functionaries—some attained high honor; some were later persecuted—than in West Germany, the Jewish communities in the East were essentially smaller right from the start.

When the Central Council was established in 1949, the Jewish communities of East Germany, numbering 1,140 members in eleven communities (aside from East Berlin), joined it. Until 1952, the Berlin Jewish community comprised both the Western and the Eastern parts of the city. The separation came only after the swing to a clearly antisemitic policy in all Eastern bloc states during the final years of Stalin's rule. In November 1952, this policy reached a climax in the Slánský show trial in Czechoslovakia. Rudolf Slánský, a former secretary-general of the Czech Communist Party, along with thirteen other, mostly Jewish, defendants, was accused of participating in a "Trotskyist-Titoist-Zionist" plot, and all were sentenced to death. Antisemitism, legitimized as anti-Zionism during the trial, was manifested even more distinctly that same year in the Soviet Union when the—again mostly Jewish—Kremlin doctors were arrested and accused of poisoning prominent politicians. East Germany explicitly approved of the Stalinist show trials and ordered concomitant measures against the few remaining Jews there. Accused of "Cosmopolitanism," several Jewish East German Communist Party functionaries were removed from their positions, many were imprisoned, and Jewish candidates were stricken from unity election slates.[13]

As a direct result of Stalinist antisemitism, the Jewish communities of East Germany combined in the *Verband der Jüdischen Gemeinden in der Deutschen Demokratischen Republik* [Association of Jewish Communities in East Germany] on July 9, 1952. Initially, the Berlin community remained united and did not join the alliance. But in that same year, its chairman, Heinz Galinski, also recognized that it was no longer possible to maintain a common institution in such different states and political systems, and moved most of the administration to West Berlin.

In the following months, the political leadership of East Germany pressured the leaders of the Jewish communities to issue a statement of loyalty equating Zionism with Fascism. Julius Meyer, chairman of the East Berlin part of the Jewish community, deputy of the People's Chamber, and undisputed leader of the Jewish community in East Germany, was unwilling to take that step and fled to the West, followed by the chairmen of the communities of Dresden, Leipzig, and Erfurt. In 1952–53, about half the Jews living in East Germany left the country.[14] The dramatic appeal of Berlin rabbi Nathan Peter Levinson to all Jews in East Germany to leave their country as fast as possible also contributed to this mass exodus. (See interview with Nathan Peter Levinson.)

The final phase of Stalin's rule can certainly be regarded as a juncture in the history of the Jews in East Germany. After 1953, the Jewish community in East Germany was reduced to a minuscule and steadily declining number of members. Moreover, most community members were loyally in tune with the Communist state and knew even

Simhat Torah—celebration in the Rykestraße Synagogue (East Berlin) with
Rabbi Riesenburger, 1953 (Bildarchiv Abraham Pisarek, Berlin)

less about Judaism than did the Jewish community in West Germany.
Aside from the communities, however, there were still a few prominent
East German Communist Party politicians of Jewish origin, and, ironi-
cally, the almost "judenrein" East Germany was probably the only coun-
try whose secretary of state for church issues (sic!), Klaus Gysi, was of
Jewish origin.

In the post-Stalin era, the East German leadership became increasingly interested in the existence of a Jewish community, even such
a small one, and gave it official support. The few hundred Jews who were
still enrolled in the Jewish communities were protected as the last speci-
mens of an extinct species, since it would not have made a good impression in world public opinion if the anti-Fascist heir of the Third Reich
were to be "judenrein."

However, official support could cover neither the cultural nor
the demographic problem of existence of the Jewish communities. A former student of the Liberal Rabbinical Seminary in Berlin, Martin Riesenburger (married to a non-Jew and, according to some accounts, never
ordained), served as rabbi in East Berlin until his death in 1965. Except for
two brief guest appearances by a Hungarian rabbi in the 1960s and an
American rabbi in the 1980s, Riesenburger had no successor. Aside from
Berlin, not a single community was capable of holding regular Sabbath
services; and even on the holidays, several communities had to join together to hold religious services. Kosher meat could be bought in East
Berlin, but (except for the diplomats of Muslim states), only a few customers were interested in it.

It was not until the final years of East Germany that clear changes were visible in Jewish life as in many other social areas. Most notable was the lively interest in Judaism evinced by the children of high Communist functionaries, who were completely alienated from Judaism, and by young Jews who were only partially of Jewish origin. Primarily in Berlin, these young people, who were often interested in secular expressions of Judaism, met in youth groups and informal gatherings, like the group *Wir für uns* [We for Us]. Nevertheless, the chairman of the East Berlin community, Peter Kirchner, predicted that his community, which numbered only about 200 members at that time, would shrink by half in the foreseeable future.[15] All the other communities of East Germany combined had even fewer members than East Berlin, most of them numbering fewer than 50 people. The number of members enrolled in the Jewish communities had shrunk from 2,600 in 1952 to 1,200 fifteen years later, and was down to 350 at the time of the dissolution of East Germany.[16] Even if—as is sometimes stated—there are ten times the number of Jews as are enrolled in the communities, the judgment of the former member of the East Berlin Academy of Science Peter Honigmann can hardly be disputed. Three years before the downfall of East Germany, Honigmann announced, "The demographic and assimilationist fate of the Jews in East Germany is sealed."[17]

4. JEWISH IDENTITY IN POSTWAR GERMANY

As we have seen before, the demographic situation in West Germany was quite different. Here the number of members has increased steadily since the 1960s. The demand that all Jews must leave Germany, repeated in Jewish circles since 1945, was refuted by the statistics. Instead of being a source of Jewish out-migration, Germany became a destination of Jewish in-migration; while, on the other hand, a growing stream of emigration was drawn from Israel, the classical country of Jewish immigration. By the 1950s, the image of Germany as only a way station to the final destination of Israel was no longer accurate. Nevertheless, decades elapsed before most Jews living in Germany openly declared a future for themselves and their children on German soil. The bad conscience of living in the country of the murderers and not immigrating to the real homeland of the Jewish people determined the identity of Jews in postwar Germany for decades.

As yet there is no systematic study of the historic development of German-Jewish identity in the postwar years, although three monographs have been devoted to specific problems of postwar German-Jewish identity in various periods. In 1964, the director of the Frankfurt Jewish youth center at the time, Walter W. Jacob Oppenheimer, wrote a dissertation on Jewish youth in Germany, analyzing 274 questionnaires administered to Jewish youth between the ages of nine and eighteen. Oppenheimer focused special attention on the dissonance among Jewish youth between their German milieu and the officially declared interest in migrating to Israel. Two-thirds of his respondents were not born in Germany, and one-third spoke a language other than German with their parents. In the mid-1960s, Yiddish and Polish were still current as colloquial languages among Jewish youth. While parents frequently gave their children German names, at home they called them by other, often Yiddish or Hebrew, names. To the question "Where would you most like to live?" 73 percent answered Israel, 18 percent the United States, but only 8 percent answered Germany.[18]

Thirteen years later, in an unpublished dissertation, Doris Kuschner reaches even more dramatic results. She interviewed 255 Jews living in Germany: 84 percent of them stated that they did not feel that Germany was their homeland; among the young people, the percentage was as high as 94.5.[19] The split personality of Jews living in Germany but identifying with Israel led the secretary-general of the Central Council of Jews in Germany, Hendrik van Dam, to reduce the situation to the following common denominator: "Today it looks as if the German-Jewish symbiosis had become a German-Jewish . . . psychosis."[20]

However, a completely different picture arises from a 1990 opinion poll of 377 Jews in West Germany, where 56 percent of the Jews living in Germany now reject the statement that Israel is their real homeland; and, despite their bond with Jewish culture, 64 percent regard themselves "above all as German."[21] Although neither the formulation of the question nor the target groups of these three opinion polls were identical, clearly, in the 1980s, a change occurred in the consciousness of the Jewish community. As the community increasingly came to be dominated by a "second" generation that was born and grew up in Germany, a stronger affirmation of life in Germany was also introduced. People who were still living in Germany after three or four decades and went on talking about the need to migrate hardly sounded credible anymore. Next to the Israeli flags and the posters of Jerusalem, documents about the local Jewish past and present were slowly making their way into the community halls; the German-Jewish heritage took center stage.

Publicly, German Jews now expressed a new self-awareness, yet they finally admitted that they had long since unpacked their bags. Scholars like Julius H. Schoeps and Michael Wolffsohn, writers like Rafael Seligmann called for a stronger identification as German Jews. Many of

Increase of the Largest Jewish Communities in Germany, 1984–1995

	1984	1995		1984	1995
Berlin	6,370	10,105	Osnabrück	80	867
Frankfurt am Main	4,685	5,934	Recklinghausen	53	863
Munich	3,982	4,964	Aachen	280	855
Düsseldorf	1,674	3,586	Offenbach	805	831
Hamburg	1,393	2,851	Mülheim	99	824
Cologne	1,241	2,466	Freiburg	381	719
Dortmund	289	2,186	Straubing	140	678
Hanover	358	2,060	Manheim	385	620
Stuttgart	704	1,474	Saarbrücken	264	604

them demanded that the Central Council of Jews in Germany be re-named the Central Council of German Jews, as a manifestation of this new awareness. But developments in subsequent years, on the other hand, seem to point in another direction. While the Jewish community in Germany has indeed been growing perceptibly since the early 1990s, two contrary tendencies that began in the eighties now stand in the way of an enhanced identification as "German Jews": the immigration of Jews from the former Soviet Union and the resurgence of extreme right-wing parties and neo-Nazi violence.

Because of migration, the official number of Jewish community members in Germany has risen from about 28,000 in 1989 to over 50,000 in 1996. Larger communities, mainly Berlin, have attracted the most immigrants, but even in smaller communities there has been considerable increase. Many small communities, which were facing a certain end, can now plan for the future once again. In several communities, like Dortmund, Hanover, Osnabrück, and Recklinghausen, the Russian migrants already constitute the vast majority of the community members (see table).

In large communities like Berlin and Düsseldorf, the situation is similar. As the Jewish communities in Germany have grown, the percentage of German Jews among their members has diminished even more. Renaming the Central Council of Jews in Germany would therefore be a clear misrepresentation of the facts and would exclude the majority of Jews living in Germany.

But even for those Jews who were born and grew up in Germany, the words "German Jew" are not so easy to utter in reunited Germany. In the 1980s, Jewish protest demonstrations were primarily against individual acts of political or cultural leaders—for example, against the visit of Helmut Kohl and Ronald Reagan to the military cemetery in Bitburg, or against the performance of Fassbinder's play *Garbage, the City, and Death* in Frankfurt in 1985. The resultant spectacularly successful protests signaled a new chapter of open political demonstrations on the part of Jewish functionaries. But ostensible verbal gaffes the following year—like that of the CSU Bundestag deputy Fellner about the payment of damages by the German Bank to the surviving slave laborers of the Flick Company ("that the Jews quickly come forward whenever money jingles in German cashboxes") or that of the Korschenbroich mayor Graf von Spree ("To balance our economy, we should have beaten a few rich Jews to death"), on the other hand—confirmed that German politicians were now more openly expressing antisemitic sentiments which had hitherto been confined to the level of private discourse.[22]

In the 1990s, however, the Jews of Germany were confronted with a new phenomenon: the entrance of radical right-wing parties in several state parliaments (the first time after the success of the NPD in the late 1960s, and now on a more frightening scale), as well as the open, almost daily violence against those seeking asylum and against foreigners living in Germany. As recently as 1994, a synagogue was set on fire in Lübeck for the first time since the November pogrom of 1938, and it was clear to the Jews living in Germany that they had also become a target, although a less visible one, of the newly risen neo-Nazis. In the absence of a clearly identifiable human objective, cemeteries and memorials became the targets of anti-Jewish violence.

5. RELIGIOUS AND CULTURAL LIFE

In 1986, Pnina Navé Levinson, representative of Liberal Judaism and literary scholar, concluded in her study of the religious life of the Jewish communities "that local Jewry lives on an island, cut off from developments in other countries, even in neighboring countries like Holland."[23] At about the same time, the Orthodox psychologist Yizhak Ahren summed up, "From a religious perspective, Germany since 1945 looks like a desert." As for its Jewish education, according to Ahren, most academically trained Jews "have remained on the level of kindergarten."[24]

In fact, Liberal and Orthodox agree on the evaluation of Jewish religious life in postwar Germany. The three major trends of Judaism that emerged in Germany in the nineteenth century—neo-Orthodox, Reform, and Conservative Jewry—steadily developed in the Western world, but in postwar Germany they practically fell into oblivion. Because of the predominance of East European community members, many synagogues mainly in southern Germany were oriented toward traditional East European variants of Jewish observance. In practice, this meant that organs were removed from synagogues or rather were no longer installed, prayer in German was banned, and partitions were erected between the men's and the women's sections. A decreasing minority maintains compliance with this external observance, which is supported by a largely secular majority, who prefer the Orthodox ritual at least on the three days a year when they attend the synagogue. On a normal Sabbath, most synagogues that still regularly hold services are gapingly empty. In the 1980s, Helmut Eschwege reported from East Germany, "today, if you go into a synagogue, forty people are there, twenty-five of them non-Jews." This could also apply to the big communities of the West, where, Yizhak Ahren stated, "We have about twelve hundred community members in Cologne, but it is a problem to get ten men together every morning."[25]

Orthodoxy in postwar Germany was just as uncreative as other religious trends in Judaism. In the 1950s, an attempt to establish a permanent *Vereinigung für thoratreues Judentum* was thwarted.[26] After most of the DPs withdrew, there was neither a yeshiva (traditional talmudic school) nor an Orthodox high school, nor a seminary for Jewish religious teachers—institutions that had existed during the Weimar Republic. Even in the early 1990s, when small groups of young Jews are beginning to return to Orthodoxy as a belated reaction to similar movements in the United States and Israel, this must not necessarily be deemed new creativity. Some of the new Orthodox Jews are doubtless impelled by an internal change, but others may be following fashion. If it was previously taboo to attract attention on the street as a Jew, this is now "in"—either by covering one's head with a skullcap, wearing ritual fringes, or using a Hebrew name instead of a German one.

At the other end of the spectrum, there was also movement in the early 1990s. In several communities, for the first time discussions took place about Liberal religious services, in which women have equal rights. Although Liberal Judaism (which comprises Reform as well as Conservative Jewry in the United States) is still less prominent in Germany than in neighboring European countries like Switzerland, Holland, and France, for the first time a (Conservative) woman rabbi has been serving in the small north German community of Oldenburg since 1995. In most large cities, Liberal religious service has been making a comeback since the early 1990s on private initiative. There are religious services with organ accompaniment in only two synagogues (Berlin Pestalozzistrasse and Saarbrücken), and even there men and women are separated.

This development does not necessarily endanger the special character of German-Jewish communities as united communities. It is true that the Jewish communities in West Germany, unlike the private congregations of the United States, are public-legal bodies to which all the Jews of a locality belong as members and taxpayers. But, with the exception of a few Orthodox "secession communities," this was also the case prior to 1933, as described above, when different synagogues were established within the so-called unified communities and where rabbis of different religious trends would officiate. It was inconceivable in the 1920s that the three rabbis in one locality would all be Orthodox, as in Munich in the nineties.

To blame the structure of the unified community (which exists unchallenged in postwar Germany, except for the small secession community of *Adass Yisroel* in Berlin) for this development is to overlook causal factors. Ignorance is rather the main cause of the stagnation of religious life in the communities. The two-hour religious instruction for Jewish students lacks not only current textbooks but also trained German-speaking teachers. In the rabbinate, the situation seems even more dramatic. After 1945, not a single rabbi with roots in postwar Germany served the German-Jewish communities. Exceptions like Uri Themal in Berlin (1968), Ady Edward Assabi in Düsseldorf (1972), and the Orthodox Rabbi Macner in Mannheim in the eighties were unable to gain a foothold and left Germany after a short time.[27] At the same time, rabbis born before the war and trained in German became increasingly rare in the eighties and nineties. Foreign rabbis shunned positions in Germany because of language problems as well as historical factors.

A similar situation emerged during the first postwar years for other essential religious functionaries in the Jewish community. If a circumcision was to be carried out, the ritual circumciser had to be brought from Strasbourg or Zurich; if kosher meat was to be slaughtered, the ritual slaughterer was flown in from London (in East Germany, from Budapest). In many communities, it is rapidly becoming more difficult to fill the ranks of the Burial Society, a post that was traditionally deemed an honor.

In 1979, the Central Council founded the College for Jewish Studies in Heidelberg. Within fifteen years, its original purpose of training rabbis and religion teachers for the Jewish communities was realized to a modest extent. Thus some of the religion teachers trained in the college are already working, but so far not a single rabbi for a Jewish community has been recruited through the college. From the beginning, the college has attracted essentially more non-Jewish than Jewish students. Its summer courses exercise a broader effect within the Jewish communities, granting about twenty community members a brief insight into the various aspects of Jewish culture each year.

Jewish primary schools exist in Munich, Frankfurt, Berlin, and most recently Düsseldorf; and since 1993, there is also a Jewish *Gymnasium* in Berlin. Whether Jewish education is firmly on the way to developing schools in Germany is not yet clear. This will depend mainly on whether these schools succeed not only in creating a Jewish milieu for their pupils (despite the fact that a few Jewish schools also have a considerable portion of non-Jewish students and teachers, and the only Jewish *Gymnasium* has a non-Jewish principal) but also on whether they can impart Jewish content. In any case, it is remarkable that, since the eighties, in most states of West Germany, many Jewish students have taken advantage of the possibility to enroll in Jewish religious teachings as an examination subject for matriculation.

After the establishment of local Jewish student organizations in the immediate postwar years, Jewish students combined in 1960 in the *Bundesverband Jüdischer Studenten in Deutschland* (BJSD) [National Association of Jewish Students in Germany]. The association, with more than a thousand members, holds seminars three or four times a year and actively engages in political discussion. The *Bund Jüdischer Jugend* [Organization of Jewish Youth], founded in the 1970s, had to dissolve after about ten years. One of the main functions of Jewish student and youth alliances—whether they admit it or not—is to provide an opportunity for men and women of marriageable age to meet. Only a minority of Jews who marry in Germany seek a Jewish spouse. Given the minuscule possibilities of selection, that is hardly surprising. In Munich, according to the principal of the local Jewish youth center, Ellen Presser, there are barely three hundred Jews between the ages of twenty-two and thirty. It is like living in a village. Sometimes people go to the "neighboring villages" of Berlin or Düsseldorf. Or to a BJSD seminar.[28]

Ever since the 1970s, Jewish students in Germany have published their own journal, first under the name of *Heshbon* [Account], and later in a different form titled *Freie Stimme* [Free voice]. Appearing irregularly and accessible to only a small circle of readers, these journals could not overcome the main problem of the German-Jewish press. Before 1933, over a hundred Jewish publications of various political, religious, and cultural orientations appeared; but in postwar Germany, there was no basis for a public Jewish discourse. After Karl Marx's death, the *Allgemeine Jüdische Wochenzeitung*, published in Düsseldorf, could not continue as an independent paper for long and became the official organ of the Central Council of the Jews in Germany. Obviously, this situation offers no latitude for criticism of the official community leadership. The Jewish journals from Munich, the German-language *Münchner Jüdische Nachrichten* [Munich Jewish news] published by Moses Lustig, and the Yiddish *Neue*

Jüdische Nachrichten [New Jewish news] published by Marian Gid, which existed until the seventies, were also loyal to the Jewish organizations and their leaders. On the other hand, because of their intellectual caliber, or rather, their polemical-critical position, *Babylon* and *Semit*, journals founded in the eighties, could not appeal to the bulk of Jewish community members. Throughout its existence, *Semit* concentrated primarily on a frontal attack against Heinz Galinski, and it seemed only natural that the journal disappeared when Galinski died. An independent Jewish journal representing critical opinions and appealing to a broad Jewish audience, like the *Jüdische Rundschau* in Switzerland, does not exist in postwar Germany.

However, an essential change is indicated in the mid-nineties. The *Allgemeine Jüdische Wochenzeitung* has become both more "Jewish" and more critical. For the first time in decades, Jewish editors are again publishing the only nationwide Jewish newspaper in Germany. It has found a young editorial staff that has grown up in postwar Germany and is increasingly devoted to the problems of community members. Less visible now are the guest commentaries by German politicians and critiques of general social topics, which had long been the basic stock of the front pages and increased even more during the brief tenure of the Israeli journalist Daniel Dagan as editor-in-chief in 1993. Turning to internal Jewish subject matter, the newspaper has become increasingly critical since Heinz Galinski's death. Even though it is still published by the Central Council, it has also opened its pages to critical voices. At the same time, however, the financial predicament has forced it to change to a biweekly.

The community papers, which contain many intellectually critical articles, have contributed to the cultural revival of the communities. A special example of this is the annual journal of the Fürth Jewish community with its rich tradition, which contains scholarly articles on local history along with news of the community. However, the paper is aimed primarily at former Fürth Jews living abroad and for a long time was even edited in England. The paper of the Association of Jewish Communities in Bavaria, which appears on the Jewish holidays, also contains longer scholarly articles and a special Yiddish-language part. In Frankfurt, the *Frankfurter Jüdische Zeitung* is the most significant independent Jewish newspaper.

In all the large communities, there are B'nai Brith lodges, as well as women's leagues, senior groups, and Zionist clubs, whose cultural productions serve primarily as social get-togethers. Adult education as well as discussions of controversial subjects are found in the programs of the Jewish adult education schools in Berlin, Frankfurt, and Munich. These institutions form the cultural backbone of the communities, include extremely prominent speakers, and have created an impressive Jewish adult education system in the three decades of their existence. But in one essential point, they differ from their predecessors, the Jewish schools of the 1920s and 1930s, which were created by Franz Rosenzweig. While Rosenzweig was mainly concerned with conveying a "lost" Jewish knowledge to assimilated Jews, today's Jewish evening schools are attended primarily by interested non-Jews.

During the 1970s and 1980s, independent "Jewish Groups," whose members fancied that they fell between all stools, emerged in opposition to the community establishment. Developing out of the student movement, they criticized the conservative community leadership and its unconditional support of every Israeli policy, especially during the war in Lebanon. At the same time, they felt rejected by their political homeland, the German Left, because of its often aggressive anti-Zionism. As "critical Jews," they tried to find a way, in informal meetings with discussions and lectures, between the established Jewish structure and the legacy of the German generation of the 1968 student protests. In unified Berlin, the *Jüdische Kulturverein* [Jewish Cultural Association] has assumed a special role; this organization, consisting primarily of a group of secular Jews from the former East Germany, presents a diversified cultural proposal.

Does the existence of these various groups indicate an incipient pluralism of Jewish life in Germany; or is it merely evidence of the flight of critical community members to a more attractive milieu? Both observations may contain some truth, but given this development, one essential factor distinguishing Jewish life in Germany from other Jewish communities must be considered. Salomon Korn, board member of the Jewish community of Frankfurt, emphasizes this specific German problematic:

> In West Germany, there is no living Jewish religious core, from which, as it were, a development stream can flow permanently from religion toward secularization; all observed scholarly and cultural activities here are no longer derivatives of living primary sources. If they did exist, the Jews living here, as in many other countries, could indulge in all kinds and "aberrations" of a secular Jewry; the disintegration inevitably associated with that, the historically recognized decline at the edges, would be compensated for by this permanent stream. But the Jews of West Germany indulge all possible derivations of Judaism, without possessing a source for this necessary stream.[29]

One manifestation of the reinforcement of a secular Jewish culture is the growing number of Jewish authors who write about Jewish subjects. They show an enormous range in style and perspective. Among the women writers, Barbara Honigmann portrayed, in her intentionally naive style, the Orthodox milieu of oriental Jews in Strasbourg, where she moved in the 1980s from East Berlin; Esther Dischereit's plays and novels, on the other hand, are closer to postmodernist feminist German writing. Very different again are the stories and novels of Irene Dische. Born in the United States to German immigrants, she was raised Protestant and continues to write in English, although her books are published mostly in German and often focus on German-Jewish characters. Among male authors, Maxim Biller and Rafael Seligmann blend disappointment about the intellectual vacuity in the Jewish community with resignation at inducing change here. As another young Jewish writer, Richard Chaim Schneider, puts it, they describe a "straggling heap clinging desperately to something it no longer possesses: a Judaism from way back when. No one shows any interest in creating a new Judaism. There is simply not enough strength for that anymore."[30] This assessment unwittingly evokes Franz Kafka's letter to his father, in which Kafka commented on the vestiges of his father's Judaism, "it was too little to be handed on to the child; it all dribbled away while you were passing it on."[31]

Kafka, who had grown up without Jewish knowledge, began to seek his lost Judaism. He became enthusiastic about Yiddish theater, studied Hebrew, and attended events at the Liberal rabbinical seminary in Berlin. Today there are once again many German Jews in Kafka's situation: branded externally by history and identification as Jews, they know little about their Judaism. Yet today, it is not antisemitism or even the shadow of the recent past that calls their Judaism into consciousness every day, but rather the immense interest in Jewish history and culture in the non-Jewish environment.

6. JEWISH CULTURE WITHOUT JEWS?

Gershom Scholem, arguably the most prominent scholar of Jewish studies in the twentieth century, once called it an irony of history that it was only after German Jewry was practically destroyed that the academic study of Judaism and the Jews—for which Jewish scholars had struggled in vain for a century—was introduced into German universities. Similar observations can be made about almost all areas of Jewish culture in postwar Germany. Jewish bookstores are flourishing in Munich and Berlin; and every year, hundreds of new books in Jewish history, literature, and religion fill their shelves. Exhibits on Jewish subjects are among the most successful enterprises of German museums. Klezmer bands and synagogue choirs of non-Jewish musicians organize concerts and festivals, exciting a non-Jewish audience over traditional East European Jewish and liturgical melodies. The kosher restaurants near the newly restored synagogue on Oranienburger Strasse of the old-new German capital have become the "in" meeting places for the intellectual elite of Berlin.

A climax of enthusiasm for Jewish culture was the exhibition *Jüdische Lebenswelten* [Patterns of Jewish Life] in Berlin during the winter of 1991–92 and its accompanying program. In no other country did curators ever succeed in putting together such an impressive and representative cross section of Jewish life and creation through the centuries and continents. The 350,000 visitors, including thousands of schoolchildren, were also visibly impressed. The curators concentrated on the creative achievement of the Jewish people, not on persecution. Hence the Holocaust was excluded, or rather treated separately in the same building. Jewish history, particularly for the organizers, was not to be portrayed as a passive history of suffering, but rather as the history of an active and creative culture. Every evening, there was an impressive program with Yiddish films, liturgical music, theatrical productions, and discussions.

Contemporary cultural life in Germany was not included in this exhibit, and for good reason. Similarly, artists for the annual *Jüdische Kulturtage* [Jewish Cultural Festival] are usually flown in—from New York, Tel Aviv, and Budapest. Only a few of the customers of the Jewish bookstores or the readers of Jewish books and the few intellectual Jewish journals are Jews. The final years of East Germany presented almost the same picture. For example, of 319 users of the East Berlin Community Library, only 23 were Jews. There was a similar proportion of Jewish participants in the *Jüdische Kulturverein*: at times, only about 10 percent of those attending were Jews. In the Leipzig synagogue choir, established in 1963, whose concerts were broadcast every other Saturday morning on Berlin Radio, the only Jewish member was the founder.[32]

Despite these facts that are well-known in West and East Germany, the dazzling golden dome of the restored synagogue on Oranienburger Strasse has blinded many observers, like one well-meaning reporter of a large Berlin newspaper. After the *Jüdische Kulturtage 1992*—still dazed by klezmer music and Anatevka romanticism—this reporter sketched a vision of "A Shtetl in the Big City of the Nineties." Clearly, he thought that exhibits and cultural festivals prove that Jewish life was back on the path to normalization. Demands to change the name of the Central Council of Jews in Germany to the Central Council of German Jews have become increasingly louder; in short, the time has come "to get away from the Holocaust fixation, put an end to the unconditional Israel orientation."[33]

That article climaxed a series of various publications of German journalists, historians, and literary scholars during the past years. Moreover, they could refer to a few German-Jewish journalists and scholars who speak of this "reincarnation" of a German-Jewish symbiosis that never existed. The flagrant lack of a vibrant internal Jewish dialogue is important, especially when Jewish voices are quoted articulating ideas that the non-Jewish side does not have the nerve to express. The public debate on the United States Holocaust Memorial Museum, which opened in Washington, D.C., on April 22, 1993, may elucidate this. While in general the German media vacillated between dispassionate approval and genuine perplexity, Jewish journalists did not mince words. Rafael Seligmann, in the *Süddeutsche Zeitung*, Professor Michael Wolffsohn in the corresponding issue of the *Frankfurter Allgemeine Zeitung* two days later, and finally Henryk M. Broder in *Der Spiegel* all expressed what had naturally constituted a taboo for others. Who else could have used such concepts as "Holocaust nostalgia society" (Seligmann) or "Shoah business" (Broder)? And only a "German-Jewish patriot" (Wolffsohn on Wolffsohn) could have condemned memorials purely and simply as sites of modern idolatry. In a penetrating analysis in the *Süddeutsche Zeitung*, another German-Jewish journalist, Josef Joffe, pointed out that indirect criticism was preferred in these cases: to prevent blasting away directly at the Holocaust sites, "hundred percent kosher grenades" were brought into play, and the memorials were declared not anti-German but anti-Jewish enemy objects, alien to the principles of true Jewish memory, which only obscure authentic Jewish identity.[34]

The rector of the College for Jewish Studies in Heidelberg, Julius Carlebach, commented on those statements: "And because the audience that can be reached is now largely non-Jewish, a safe shield has been adopted. Where hatred is expressed, they imagine that their own Jewishness is the qualification that makes it possible to assault everything Jewish in style and attitude, something no German who writes about Jews can indulge in these days."[35] This predilection makes it difficult in fact to be a "critical" Jewish voice in Germany. Willy-nilly, the moment one reveals his identity as a Jew, one becomes a token Jew. Or, as the writer Esther Dischereit put it self-critically, "To write in Jewish in front of a German-German audience has a slatternly prostituting air about it—like a woman getting undressed in front of the eyes of men, I know."[36]

As for non-Jews, well-meaning efforts to "assimilate" their own past and "refurbish" the orphaned German-Jewish heritage are often just as painful. Surely the German railroad administration meant well when it named one of its new intercity trains for Anne Frank. We can only hope they were sensitive enough not to put the Anne Frank Express on the Frankfurt-Warsaw line. But what is most impressive is that no one even seems to notice the tragic irony of such a name. Occasionally, the "good intentions" also have a more humorous aspect, as in the case of the mayor of a small Bavarian town who held a buffet for Brotherhood Week. For this occasion, he ordered extra kosher meat from Munich, which was served with cheese in sandwiches. Or the resolute speaker of the Berlin House of Deputies who, at the memorial for Heinz Galinski, kept talking about the "Jewish God Jahweh," not noticing the Orthodox rabbi sinking deeper into his chair at the sacrilege of mentioning the divine name at a Jewish funeral. If German Jews were once suspected of appearing more German than the Germans, many non-Jews are now trying to be more Jewish than the Jews.

There are also more egregious cases of German-Jewish role changes, as illustrated by two examples from the still divided Germany. Karin Mylius, daughter of a former member of an SS Special Unit, managed to get elected to the board of the Jewish community of Halle in 1969, through a clever intrigue and without ever converting to Judaism. During her twenty-five years in this office, she systematically destroyed whatever was left of Jewish life in the city, adopted the hardly appropriate title of doctor of theology, buried her father in rabbinical robes under a Star of David, and offered non-Jews "sample prayers" in an imaginary language. Her son Frank Chaim evinced a unique and precocious interest in Jewish matters by smashing synagogue windows and scrawling swastikas; this, however, did not prevent his mother from sending him to the Budapest rabbinical school to be trained as a cantor, and having him apply to the Jewish communities to serve in that capacity.[37] In 1993, an Israeli press report stated that not a single member of the board of the Magdeburg Jewish community was a Jew. Here, Max Frisch's Andri—the Jew who is not a Jew but is considered by his milieu to be a Jew— becomes living satire.

Such perversions of Jewish life were not limited to the East. In Cologne, in the 1980s, a bizarre murder caused a sensation. A student of Jewish studies who had converted to Judaism shot and killed her non-Jewish professor and wounded several other lecturers and fellow students in the institute building. She claimed as her motive that non-Jews were forbidden to engage in Jewish scholarship.

While non-Jews and new Jewish converts demonstrate a need to be more Jewish than their Jewish compatriots, Jews are supposed to demonstrate a German character. Hence films about Jews as German patriots are screened and plays about Jews in the German army are staged. Even the soul of Heinz Galinski, may he rest in peace, was not impervious to being gathered in by German patriotism. Shortly before the memorial ceremony, when the first honors appeared in the Berlin newspapers, one tabloid believed it best to honor the chairman of the Jewish community by turning the man—whose harsh words with friends often caused ill feeling—from an Auschwitz survivor into the model German bourgeois. The city had lost a great Berliner, who had participated in many things but was moved when his Hertha soccer team played and liked nothing better than breeding cactus at home. If this metamorphosis were not enough, he subsequently also had to be anointed with holy water: an oversize cross was resplendent next to his name on the front page of that edition.[38] The responsible journalists were doubtless aware of what they were doing—and they probably acted out of good intentions, knowing full well that Galinski would be accepted by their readers only if he were "one of us." In other words, there is still a great demand for German Jews among the public, but they must also be good Germans.

Despite this rather unattractive description of Jewish life in Germany on the eve of the millennium, there is also legitimate hope for a more optimistic future. Two developments that have no connection to speak of run parallel to one another: On the one hand, since the 1980s, a change of consciousness has emerged among young German Jews who are unmistakably and increasingly trying to express their Jewish identity within the framework of a general "ethnic revival." On the other hand, institutions necessary for the construction of a living culture do exist but do not attract much of a Jewish audience. The immigration of Jews from the former Soviet Union could form the connecting link between these two developments. Instead of a turning outward with shrill tones, there now appears a need to make the even "less Jewish" immigrants into "real Jews," and in the process, one often encounters one's own Judaism. It is only because of this recent development that a small community like Wuppertal employs its own rabbi, that evening courses for Jewish adults are held in the Bavarian town of Weiden, that Liberal religious services take place for the first time in Heidelberg, and in other places people are explaining the prayers to the worshipers for the first time. Ostensibly, this is supposed to make integration easy for the new members of the community; in fact, however, the old members of the community profit from it to the same degree.

This process of self-discovery is hardly a retreat to the old society. In a proportion of the population of 0.1 percent, talk of the danger of ghettoization is absurd. This development is necessary for survival precisely so that Jewish identity is defined not solely by a negative demarcation from the surrounding society but rather as the expression of a positive knowledge of Jewish culture, whether religious or secular. If German Jews were henceforth to be seriously interested in their own history, they would also discover that their "search for a lost Judaism" is absolutely nothing new. Franz Rosenzweig clearly understood that if German Jews became aware of their Judaism, it would make them not only better Jews but also better Germans. In the framework of a systematic renewal of Jewish adult education, in 1920, he established the *Freie Jüdische Lehrhaus*, whose function was formulated in 1923 by one of its teachers, the physician Richard Koch, in words that sound almost prophetic:

> We separate ourselves from no one of goodwill. Nor from the non-Jewish world, the nations among whom we do not live, but rather to whom we belong, as we are, with what we love and want. May our road onward with them not again be a road of suffering, as it has been for such long stretches. But if our historical suffering should recur someday, then we want to know why we suffer; we do not want to die like animals, but like humans who know what is good and what is bad. . . . Often enough others and we ourselves have told us that we are Jews, that we have faults and virtues. The Lehrhaus shall teach us why and for what purpose we are [Jews].[39]

Fifty years after its reestablishment, the Jewish community in Germany has reached a turning point. Contrary to all the forebodings of the early postwar years, the number of its members is higher today than at any time since the war. Despite increasing neo-Nazi tendencies, despite recently damaged synagogues and memorials, united Germany will definitely not be a Germany without Jews. The big question on the eve of the next millennium is whether there will again be a Jewish life among the Jews of Germany, whether they will know "why and how" they identify themselves as Jews.

IV.

Interview with Ignatz Bubis, President of the Central Council of the Jews in Germany, on the Situation of German Jewry (July 1994)

IGNATZ BUBIS was born to Polish-Jewish parents in then German Breslau in 1927. Together with his family he moved to Polish Deblin after the Nazi rise to power. Surviving ghetto and concentration camp, he settled as a businessman in postwar Germany. He has been living in Frankfurt am Main since 1956. As one of the leading real estate owners in Frankfurt he was a primary target of social protests in the 1970s and was identified as the anonymous "rich Jew" in Rainer-Werner Fassbinder's controversial play, *Der Müll, die Stadt und der Tod*. Together with other members of the Jewish community, Bubis helped to prevent the staging of this play by demonstrating on the occasion of the planned opening of the show in 1985. He has been active for more than two decades in Jewish communal politics in Frankfurt and was elected in 1992 as the successor of Heinz Galinski, to lead the Central Council of Jews in Germany. Ever since, he has been a prominent and popular figure among the German public, whose integrity and openness have earned him appreciation from virtually all political camps. At the same time he is an active member of the Liberal Party and led their slate in the 1997 elections to the Frankfurt City Council. For two autobiographical accounts of his experiences (in German), see *I Am a German Citizen of the Jewish Faith* (1993) and *I Am Not Finished Yet* (1996).

Are you pleased with the title of your autobiography, Deutscher Staatsbürger jüdischen Glaubens *[I am a German citizen of the Jewish faith]?*

Yes, I even insisted on this title. With this title, I wanted to make non-Jews aware that a great many Jews living here have been Germans for centuries. It is still the case that a lot of Jews are considered foreigners.

There is no doubt now, after the immigration from the former Soviet Union, it's undeniable, that the majority of the current Jewish society is not of German origin, but we also have a part that is rooted here in Germany.

What about the second part of this phrase, the definition of Judaism as faith?

I would define Judaism primarily as faith. There is also the Jewish people. And now this is what happens: Everybody who converts to Judaism is part of the Jewish people. Or—what happens with somebody who leaves Judaism, converts to Christianity—is he or are his children still part of the Jewish people? Judaism is a mixture of peoplehood and religion, and it's hard to separate one from the other.

If we define Judaism on a religious-cultural level, how do you judge the present situation of Judaism in Germany? Do you see a certain flourishing of Jewish culture?

No, I am very cautious here. If we're talking about Jewish culture today, which does have a certain attraction here, it is more an attraction out of curiosity among non-Jews, maybe even curiosity about the exotic, but not a genuine, profound interest. Not even among the Jews is there a genuine interest in Jewish culture, maybe a little nostalgia. I note this when we have a performance of klezmer music in Frankfurt, with Jewish theater, etc.—you see people over sixty and non-Jews, because for them it's something exotic. When my daughter speaks Yiddish with her grandmother, for example, it's more as a lark, not out of any profound interest.

You write in your book that, after Rabbi Lichtigfeld (in Frankfurt during the 1960s), there was no rabbinical personality in Germany. How would you imagine such a rabbinical personality in Germany?

I would imagine a rabbinical personality, you know—when he comes through the door, people respect him. Rabbis can acquire this respect only themselves through their authority, their knowledge, and their behavior.

Can a woman also achieve this respect—a woman rabbi, as is quite common in America?

No, in my view, no. Even though Judaism is increasingly secular and reform.

But the reform movement and secularization are two different things. This is a redefinition of the Jewish religion.

Yes, you're right. And I also believe that the Conservative movement, which is widespread even in Israel, will prevail in Germany too in the long run. But the survival of Judaism for two thousand years of Diaspora was possible only because, in these two thousand years, it didn't reform.

How do you judge the current efforts in many communities to achieve greater religious variety?

I have no problem at all with Liberal religious services if they are within the homogeneous communities—but it has to happen under the umbrella of unity.

How do you see the function of the College for Jewish Studies in this connection?

I would expect more from a College for Jewish Studies, at least the training of a greater number of qualified teachers of religion. As yet, it is primarily an educational institution for interested non-Jews. But maybe that's because Jewish youth in Germany unfortunately aren't very interested in religious life or don't have much desire to be teachers or rabbis.

Given the situation you described, how do you judge the future of the Jewish community?

I am not very optimistic. The Russian immigrants have given the numbers of the communities a tremendous boost. I don't know how long they will stay in the communities. Not very many impulses for Judaism will come from them.

Isn't it a task of the communities to do more here?

Here in fact too little happens to lead them to Judaism. The Israelis say that when somebody with no notion of Judaism comes to Israel, he'll become a Jew. But when somebody who has no notion of Judaism comes to Germany, Judaism gets lost; that's true in a certain sense.

Is it your opinion, therefore, that in the future there will be Jews in Germany but no living Judaism?

There will be a living Judaism, but of a minority. So today (1994), including the immigration, there are 43,000 of us Jews in Germany; maybe the number will reach 50–60,000 some day. But living Judaism will be limited to a small group, I'm afraid: to Munich, Frankfurt, Berlin, Düsseldorf, Cologne, and now I have to think about it some more. I am very pessimistic, and I must say we should be much more active in this direction.

Do you have any concrete proposals for that?

Yes, I don't think we have enough religion teachers and rabbis. Rabbis who regard it as a calling—not a profession. We have a few rabbis who regard it as a profession, but not as a calling. And the others don't want to come to Germany.

How would you want this situation to change?

I don't know. I really don't know. You know, in the last two years, since I have been the chairman of the Central Council, I have been more concerned with political issues than with internal Jewish affairs. I hope the political situation will calm down, so that I will have more time again for Jewish issues.

Appendix

BIBLIOGRAPHICAL ESSAY

Titles mentioned in the bibliographical essay have been noted in short form in the notes. Yiddish and Hebrew titles have been transcribed into Latin letters according to standard rules but deviate if the original has been published in Latin letters.

In the absence of a complete bibliography on the subject, the current bibliography of the Leo Baeck Institute Year Book offers the most comprehensive survey. A collection of the most important titles is in Eva-Maria Timme, "Bibliographie zur Nachkriegsgeschichte der Juden in Deutschland," in Andreas Nachama and Julius H. Schoeps, eds., *Aufbau nach dem Untergang: Deutsch-jüdische Geschichte nach 1945* (Berlin, 1992), pp. 427–436. Source material for the first postwar years is scattered in several archives in Germany, Israel, and the United States. Most Jewish communities in Germany have their own archive, a few of which have been collected in the Heidelberg *Zentralarchiv zur Erforschung der Geschichte der Juden in Deutschland* [Central Archive for Research of the History of the Jews in Germany] since the early 1990s. An important source for Jewish life in the postwar period is the German-Jewish press. The *Allgemeine Jüdische Wochenzeitung*, founded in 1946 (under changing titles), and published since 1973 by the Central Council of Jews in Germany, has been of central significance. Important articles on contemporary German-Jewish history are mainly in the intellectual forum *Babylon*, which has appeared since 1986. The *Tribüne*, published since 1962, and *Emuna*, which appeared between 1966 and 1975, are devoted to the Christian-Jewish dialogue and relations with Israel. Three journals of recent origin have a scholarly character: *Menora* of the Steinheim Institute in Duisburg, *Trumah* of the College for Jewish Studies in Heidelberg, and *Aschkenas*, which is devoted especially to German-Jewish history. All three journals also include articles on Jewish life in postwar Germany.

INTRODUCTORY LITERATURE

A comprehensive study of the reconstruction of Jewish life in postwar Germany has not yet been done. The most valuable monograph on the construction phase is still the unpublished dissertation of Harry Maor, "Über den Wiederaufbau der jüdischen Gemeinden in Deutschland seit 1945" (Mainz,

1960). *Jüdisches Leben in Deutschland seit 1945*, ed. Micha Brumlik et al. (Frankfurt am Main, 1986) presents the lectures of a conference on various aspects of Jewish life in postwar Germany. A more recent collection is Michal Y. Bodemann, ed., *Jews, Germans, Memory: Reconstruction of Jewish Life in Germany* (Ann Arbor, 1996). Monika Richarz offers a summary, "Jews in Today's Germanies," *Year Book of the Leo Baeck Institute* 30 (1985): 265–274; as does Lynn Rapaport in "The Cultural and Material Reconstruction of the Jewish Communities in the Federal Republic of Germany," in *Jewish Social Studies* 49 (1987): 137–154. Thus far, the only comprehensive German monograph on this subject is Erica Burgauer, *Zwischen Erinnerung und Verdrängung—Juden in Deutschland nach 1945* (Reinbek, 1993). For the flaws of this work, however, see the critical review by Stefan Rohrbacher, "Am grossen Thema kläglich gescheitert," in *Aufbau*, January 21, 1994. On the problems of the study by the American anthropologist Michael Cohn, *The Jews in Germany, 1945–1993: The Building of a Minority* (Westport and London, 1994), see my criticism, "Neues Leben—oder nur ein trügerischer Glanz?" in *Frankfurter Allgemeine Zeitung*, December 14, 1994, p. 15. While an adequate portrait of postwar Jewish history in Germany is still a desideratum of research, numerous important studies of individual aspects have appeared.

JEWISH DISPLACED PERSONS

An effective summary of the situation of the Jewish DPs is offered by the recent monograph of Angelika Königseder and Juliane Wetzel, *Lebensmut im Wartesaal. Die jüdischen DPs im Nachkriegsdeutschland* (Frankfurt am Main, 1994). Wetzel previously published the important local study *Jüdisches Leben in München 1945–1951. Durchgangsstation oder Wiederaufbau?* (Munich, 1987). The British Occupation Zone is the focus of Wolfgang Jacobmeyer's "Jüdische Überlebende als 'Displaced Persons,'" in *Geschichte und Gesellschaft* 9 (1983): 429–444; as well as of Ursula Büttner's *Not nach der Befreiung. Die Situation der deutschen Juden in der britischen Besatungszone 1945–1948* (Hamburg, 1986); and Hagit Lavsky, "The Day After: Bergen-Belsen from Concentration Camp to the Centre of Jewish Survivors in Germany," in *German History* 11 (1993): 36–59. On the situation in Austria, see Thomas Albrich, *Exodus durch Österreich. Die jüdischen Flüchtlinge 1945–1948. Innsbrucker Studien zur Zeitgeschichte*, vol. 1 (Innsbruck, 1987). These works are thorough analyses of the existing archival materials on the subject of Jewish Displaced Persons, but (with the exception of Lavsky) they exclude Hebrew and Yiddish sources (unless the Yiddish camp newspapers were printed in Latin letters). This is also true of the general surveys of the DPs in postwar Germany. The two most important are: Wolfgang Jacobmeyer, *Vom Zwangsarbeiter zum heimatlosen Ausländer. Die Displaced Persons in Westdeutschland 1945–1951* (Göttingen, 1985); and Mark Wyman, *DP: Europe's Displaced Persons, 1945–1951* (Philadelphia, 1989). In this connection, we should also mention Kurt

R. Grossmann, *The Jewish D.P. Problem, Its Origins, and Liquidation* (New York, 1961). Among the many articles by Abraham Peck on the situation of Jewish DPs in postwar Germany, the following are especially noteworthy: "Zu den Anfängen jüdischen Lebens nach 1945," in Andreas Nachama and Julius H. Schoeps, eds., *Aufbau nach dem Untergang: Deutsch-jüdische Geschichte nach 1945* (Berlin, 1992), pp. 225–238; and "Jewish Survivors of the Holocaust in Germany: Revolutionary Vanguard or Remnants of a Destroyed People?" in *Tel Aviver Jahrbuch für Geschichte* 19 (1990): 33–45. *She'erit Hapletah, 1994–1948: Rehabilitation and Political Struggle* (Jerusalem, 1985), edited by Yisrael Gutman and Avital Saf, covers the fate of Jewish DPs in and beyond Germany. A rare example of a short contemporary portrait of a small DP community is Moisze Steinberg, *Di Jidn in Hof* (Hof, 1947).

More recent Israeli studies, concentrating to a large extent on internal Jewish aspects, investigate the Hebrew and Yiddish sources as well. The most outstanding of these is the work of Yehuda Bauer, as in his monographs *Flight and Rescue: Brichah* (New York, 1970) on the illegal immigration of Jewish DPs to Palestine; and *Out of the Ashes: The Impact of American Jews on Post-Holocaust European Jewry* (New York, 1989). Bauer's article "The Initial Organization of the Holocaust Survivors in Bavaria," in *Yad Vashem Studies* 8 (1970): 127–157, also presents important findings. Foremost among the dissertations at the Hebrew University is Zeev Mankovitz, "The Politics and Ideology of Survivors of the Holocaust in the American Zone of Germany, 1945–1946" (Hebrew University, Jerusalem, 1987; in Hebrew). A more recent German dissertation also devoted to internal Jewish aspects is Jacqueline Dewell-Giere, "Wir sind unterwegs, aber nicht in der Wüste. Erziehung und Kultur in den jüdischen Displaced Persons-Lagern der amerikanischen Zone im Nachkriegsdeutschland 1945–1949" (University of Frankfurt am Main, 1992). Judith Tydor Baumel, "Kibbutz Buchenwald and Kibbutz Hafetz Hayyim: Two Experiments in the Rehabilitation of Jewish Survivors in Germany," *Holocaust and Genocide Studies* 9 (1995): 231–249, is also a valuable and detailed study. An illustrated account of Jewish life in the DP camp is Rachel Salamander and Jacqueline Giere, *Ein Leben aufs Neu. Das Robinson-Album. Juden auf deutschem Boden 1945–1948* (Vienna, 1995).

The period right after the Liberation in Dachau is the subject of the first volume of the *Dachauer Hefte. Studien und Dokumente zur Geschichte der nationalsozialistischen Konzentrationslager* 1 (1985). On the issue of the self-assessment of the DPs, see Michael Brenner, "Wider den Mythos der 'Stunde Null'— Kontinuitäten im innerjüdischen Bewußtsein und deutsch-jüdischen Verhältnis nach 1945," in *Menora* 3 (1992): 155–181. The contemporary article by Koppel S. Pinson, "Jewish Life in Liberated Germany," in *Jewish Social Studies* 9 (1947): 101–126, is very informative. The last two chapters of Lucy S. Dawidowicz's autobiography, *From That Place and Time: A Memoir, 1938–1947* (New York and London, 1989), describe the cultural situation among the Displaced Persons as well as the issue of the restitution of cultural properties. The DP press is documented in a Hebrew monograph: Tsemah Tsamriyon, *The Press of the Holocaust Survivors in Germany as an Expression of Their Problems* (Tel Aviv, 1970; in Hebrew). See also the list of about a hundred Jewish journals by Zosa Szajkowski, "The Jewish Press in Germany, Austria, Italy, and Sweden," in *YIVO-Bleter* 28 (1946; in Yiddish): 397–408. Gerd Korman used archival sources to detail the history of the printing of the Heidelberg Talmud in "Survivors' Talmud and the U.S. Army," in *American Jewish History* 73 (1984): 252–285.

Works dealing with the rabbis and chaplains entrusted with the care of the Jewish DPs are: Louis Barish, ed., *Rabbis in Uniform* (New York, 1970); and more recently, Alex Grobman, *Rekindling the Flame: American Jewish Chaplains and the Survivors of European Jewry, 1944–1948* (Detroit, 1993). The memoir of an American chaplain, George Vida, *From Doom to Dawn: A Jewish Chaplain's Story of Displaced Persons* (New York, 1967), is an important document. New source materials have been analyzed in two articles by Julius Carlebach and Andreas Brämer, "Flight into Action as a Method of Repression: American Military Rabbis and the Problem of Jewish Displaced Persons in Postwar Germany," *Jewish Studies Quarterly* 2 (1995): 76; and "Rabbiner in Deutschland—die ersten Nachkriegsjahre," in Julius Carlebach, ed., *Das aschkenasische Rabbinat. Studie über Glaube und Schicksal* (Berlin, 1995), pp. 225–234.

In *America and the Survivors of the Holocaust* (New York, 1982), Leonard Dinnerstein presents the most thorough analysis of American policy vis-à-vis the Jewish DPs. British policy concerning the DPs in light of the British Mandate in Palestine is the subject of Arieh J. Kochavi, "The Displaced Persons' Problem and the Formulation of British Policy in Palestine," in *Studies in Zionism* 10 (1989): 31–48. The tripartite relationship of England–Palestine–DPs in Germany is the focus of Horst Siebecke's popular history, *Die Schicksalsfahrt der "Exodus 47"* (Munich, 1984; paperback ed., Frankfurt am Main, 1987). A lesser known chapter of the relations between Germany, or rather, the Jewish DPs living in Germany, and Israel appears in the essay by Yeshayahu A. Jelinek, "Like an Oasis in the Desert: The Israeli Consulate in Munich, 1948–1953," in *Studies in Zionism* 9 (1988): 81–98. For the dissolution of the last DP camp and its consequences for those concerned, see Johannes Menke, *Die soziale Integration jüdischer Flüchtlinge des ehemaligen Regierungslagers "Föhrenwald" in den drei westdeutschen Großstädten Düsseldorf, Frankfurt und München* (Hamburg, 1960).

Memoirs of documentary value are in the collection *Belsen* (Tel Aviv, 1957), published by the Irgun She'erit hapleyta mi'ha-esor ha'briti; as well as in Yaffa Eliach and Brana Gurewitsch, eds., *The Liberators: Eyewitness Accounts of the Liberation of Concentration Camps*, vol. 1 (New York, 1981), and in Zalman Grinberg, *Shuchrarnu mi-Dachau* (Herzliya, 1948; in Hebrew). The factually based novel of Leo W. Schwarz, *The Redeemers* (New York, 1953), also has some documentary value. The portrait of a large DP camp is in Simon Schochet, *Feldafing* (Vancouver, 1983). The letters of the commander of the Landsberg DP camp, Irving Heymont, *Among the Survivors of the Holocaust, 1945: The Landsberg DP*

Letters of Major Irving Heymont, U.S. Army (Cincinnati, 1982), are especially interesting. Finally, two contemporary works on the DP problem should be mentioned: in 1946, Zorach Wahrhaftig composed a comprehensive interim report on the situation of the Jewish DPs for the Institute of Jewish Affairs: *Uprooted: Jewish Refugees and Displaced Persons after Liberation* (New York, 1946). Julius Posner, *In Deutschland 1945–1946* (Jerusalem, 1947) is the travel account of a Jewish emigrant returning to postwar Germany.

RESTORATION OF GERMAN-JEWISH COMMUNITIES

The new beginning of Jewish life has produced several scholarly works on individual communities. Along with the above-mentioned monograph by Juliane Wetzel on Munich, this is usually done in the form of a succinct "epilogue" to a comprehensive history of the community or a special chapter in general histories of cities in the postwar era. Only the most important examples will be cited here. A few essays on Jewish life in postwar Berlin, with special emphasis on Heinz Galinski, are in Andreas Nachama and Julius H. Schoeps, eds., *Aufbau nach dem Untergang: Deutsch-jüdische Geschichte nach 1945* (Berlin, 1992). In this volume, Hermann Simon deals with an unknown chapter of the restoration period in Berlin, "Die Jüdische Gemeinde Nordwest—Eine Episode aus der Zeit des Neubeginns jüdischen Lebens in Berlin nach 1945," pp. 274–284. For Hamburg, there are two valuable articles: Ina S. Lorenz and Jörg Berkemann, "Kriegsende und Neubeginn. Zur Entstehung der neuen Jüdischen Gemeinde in Hamburg 1945–1948," pp. 633–656, in Arno Herzig, ed., *Die Juden in Hamburg 1590–1990* (Hamburg, 1991); and Ursula Büttner, "Rückkehr in ein normales Leben? Die Lage der Juden in Hamburg in den ersten Nachkriegsjahren," ibid., pp. 613–632. A successful documentation is Günther Bernd Ginzel, "Die Phasen der Etablierung einer Jüdischen Gemeinde in der Kölner Trümmerlandschaft," in Jutta Bohnke-Kollwitz et al., eds., *Köln und das rheinische Judentum. Festschrift Germania Judaica* (Cologne, 1984), pp. 445–461. The postwar Frankfurt Jewish community is sketched by Cilly Kugelmann, "Juden in Frankfurt nach 1945," in Rachel Heuberger and Helga Krohn, eds., *Hinaus aus dem Ghetto . . . Juden in Frankfurt am Main, 1800–1950* (Frankfurt am Main, 1988), pp. 195–205; and Salomon Korn, "Die 4. Jüdische Gemeinde in Frankfurt am Main. Zukunft oder Zwischenspiel?" in Karl E. Grözinger, ed., *Judentum im deutschen Sprachraum* (Frankfurt am Main, 1991), pp. 409–433.

Smaller communities are studied by Pedro Wagner, "Neubildung der Synagogengemeinde Bonn," in H. Linn, ed., *Juden an Rhein und Sieg* (Siegburg, 1983), pp. 381–397; and A. Epstein, "Nach dem Nationalsozialismus—1945 bis heute," in F. Schütz, ed., *Juden in Mainz* (Mainz, 1978), pp. 91–97. Larger regions are portrayed in Zvi Asaria, *Die Juden in Niedersachsen von den ältesten Zeiten bis zur Gegenwart* (Leer, 1979), pp. 539–635; and Wolf-Arno Kropat, "Jüdische Gemeinden. Wiedergutmachung, Rechtsradikalismus und Antisemitismus nach 1945," in *900 Jahre Geschichte der Juden in Hessen* (Wiesbaden, 1983). See also the series of my articles on Jewish communities in postwar Germany in the *Allgemeine Jüdische Wochenzeitung* between November 1984 and February 1985.

The attitude of the German population toward the Jews was analyzed in several articles by Frank Stern, based on his pathbreaking monograph, *The Whitewashing of the Yellow Badge: Antisemitism and Philosemitism in Postwar Germany* (Oxford, 1992). For Bavaria, see Constantin Goschler, "The Attitude towards Jews in Bavaria after the Second World War," in *Year Book of the Leo Baeck Institute* 36 (1991): 443–458. There are several essays on related subjects in Werner Bergmann and Rainer Erb, eds., *Antisemitismus in der politischen Kultur nach 1945* (Opladen, 1990).

Rolf Rendtorff and Hermann Henrix have drawn up a comprehensive and carefully selected documentation on Christian-Jewish relations after 1945: *Die Kirchen und das Judentum. Dokumente von 1945 bis 1985* (Paderborn and Munich, 1987). The interviews Ronald Webster conducted with Jewish returnees form the basis of his article "Jewish Returnees to West Germany after 1945: Why They Returned and How They Fared," in *YIVO Annual* 21 (1992): 33–66.

Basic works for the issue of reparations are the seven-volume survey, *Die Wiedergutmachung nationalsozialistischen Unrechts durch die Bundesrepublik Deutschland*, published by the West German Ministry of Finance in cooperation with Walter Schwarz (Munich, 1974–); and the collection, *Wiedergutmachung in der Bundesrepublik Deutschland*, edited by Ludolf Herbst and Constantin Goschler (Munich, 1989). A special aspect was investigated by Ronald W. Zweig, *German Reparation and the Jewish World: A History of the Claims Conference* (Boulder and London, 1987).

Jewish Identity and the Establishment of Jewish Life

Two dissertations in the 1960s and 1970s deal with Jewish identity in postwar Germany. One is Walter W. Jacob Oppenheimer, *Jüdische Jugend in Deutschland* (Munich, 1967); the other is the unpublished work by Doris Kuschner, "Die jüdische Minderheit in der Bundesrepublik Deutschland" (Cologne, 1977). A sociological investigation that touched on only a few aspects of Jewish life is Alphons Silbermann and Herbert Sallen, *Juden in Westdeutschland. Selbstbild und Fremdbild einer Minorität* (Cologne, 1992). Peter Sichrovsky's *Strangers in Their Own Land: Young Jews in Germany and Austria Today* (New York, 1986)—originally published as *Wir wissen nicht was morgen wird, wir wissen wohl was gestern war* (Cologne, 1985)—is not representative but is nevertheless informative as testimony of individual feelings about Jewish life. The same is true of the brief portraits in Henryk M. Broder and Michel R. Lang, eds., *Fremd im eigenen Land. Juden in der Bundesrepublik* (Frankfurt am Main, 1979); and of the interviews in Susann Heenen-Wolff, *Im Land der Täter. Gespräche mit überlebenden Juden* (Frankfurt am Main, 1994).

There is a relatively extensive literature on Jews in East Germany. One of the first works in this field is the unpublished dissertation of G. E. Thompson, "The Political Status of the Jews in the German Democratic Republic" (University of Iowa, 1967). A collection of sermons by the only long-term rabbi in East Germany, from 1949 to 1958, is Martin Riesenburger, *Also spricht Dein Bruder* (Berlin, 1958). The collection, *Juden in der DDR. Geschichte—Probleme—Perspektiven* (Duisburg, 1988), edited by Siegfried Arndt et al., takes account of more recent tendencies. Interestingly, in her above-mentioned study, Erica Burgauer devotes more space to the Jews of East Germany than to the Jews of West Germany during the first four years after the war. Nora Goldenbogen analyzes the antisemitism of the late Stalinist period in East Germany in her essay "'Säuberungen' und Antisemitismus in Sachsen 1949 und 1953," in *Historische Blätter aus Politik und Geschichte* 1992, pp. 19–25. Two collections of interviews are illuminating. Robin Ostow published her book, *Jews in Contemporary East Germany: The Children of Moses in the Land of Marx* (New York, 1989), when the DDR still existed; while Vincent von Wroblewsky's *Zwischen Thora und Trabant. Juden in der DDR* (Berlin, 1993) appeared only after the Wall came down. In his autobiography, *Fremd unter meinesgleichen. Erinnerungen eines Dresdner Juden* (Berlin, 1991), Helmut Eschwege reports on the experiences of an "uncomfortable" Jew in four decades of East Germany.

The first phase of rebuilding Jewish life in West Germany is documented in several contemporary collections. The liveliest of these are Heinz Ganther, ed., *Almanach. Die Juden in Deutschland 1951/52* (Hamburg, 1951); and the yearbook *Israel und Wir*, published in 1966 and 1970 by the Jewish National Fund, Keren Hayesod. Sketches of Jewish life in the larger communities as well as the most important Jewish organizations in reunited Germany are contained in the collections by Uri R. Kaufmann, ed., *Jewish Life in Germany Today* (Bonn, 1994); and Wolfgang Benz, ed., *Zwischen Antisemitismus und Philosemitismus. Juden in der Bundesrepublik* (Berlin, 1991). A similar subject is treated in the work published by the Bundeszentrale für politische Bildung in the early 1990s, *Deutsche Juden—Juden in Deutschland* (n.d.). Several essays on the situation of the Jews in Germany in the early 1990s are collected in *Judaica. Beiträge zum Verständnis des jüdischen Schicksals in Vergangenheit und Gegenwart* 49/1 (March 1993). On a more popular level, the special issue of *Der Spiegel* on *Juden und Deutsche* 2/1992, including an article by Wolfgang Benz, "Juden im Nachkriegsdeutschland," pp. 47–53, focuses on the same subject. On the immigration and integration of Russian Jews, see Julius H. Schoeps, Willi Jasper, and Bernhard Vogt, eds., *Russische Juden in Deutschland. Integration und Selbstbehauptung in einem fremden Land* (Weinheim, 1996).

Jewish youth is treated in the conference volumes *Die Zukunft unserer Gemeinden. Jugend- und Kulturtagung des Zentralrats der Juden in Deutschland*, edited by Alexander Ginsburg (Düsseldorf, 1977), and *Junge Juden in Deutschland*, edited by Ellen Presser and Bernhard Schossig (Munich, 1991). Jewish religious life in West Germany has not yet been analyzed thoroughly. A brief summary of the religious problematic with a documentary appendix is presented by Pnina Navé Levinson, "Religiöse Richtungen und Entwicklungen in den Gemeinden," in *Jüdisches Leben in Deutschland seit 1945*, pp. 140–171. A testimony of religious culture is the volume of sermons by Nathan Peter Levinson, *Ein Rabbiner in Deutschland, Aufzeichnungen zu Religion und Politik* (Gerlingen, 1987). On the Jewish press, see Ralph Giordano, ed., *Narben, Spuren, Zeugen. Fünfzehn Jahre Allgemeine Jüdische Wochenzeitung in Deutschland* (Düsseldorf, 1961); and Karl Marx, ed., *Zwanzig Jahre Allgemeine. Dokumentation und Echo* (Düsseldorf, 1966). On the most committed Jewish woman politician in postwar Germany, an informative work is the memorial book edited by Hans Lamm for *Jeannette Wolff. Mit Bibel und Bebel* (Bonn, 1980). The most important social welfare institution of Jewish life in Germany is documented in Bertold Scheller, *Die Zentralwohlfartsstelle der Juden in Deutschland. Eine Selbstdarstellung* (Frankfurt am Main, 1987).

The architectural legacy of Jewish life is the subject of Thea Altaras, *Synagogen in Hessen—was geschah nach 1945?* (Königstein i.Ts., 1988). Synagogue architects of the postwar period have also produced theoretical essays, as, for example: Salomon Korn, "Zur Geschichte der Synagogal-Architektur in der Nachkriegszeit," in Andreas Nachama and Julius H. Schoeps, eds., *Aufbau nach dem Untergang: Deutsch-jüdische Geschichte nach 1945* (Berlin, 1992), pp. 187–214; and Hermann Zvi Guttman, *Vom Tempel zum Gemeindezentrum: Synagogen im Nachkriegsdeutschland* (Frankfurt am Main, 1989).

The relation of Jewish society in other countries to Germany and its Jews was studied by Shlomo Shafir with the example of the World Jewish Congress: "Der Jüdische Weltkongress und sein Verhältnis zu Nachkriegsdeutschland (1945–1967)," in *Menora* 3 (1992): 210–237. The memoir of the former Israeli ambassador in Bonn Yohanan Meroz, *In schwieriger Mission* (Frankfurt am Main, 1986), is an important personal document. For an earlier phase, see the memoirs of Nahum Goldmann, *Mein Leben als deutscher Jude* (Munich and Vienna, 1980).

Subjective descriptions of Jewish life through the eyes of foreign Jewish observers are Leo Katcher, *Post-Mortem: The Jews in Germany Today* (New York, 1968); and Karen Gershon, *Postscript: A Collective Account of the Lives of Jews in West Germany since the Second World War* (London, 1969). Accounts of American Jewish women in the 1980s include Jane E. Gilbert, *Ich mußte mich vom Haß befreien. Eine Jüdin emigriert nach Deutschland. Ein Lebensbericht* (Munich, 1989); and Susan Neiman, *Slow Fire: Jewish Notes from Berlin* (New York, 1992).

Postwar German-Jewish literature in the interim has also been the subject of scholarly essays: Sander L. Gilman is the leading scholar in this area and has published a monograph, *Jews in Today's German Culture* (Bloomington, 1994), as well as a collection with Karen Remmler: *Reemerging Jewish Culture in Germany: Life and Literature since 1989* (New York, 1994). Important literary texts have been collected, as an anthology, in Elena Lappin, ed., *Jewish Voices, German Words: Growing Up in Postwar Germany and Austria* (North Haven, 1994). Anat Feinberg deals with dramatic literature in *Wiedergutmachung im Programm: Jüdisches Schicksal im deutschen Nachkriegsdrama* (Cologne, 1988).

Reflections of quite varying quality on German-Jewish life in the postwar era and German-Jewish relations include: Michael Wolffsohn, *Eternal Guilt? Forty Years of German-Jewish-Israeli Relations* (New York, 1993), and *Verwirrtes Deutschland? Provokative Zwischenrufe eines deutsch-jüdischen Patrioten* (Munich, 1993); and Julius H. Schoeps, *Leiden an Deutschland. Vom antisemitischen Wahn und der Last der Erinnerung* (Munich, 1990). Rafael Seligmann offers little of substance in *Mit beschränkter Hoffnung. Juden, Deutsche, Israelis* (Hamburg, 1991). There are provocative essays in Henryk M. Broder's volumes, *Ich liebe Karstadt und andere Lobreden* (Augsburg, 1987), *Erbarmen mit den Deutschen* (Hamburg, 1993), and *Schöne Bescherung! Unterwegs im Namen Deutschlands* (Augsburg, 1994); the same is true of Eike Geisel, *Die Banalität der Guten. Deutsche Seelenwanderungen* (Berlin, 1992). Lea Fleischmann's account of an emigration from Germany, *Dies ist nicht mein Land. Eine Jüdin verläßt die Bundesrepublik* (Hamburg, 1980), was a sensation when it came out. The most representative collection of contemporary Jewish voices in Germany is Susan Stern, *Speaking Out: Jewish Voices from United Germany* (Carol Stream, Ill., 1995). Laura Waco, *Von zu Hause wird nichts erzählt* (Munich, 1996) gives a lively impression of a Jewish childhood in the Germany of the 1950s and 1960s.

For the controversy about the Bitburg visit, see the collection by Geoffrey Hartman, ed., *Bitburg in Moral and Political Perspective* (Bloomington, 1986). The 1985 theater scandal in Frankfurt is the subject of E. Kiderlen, ed., *Fassbinders Sprengsätze, Deutsch-jüdische Normalität*, Pflasterstrand Flugschrift 1 (Frankfurt am Main, 1985). The smouldering conflict of a few years later about the development of the Judengasse is documented in Michael Best, ed., *Der Frankfurter Börneplatz. Zur Archäologie eines politischen Konflikts* (Frankfurt am Main, 1988). Richard Chaim Schneider, *Zwischenwelten. Ein jüdisches Leben im heutigen Deutschland* (Munich, 1994) is an informative mixture of self-analysis and an analysis of the situation of the Jews in reunited Germany. The autobiographical conversation between Edith Kohn and Ignatz Bubis, *Ich bin ein deutscher Staatsbürger jüdischen Glaubens* (Cologne, 1993) was the first autobiographical document of a leader of the Central Council of the Jews in Germany, followed by his more detailed *Damit bin ich längst noch nicht fertig* (Frankfurt am Main, 1996) and two memoirs of younger Frankfurt Jews active in political life and Jewish community affairs: Michel Friedman, *Zukunft ohne Vergessen. Ein jüdisches Leben in Deutschland* (Cologne, 1995), and Micha Brumlik, *Kein Weg als Deutscher und Jude* (Munich, 1996). The longest-serving rabbi in postwar Germany, Nathan Peter Levinson, published his memoirs recently: *Ein Ort ist, mit wem du bist. Lebensstationen eines Rabbiners* (Berlin, 1996).

Notes

I. HISTORICAL OVERVIEW

1. Liberated—But Not Free

1. Filip Müller, *Eyewitness Auschwitz: Three Years in the Gas Chambers,* trans. Susanne Flatauer (New York, 1979), p. 166.

2. Jenny Spritzer, "Der letzte Marsch," in Gerhard Schoenberner, ed., *Wir haben es gesehen: Augenzeugenberichte über die Judenverfolgung im Dritten Reich* (Wiesbaden, 1981), pp. 388–389.

3. Eugen Kogon, *The Theory and Practice of Hell,* trans. Heinz Norden (New York, 1976), p. 248.

4. Barbara Distel, "Die Befreiung des KZ Dachau," *Dachauer Hefte* 1 (1985): 4–5.

5. Kogon, *The Theory and Practice of Hell,* p. 359.

6. Eberhard Kolb, "Das Lager Bergen-Belsen. Eine Skizze der Lagerentwicklung," in Landesverband der Jüdischen Gemeinden von Niedersachsen, ed., *Von der Knechtschaft in die Befreiung. Bergen-Belsen 1945/1970,* p. 25.

7. Distel, "Die Befreiung des KZ Dachau," p. 4.

8. Toni Siegert, *30,000 Tote mahnen! Die Geschichte des Konzentrationslagers Flossenbürg und seiner 100 Aussenlager von 1938 bis 1945,* 3d ed. (Weiden, 1987), p. 56.

9. For a list of all the death marches from Flossenbürg and its outside camps, see Peter Heigl, *Konzentrationslager Flossenbürg in Geschichte und Gegenwart* (Regensburg, 1989), pp. 40–43.

10. Michael Brenner, *Am Beispiel Weiden: Jüdischer Alltag im Nationalsozialismus* (Würzburg, 1983), p. 148.

11. Kolb, "Das Lager Bergen-Belsen," p. 25.

12. Distel, "Die Befreiung des KZ Dachau," p. 11.

13. Wolfgang Benz, "Zwischen Befreiung und Heimkehr. Das Dachauer Internationale Häftlings-Komitee und die Verwaltung des Lagers im Mai und Juni 1945," in *Dachauer Hefte,* vol. 1 (1985), pp. 39–40.

14. *Report on the Situation of the Jews in Germany. October/December, 1945* (Geneva, 1946), p. 33. The report concluded that the Jewish survivors "are still

robbed of their freedom. They are systematically refused human rights. No one is concerned about their individuality and no one restores their self-respect" (p. 17).

15. *New York Times*, September 30, 1945, p. 38.

16. On the number of Jewish survivors in Germany after the end of the war, see Jacobmeyer, "Jüdische Überlebende als 'Displaced Persons,'" p. 421 n. 1.

17. *Report on the Situation of the Jews in Germany. October/December, 1945.*

18. David Max Eichhorn, "Sabbath-Gottesdienst im Lager. Bericht des US-Militärrabbiners über die erste Maiwoche 1945," in *Dachauer Hefte*, vol. 1 (1985), p. 213; Jacobmeyer, "Jüdische Überlebende," p. 446; Asaria, *Die Juden in Niedersachsen*, p. 556.

19. Bauer, *Flight and Rescue: Brichah*, p. 61; and "The Initial Organization," p. 145.

20. *Der Weg*, June 6, 1946.

21. Heymont, *Among the Survivors*, p. 5.

22. Eichhorn, "Sabbath-Gottesdienst im Lager," p. 211.

23. Vida, *From Doom to Dawn*, p. 25.

24. *Undzer Hofenung*, December 13, 1946.

25. Dinnerstein, *America and the Survivors of the Holocaust*, p. 33.

26. Vida, *From Doom to Dawn*, p. 26.

27. Quoted in Dinnerstein, *America and the Survivors of the Holocaust*, p. 62.

28. Heymont, *Among the Survivors*, p. 5.

29. Wahrhaftig, *Uprooted*, p. 39.

30. Schwarz, *The Redeemers*, pp. 27–28. Patton was removed by General Truscott in September 1945. See Bauer, "The Initial Organization," p. 142.

31. Quoted in United States Holocaust Museum, ed., *1945: The Year of Liberation* (Washington, 1945), p. 195.

32. Quoted in Jacobmeyer, "Jüdische Überlebende," p. 423.

33. Yisrael Gutman and Shmuel Krakowski, *Unequal Victims: Poles and Jews during World War Two* (New York, 1986), pp. 370–374.

34. Wahrhaftig, *Uprooted*, p. 39.

35. Jacobmeyer, "Jüdische Überlebende," pp. 436–437.

36. Dinnerstein, *America and the Survivors of the Holocaust*, pp. 278–279.

37. Jacobmeyer, "Jüdische Überlebende," p. 444.

38. Ibid. p. 449.

2. Culture behind Barbed Wire

1. Rosensaft, "Our Belsen," in *Belsen*, pp. 47–48.

2. Ibid., pp. 34–35.

3. Dawidowicz, *From That Place and Time*, p. 290.

4. Heymont, *Among the Survivors*, p. 42.

5. *Undzer Veg*, October 12, 1945, p. 1.

6. Dewell-Giere, "Wir sind unterwegs," pp. 273–289.

7. B. Kossowski, *Bibliografie fun die jiddische oisgabes in der britischer Son fun Dajtschland, 1945–1950* (Bergen-Belsen, 1950).

8. Published by the *Centrale fun die Warszewer Landsmanszaftn in der US Zone in Dajczland* (Munich, 1948).

9. Pinson, "Jewish Life in Liberated Germany," p. 121; cf. Dawidowicz, *From That Place and Time*, pp. 312–326.

10. Mordechai Bernstein, "Die kulturelle Tätigkeit der Shearit Haplei-tah," in Hans Lamm, ed., *Vergangene Tage. Jüdische Kultur in München* (Munich and Vienna, 1982), p. 370.

11. Jewish Brigade: A Jewish military unit from Palestine in the British army that saw service in Egypt, northern Italy, and northwest Europe between 1944 and 1946. The Brigade played an important part in the care of Jewish survivors in postwar Europe.

12. Asaria, *Die Juden in Niedersachsen*, pp. 550–551; and Manfred Lu-bliner, "Jewish Education in Belsen," in *Belsen*, p. 157.

13. Wahrhaftig, *Uprooted*, p. 53.

14. Dewell-Giere, "Wir sind unterwegs," p. 103.

15. Ibid., p. 332.

16. Analysis of the index cards of Jewish DPs, Archiv der Israelitischen Kultusgemeinde Weiden.

17. Stefan Schwarz, *Die Juden in Bayern im Wandel der Zeiten* (Munich and Vienna, 1963), p. 314.

18. Leo Srole, "Why the DPs Can't Wait," *Commentary*, January 1947, p. 18.

19. Asaria, *Die Juden in Niedersachsen*, p. 555. Schwarz Collection, YIVO Archive (New York), File 434, p. 1241. Cf. Yad Vashem Archive, Jerusalem, M-1/P44.

20. Memorandum of Rosenberg, February 27, 1946, p. 11. American Joint Distribution Committee Archives, New York, AR 4564.406.

21. Schwarz, *Die Juden in Bayern*, p. 314.

22. Gerd Korman, "Survivors' Talmud and the U.S. Army," *American Jewish History* 73 (1984): 252–285.

23. Pinson, "Jewish Life in Liberated Germany," p. 111.

24. Srole, "Why the DPs Can't Wait," p. 19.

25. Asaria, *Die Juden in Niedersachsen*, p. 556.

26. Ibid., p. 557.

27. Israel Blumenfeld, ed., *Pessach Buch 5706–1946. Zum ersten Be-freiungs- und Frühlingsfest der Überreste Israels in Europa*, 2d ed. (Giessen, 1948), pp. 12–15.

28. *Der Weg*, February 21, 1946.

29. Dawidowicz, *From That Time and Place*, p. 305.

30. Ibid.

31. Archive of the Leo Baeck Institute (New York), AR 2371, "Jüdisches Theater III."

32. Samy Feder, "The Yiddish Theatre of Belsen," in *Belsen*, pp. 137–139; Asaria, *Die Juden in Niedersachsen*, p. 554.

33. *Undzer Veg*, January 4, 1946.

34. See, for example, *Undzer Hofenung*, July 5, 1946, p. 6.

35. *Undzer Moment*, August 13, 1947, p. 6.

36. Schwartz Collection, YIVO Archive (New York), File 160.

37. M. Levin, ed., *Kibbuts Buchenwald* (Tel Aviv, 1946), p. 39.

3. Autonomy and Emigration

1. Rosensaft, "Our Belsen," in *Belsen*, p. 27.

2. Ibid., pp. 28–29.

3. Pinson, "Jewish Life in Liberated Germany," p. 126.

4. For Rosensaft, see Bauer, *Flight and Rescue: Brichah*, p. 72; and Schwarz, *The Redeemers*, p. 32.

5. *Undzer Hofenung*, November 22, 1946, p. 5.

6. Schwarz, *Die Juden in Bayern*, p. 313.

7. Juliane Wetzel, "Lebensmut im Wartesaal. Der Wiederaufbau der Israelitischen Kultusgemeinde und des jüdischen Lebens in München 1945–1949," in Friedrich Prinz, ed., *Trümmerzeit in München. Kultur und Gesellschaft einer deutschen Großstadt im Aufbruch 1945–1949* (Munich, 1989), p. 143.

8. Bauer, *Flight and Rescue: Brichah*, p. 73.

9. In Landsberg, the overwhelming majority of the camp committees consisted of Lithuanian and Latvian Jews. See Heymont, *Among the Survivors*, p. 14.

10. Ibid., p. 62.

11. Bauer, "The Initial Organization," p. 145.

12. Ibid., pp. 142–159.

13. For the "Jewish Infantry Brigade Group," see Bauer, *Flight and Rescue: Brichah*, pp. 62–68.

14. Rosensaft, "Our Belsen," in *Belsen*, p. 26.

15. Heymont, *Among the Survivors*, pp. 65–66.

16. Michael Marrus, *The Unwanted: European Refugees in the Twentieth Century* (New York and Oxford, 1985), p. 334.

17. Quoted in Siebecke, *Die Schicksalsfahrt der "Exodus 47,"* pp. 211ff.

18. The Jewish Committee in the Bavarian Neunburg vorm Walde was the first to call for a hunger strike. See *Undzer Moment* (Regensburg), August 13, 1947, p. 6; August 29, 1947, p. 1.

19. Dinnerstein, *America and the Survivors of the Holocaust*, p. 288.

20. Pinson, "Jewish Life in Liberated Germany," pp. 116–117.

21. Schwarz, *The Redeemers*, p. 291.

22. *Undzer Veg*, September 5, 1946, p. 3.

23. *Undzer Veg*, April 1, 1949.

24. *Undzer Veg*, January 20, 1950, p. 7.

25. Maor, "Über den Wiederaufbau jüdischer Gemeinden," p. 24.

4. *Yekkes and Ostjuden*

1. Menke, *Die soziale Integration jüdischer Flüchtlinge*, pp. 27 and 75.

2. *Verzeichnis der nach der Befreiung durch die Alliierten in Berlin befreiten Juden* (Berlin, 1947).

3. Berlin Jewish community, *Arbeitsbericht 1945–1946*, Addendum I.

4. Hans Winterfeldt, "Deutschland. Ein Zeitbild, 1926–1945," unpublished MS, Archive of the Leo Baeck Institute, New York, ME 690, pp. 401–402.

5. Letter of July 31, 1945, in collection of letters, *Organization of the Jews from Wuerttemberg*, p. 8, Archive of the Leo Baeck Institute, New York, Leopold Levi Col., AR 7041, Box 1, Folder 7.

6. Epstein, "Nach dem Nationalsozialismus—1945 bis heute," p. 92.

7. Oskar Wolfsberg-Aviad, *Die Drei-Gemeinde. Aus der Geschichte der jüdischen Gemeinde Altona-Hamburg-Wandsbek* (Munich, 1960), p. 134.

8. Ginzel, "Die Phasen der Etablierung einer Jüdischen Gemeinde in der Kölner Trümmerlandschaft."

9. Pedro Wagner, "Neubildung der Synagogenmeinde Bonn," in H. Linn, *Juden an Rhein und Sieg*, p. 383.

10. Epstein, "Nach dem Nationalsozialismus—1945 bis heute," p. 92.

11. Ina Lorenz and Jörg Berkemann, "Kriegsende und Neubeginn. Zur Entstehung der neuen Jüdischen Gemeinde in Hamburg 1945–1948," in Arno Herzig, ed., *Die Juden in Hamburg 1590–1990* (Hamburg, 1991), p. 636.

12. *Jüdisches Gemeindeblatt für die Britische Zone*, February 5, 1947.

13. Paul Baruch, "Wie es nach 1945 in Nürnberg war," in *Gemeindeblatt der Israelitischen Kultusgemeinde Nürnberg*, vol. 1 (1967–68)–vol. 2 (1968–69), 1–11. Installment.

14. Maor, *Über den Wiederaufbau*, p. 19.

15. *Der Weg*, July 26, 1946.

16. *Jüdisches Gemeindeblatt für die Nord-Rheinprovinz und Westfalen*, July 10, 1946, p. 4.

17. Juliane Wetzel, "Lebensmut im Wartesaal. Der Wiederaufbau der Israelitischen Kultusgemeinde und des jüdischen Lebens in München 1945–1949," in Friedrich Prinz, ed., *Trümmerzeit in München. Kultur und Gesellschaft einer deutschen Großstadt im Aufbruch 1945–1949* (Munich, 1989), p. 143.

18. Asaria, *Die Juden in Niedersachsen*, p. 585.

19. Letters of the "Aktionskomitee zur Vorbereitung demokratischer Wahlen in der Israelitischen Kultusgemeinde Augsburg," January 1954, Archive of the Leo Baeck Institute, New York, AR 5890/3.

20. *Jüdisches Gemeindeblatt*, December 3, 1948, p. 3.

21. *Der Weg*, March 1, 1946, p. 3.

22. Ibid. p. 2.

23. *Jüdisches Gemeindeblatt für die Nord-Rheinprovinz und Westfalen*, November 9, 1946.

24. Knud C. Knudsen, ed., *Welt ohne Hass. Aufsätze und Ansprachen zum 1. Kongress über bessere menschliche Beziehungen in München* (Berlin, Hamburg, and Stuttgart, n.d.), pp. 158–161.

25. *Der Weg*, April 5, 1946, p. 3.

26. *Der Weg*, February 21, 1946.

27. *Conference on the Future of the Jews in Germany*, pp. 13–15.

28. In fact, up to 1950, at least a thousand DPs had married German women. See Peck, "Jewish Survivors of the Holocaust in Germany," p. 41.

29. Asaria, *Die Juden in Niedersachsen*, pp. 559–560. This resolution was also against the membership of Jews in Jewish community organizations who "still enter into marriage with non-Jews today," and declared, "New acceptance of converts does not take place for the time being."

30. Gershon, *Postscript*, pp. 76 and 81.

31. Hans Winterfeldt, "Deutschland. Ein Zeitbild, 1926–1945," unpublished MS, Archive of the Leo Baeck Institute, New York, ME 690, p. 401.

32. Büttner, *Not nach der Befreiung*, pp. 16–17.

33. Scheller, *Die Zentralwohlfahrtsstelle*, p. 47.

34. Ginzel, "Die Phasen der Etablierung einer Jüdischen Gemeinde in der Kölner Trümmerlandschaft," pp. 452–454.

35. Hermann Simon, "Die Jüdische Gemeinde Nordwest—Eine Episode aus der Zeit des Neubeginns jüdischen Lebens in Berlin nach 1945," in *Aufbau nach dem Untergang*, pp. 274–284.

36. Ursula Büttner, "Rückkehr in ein normales Leben? Die Lage der Juden in Hamburg in den ersten Nachkriegsjahren," p. 619.

5. Victims and Defeated

1. *Der Weg*, April 15, 1946, p. 4; and March 22, 1946, p. 2.

2. Julius Posner, *In Deutschland 1945–1946* (Jerusalem, 1947), p. 115.

3. Ruth Klüger, *Weiterleben. Eine Jugend* (Göttingen, 1992), p. 208.

4. *Jüdisches Gemeindeblatt für die Nord-Rheinprovinz und Westfalen*, November 26, 1946.

5. *Jüdisches Gemeindeblatt*, March 4, 1949, p. 1.

6. *Jüdisches Gemeindeblatt für die Nord-Rheinprovinz und Westfalen*, May 24, 1946, p. 18.

7. Schwarz, *The Redeemers*, p. 106.

8. *Der Weg*, March 29, 1946, p. 2.

9. Press report of the "Council of Liberated Jews in the American Occupied Zone of Germany," April 1, 1946, Schwartz Collection, YIVO Archive,

New York, File 460. This same press report calls a similar incident in Fürth "a resettlement campaign on the Nazi pattern."

10. Asaria, *Die Juden in Niedersachsen*, p. 607.

11. *Neue Zeitung*, August 11, 1949.

12. Y. Michal Bodemann, "Staat und Minorität. Antisemitismus und die gesellschaftliche Rolle der Juden in der Nachkriegszeit," in *Antisemitismus in der politischen Kultur nach 1945*, pp. 328–330.

13. Municipal Court of Memmingen, File Reference C 312/48 (1948). Quoted in *Jüdisches Gemeindeblatt*, January 14, 1949, p. 5, under the headline "Ritual Murder 1948."

14. *Neue Welt. Mitteilungsblatt der Jüdischen Gemeinden in Bayern*, no. 1, mid-September 1947, p. 6. The rumor was corrected by the putative victim himself after the "missing person" showed up again.

15. *Mitteilungsblatt für die jüdischen Gemeinden der Nord-Rheinprovinz*, June 7, 1946, p. 25.

16. Quoted in *Süddeutsche Zeitung*, October 7, 1947.

17. Quoted in Goschler, "Der Fall Philipp Auerbach. Wiedergutmachung in Bayern," in *Wiedergutmachung in der Bundesrepublik Deutschland*, p. 81.

18. Constantin Goschler, "The Attitude towards Jews in Bavaria after the Second World War," *Yearbook of the Leo Baeck Institute* 36 (1991): 450.

19. *Undzer Hofenung*, August 2, 1946, p. 3.

20. *Neue Welt*, no. 5, beginning of December 1947, p. 5.

21. *Der Spiegel*, July 26, 1947, p. 4. A listing of antisemitic incidents in German railroads is in the newspaper *Neue Welt. Mitteilungsblatt der Jüdischen Gemeinden in Bayern*, no. 1, mid-September 1947, p. 11.

22. *Jüdisches Gemeindeblatt für die Nord-Rheinprovinz und Westfalen*, September 26, 1946.

23. *Allgemeine Jüdische Wochenzeitung*, July 20, 1951, p. 7.

24. Cf. Frank Stern, "Wider Antisemitismus—für christlich-jüdische Zusammenarbeit. Aus der Entstehungszeit des Koordinierungsrats," *Menora* 3 (1992): 182–209.

25. Rendtorff and Henrix, *Die Kirchen und das Judentum*, p. 528.

26. Ibid., p. 530.

27. Ibid., p. 542.

28. Ibid., p. 239.

29. *Verzeichnis der nach der Befreiung durch die Aliierten in Berlin befreiten Juden* (Berlin, 1947).

30. *Der Weg*, August 29, 1947, p. 3.

31. *Undzer Moment*, September 28, 1947, p. 5.

32. *Der Weg*, July 19, 1946, p. 1.

33. See Richarz, "Jews in Today's Germanies," pp. 268–69.

34. For the history of the *Allgemeine Jüdische Wochenzeitung*, see E. G. Lowenthal, "Vom 'Gemeindeblatt' zur 'Allgemeinen,'" *Allgemeine Jüdische Wochenzeitung*, May 16, 1986, pp. 3–4.

35. Hans Lamm, "Über die innere und äussere Entwicklung des deutschen Judentums im Dritten Reich" (unpublished diss., Erlangen 1951), pp. 273–274.

36. Maor, "Über den Wiederaufbau," p. 39.

37. Ludolf Herbst, "Einleitung," in *Wiedergutmachung in der Bundesrepublik Deutschland*, p. 22.

38. Ben Ephraim, "Der steile Weg zur Wiedergutmachung," in Ganther, *Almanach*, pp. 293–294.

39. Ibid., p. 296.

40. *Conference on the Future of the Jews in Germany*, p. 56.

41. Archive of the Leo Baeck Institute, New York, Collection Council of Jews from Germany, AR 5890/II.

42. Ibid.

43. *Aufbau*, February 5, 1954, p. 8.

44. "The project of the status of the 'Union of Liberated Jews in the American Occupied Zone' which is going to be founded is rejected by the communities as not binding for them. They are the juridical heirs of the local Jewish communities before 1933 and decline therefore also the financial claims of the Union to the Jewish assets in the U.S. zone." Resolution signed by representatives of the Jewish communities in Munich, Nuremberg, Fürth, Würzburg, the Israelite Religious Federation of Württemberg, the Supreme Council of the Israelites of Baden, and the "Reichsvereinigung der Juden in Deutschland" (*sic!*), Schwartz Collection, YIVO Archive, New York, Folder 112.

45. *Neue Jüdische Zeitung*, September 9, 1953.

46. Ben Ephraim, "Der steile Weg zur Wiedergutmachung," in Ganther, *Almanach*, pp. 296–299.

47. Lucy Dawidowicz, *From That Place and Time*, pp. 312–315.

6. *The Establishment of Jewish Life*

1. *Resolutions Adopted by the Second Plenary Assembly of the World Jewish Congress, Montreux June 27th–July 6th, 1948* (London, 1948), p. 7.

2. H. Ingster, in the *Jüdisches Gemeindeblatt für die Britische Zone*, March 19, 1947.

3. *Jewish Frontier*, May 1951, pp. 18–21.

4. Schalom Adler-Rudel, quoted in Posner, *In Deutschland 1945–46*, p. 115.

5. Quoted in Zachariah Schuster, "Must the Jews Quit Europe? An Appraisal of the Propaganda for Exodus," *Commentary*, December 1945, p. 9.

6. Samuel Gringauz, "Jewish Destiny as the DPs See It," *Commentary*, December 1947, p. 505.

7. Quoted in Pinson, "Jewish Life in Liberated Germany," p. 114 n. 12.

8. *Der Weg*, July 4, 1947.

9. *Jüdisches Gemeindeblatt für die Nord-Rheinprovinz und Westfalen*, May 24, 1946.

10. *Allgemeine Jüdische Wochenzeitung*, July 20, 1951, p. 1.

11. Maor, "Über den Wiederbau," p. 96.

12. Matthew Kalman, *The Kids Are Alright: Chapters in the History of the World Union of Jewish Students* (Jerusalem, 1986), p. 35.

13. Resolutions of Fourteenth WUJS Congress, p. 2. Archive of the World Union of Jewish Students, Jerusalem.

14. E. G. Lowenthal, "Three Years with the Jews in Germany," *Commentary*, May 1950, p. 749.

15. *Jewish Monthly*, August 1948, p. 297.

16. *Der Weg*, June 27, 1947, p. 1.

17. Pnina Navé Levinson, "Religiöse Richtungen und Entwicklungen in den Gemeinden," in *Jüdisches Leben in Deutschland seit 1945*, p. 150.

18. Levinson, *Ein Rabbiner in Deutschland*, p. 111.

19. Oskar Wolfsberg-Aviad, *Die Drei-Gemeinde. Aus der Geschichte der jüdischen Gemeinde Altona-Hamburg-Wandsbek* (Munich, 1960), p. 139.

20. Siegbert Neufeld, "Die Gründung der Rabbinerkonferenz in Deutschland," *Udim* 1 (1970): 105–107.

21. Maor, "Über den Wiederaufbau," p. 103.

22. *Nachrichten für den jüdischen Bürger Fürths*, September 1971, pp. 3–9.

23. Navé Levinson, "Religiöse Richtungen und Entwicklungen," p. 151.

24. *Der Weg*, June 28, 1946, p. 1.

25. Nathan Peter Levinson, "Conversion or Camouflage? An Account of Proselytism in Post-War Germany," *Judaism*, 1955, pp. 352–359.

26. *Conference on the Future of the Jews in Germany*, pp. 16–17. This percentage remained about the same at the end of the 1950s. See Maor, "Über den Wiederaufbau," p. 105.

27. Jüdische Gemeinde Berlin, *Arbeitsbericht 1945–46*, p. 10.

28. *Conference on the Future of the Jews in Germany*, p. 12.

29. Ibid., p. 34.

30. See Scheller, *Die Zentralwohlfahrtsstelle*, p. 51.

31. *Arbeitsbericht*, pp. 4–5.

32. Ibid., pp. 6–7.

33. *Conference on the Future of the Jews in Germany*, p. 18.

34. *Jüdisches Gemeindeblatt für die Nord-Rheinprovinz und Westfalen*, May 24, 1946.

35. Hugo Oppenheimer, "Jean Mandel—Sixty Years," *Nachrichten für den jüdischen Bürger Fürths*, September 1971, pp. 15–17.

36. *Conference on the Future of the Jews in Germany*, p. 5.

37. Ibid., p. 21.

38. Ibid., p. 23.

39. Ibid., p. 43.

40. Hans Lamm, "Über die innere und äussere Entwicklung des deutschen Judentums im Dritten Reich" (unpublished diss., Erlangen 1951), p. 252.

41. Minutes of the meeting of the *Zentralrat* of January 7, 1951, in Hamburg, Archive of the *Allgemeine Jüdische Wochenzeitung*, Bonn, p. 3.

II. WITNESS ACCOUNTS

1. The Werewolf was a paramilitary auxiliary of the Wehrmacht set up in the closing days of World War II, when Germany was on the brink of defeat.

2. Max A. Braude (b. 1913 in Pennsylvania) was the highest-ranking Jewish chaplain with the U.S. armed forces in Europe. After the war, he was in charge of the welfare of the Displaced Persons. He later served as director of the World ORT Union and director-general of its international office in Geneva.

3. Yekutiel Yehuda Halberstam (b. 1904), the "Klausenburg Rebbe," was a descendant of the Zanz dynasty and one of the most respected Hasidic rebbes who survived the Holocaust. He was the first rabbi to establish a yeshiva in a German DP camp. During his stay in Föhrenwald, he was the director of the Central Committee of *She'erit ha-pleyta*. After his emigration, he reestablished his court in the Williamsburg section of Brooklyn, and in 1956 he founded the settlement of Kiryat Zanz in Israel.

4. Hans Habe (pseudonym of János Békassy) was born in Budapest in 1911. After escaping from a German POW camp in 1940, he served in the U.S. armed forces. In 1945, he founded the Munich *Neue Zeitung*. He became a celebrated novelist in postwar Germany and died in Switzerland in 1977.

5. In July 1945, the Western Allied troops moved out of Saxony and other parts of what was to become the Soviet Occupation Zone, in exchange for control of the three Western sectors of Berlin.

6. John Jay McCloy (1895–1989) was the high commissioner for Germany between 1949 and 1952, after serving as president of the World Bank.

7. The *Volkssturm* was a fighting organization formed by the Germans in September 1944, consisting of men and boys unfit for regular service.

8. The exterior of the Westend Synagogue survived the war. It was restored and served as the largest synagogue in postwar Frankfurt.

9. Steven S. Schwarzschild (1924–1989) had left Germany in 1939. He returned to Berlin in 1948 at the request of the World Union of Progressive Judaism as rabbi of the Liberal community. After his return to the United States, he was the editor of the journal *Judaism* and a professor of philosophy and Judaic studies at Washington University, St. Louis.

10. Rabbi Michael Munk, the son of Rabbi Ezra Munk of the Orthodox Adass Jisroel congregation of Berlin, returned only briefly to his hometown and lived as a Jewish educator in the United States.

11. Leo Baeck (1873–1956) was a Liberal rabbi, a professor at the Liberal rabbinical seminary in Berlin, and the undisputed spiritual and communal leader of German Jews during the years of Nazi persecution. When the *Reichsvertretung der deutschen Juden in Deutschland* was formed in 1933, Baeck became its president and retained this office until the dissolution of its successor organization, the *Reichsvereinigung*, in 1943. He refused to leave Germany as long as there were Jews left there. In 1943 he was deported to Theresienstadt, where he continued to serve as a spiritual leader of the remnant of German Jewry. After his liberation in 1945, he lived in London, with regular periods of teaching at the Hebrew Union College in Cincinnati. Eugen Täubler (1879–1953), a childhood friend of Baeck's from their days together in the Prussian province of Posen, was one of the most celebrated scholars of classical and Jewish studies in Weimar Germany. He taught ancient history at the universities of Zurich and Heidelberg and became Baeck's colleague at the Berlin Hochschule (renamed *Lehranstalt* by the Nazis) between 1935 and 1938. After immigrating to the United States, he taught at Hebrew Union College in Cincinnati.

12. Hans Rosenthal (1925–1987), perhaps the best-known Jew in post-war Germany, was one of the most popular German television masters-of-ceremony. Rosenthal, who had survived the war in hiding in Berlin, was actively engaged in Jewish community affairs after the war.

13. *Garbage, the City, and Death,* (*Der Müll, die Stadt und der Tod*), a controversial play by the late film director Rainer Werner Fassbinder, was scheduled to open at the Frankfurt Schauspielhaus on October 30, 1985. The performance was successfully prevented after an onstage demonstration organized by members of the local Jewish community, including its president, Ignatz Bubis. The demonstrators claimed that the play, whose main character was a real estate speculator, designated as "the Rich Jew" (allegedly a reference to Bubis himself), was very antisemitic and unfit for production in Germany.

14. Ernst Lemmer (1898–1970) was a liberal member of the Reichstag in Weimar Germany and a cofounder of the Christian Democratic Union (CDU) in 1945. He served as cabinet minister under Konrad Adenauer in the 1950s and 1960s. Theodor Heuss (1884–1963) was a liberal publicist and member of the Reichstag in Weimar Germany. He was the first president of the Federal Republic of Germany between 1949 and 1959.

15. Hans-Joachim Schoeps (1909–1980), the founder of the German nationalist Jewish youth group *Vortrupp* in 1933, was a disputed figure because of his conviction that German Jews could come to terms with the National Socialists. After his return from Swedish exile, he became a professor of intellectual history at the University of Erlangen in 1947.

III. Five Decades of Jewish Life in Postwar Germany

1. *Der Spiegel*, February 14, 1951, p. 10.

2. *Der Spiegel*, May 9, 1951, pp. 11–13. See previous report in *Der Spiegel*, August 9, 1947, p. 6.

3. *Der Spiegel*'s press campaign against Auerbach had its prologue in a libel suit Auerbach had filed against the news magazine a few months previously, for antisemitic undertones that had been insinuated in an article on Jews and the black market, in *Der Spiegel* of July 13, 1950. See Archive of the *Allgemeine Jüdische Wochenzeitung*, Bonn, 01.85.

4. Statement of the board of the *Zentralrat der Juden in Deutschland*, February 25, 1951, Archive of the *Allgemeine Jüdische Wochenzeitung*, Bonn.

5. Ben Ephraim, "Der steile Weg zur Wiedergutmachung," in Ganther, *Almanach*, p. 325.

6. *Allgemeine Jüdische Wochenzeitung*, August 22, 1952.

7. Bodemann, "Staat und Ethnizität: Der Aufbau der jüdischen Gemeinden im kalten Krieg," in *Jüdisches Leben in Deutschland*, p. 65. In the same volume, see Hans Jakob Ginsburg, "Politik danach—Jüdische Interessenvertretung in der Bundesrepublik," pp. 108–118.

8. Hans Lamm, ed., *Vergangene Tage. Jüdische Kultur in München* (Munich and Vienna, 1982); Stefan Schwarz, *Die Juden in Bayern im Wandel der Zeiten* (Munich and Vienna, 1963).

9. Henryk M. Broder, "Rehabilitiert Werner Nachmann," in Nachama, *Aufbau im Untergang*, p. 299.

10. Maor, "Über den Wiederaufbau," pp. 39–43.

11. Ibid., pp. 53–55.

12. There is a detailed list in Salomon Korn, "Zur Geschichte der Synagogal-Architektur in der Nachkriegszeit," in Nachama, *Aufbau im Untergang*, p. 212.

13. Burgauer, *Zwischen Erinnerung und Verdrängung*, p. 178.

14. Ibid., pp. 180–181.

15. Ostow, *Jews in Contemporary East Germany*, p. 20.

16. Mertens, "Schwindende Minorität. Das Judentum in der DDR," in *Juden in der DDR*, pp. 136, 149.

17. Peter Honigmann, "Über den Umgang mit Juden und jüdischer Geschichte in der DDR," in *Juden in der DDR*, p. 121. In the same article, Honigmann puts the total number of Jews living in East Berlin in 1986 at about two thousand.

18. Oppenheimer, *Jüdische Jugend in Deutschland*, p. 148.

19. Kuschner, "Die jüdische Minderheit in der Bundesrepublik Deutschland," pp. 126 and 172.

20. Quoted in ibid., p. 97.

21. Silbermann and Sallen, *Juden in Westdeutschland*, pp. 104–105.

22. Quoted in Burgauer, *Zwischen Erinnerung und Verdrängung*, p. 94.

23. Pnina Navé Levinson, "Religiöse Richtungen und Entwicklungen in den Gemeinden," in *Jüdisches Leben in Deutschland seit 1945*, p. 141.

24. Sichrovsky, *Wir wissen nicht was morgen wird*, pp. 164–165.

25. Ibid., p. 166.

26. Peter Honigmann, "Die Gründung der 'Vereinigung für Thoratreues Judentum' 1954 in Fürth," in *Nachrichten für den jüdischen Bürger Fürths*, September 1994, pp. 38–41.

27. For the conflict between Themal and the Jewish community of Berlin, see *Berliner Morgenpost*, December 3, 1970.

28. Ellen Presser, "Integrated, But Apart," in Kaufmann, ed., *Jewish Life in Germany Today*, p. 52.

29. Korn, "Die 4. jüdische Gemeinde in Frankfurt am Main," pp. 424–425.

30. Schneider, *Zwischenwelten*, p. 151.

31. *The Basic Kafka*, ed. Erich Heller (New York: Washington Square Press, 1979), p. 217.

32. Mertens, "Schwindende Minorität. Das Judentum in der DDR," in *Juden in der DDR*, p. 140; Königseder and Wetzel, *Lebensmut im Wartesaal*; and Burgauer, *Zwischen Erinnerung und Verdrängung*, p. 161.

33. *Tagesspiegel*, November 30, 1992.

34. *Süddeutsche Zeitung*, April 22, 1993.

35. Julius Carlebach, "Jüdische Geistigkeit und Kultur in der Bundesrepublik," in Wolfgang Benz, ed., *Zwischen Antisemitismus und Philosemitismus: Juden in der Bundesrepublik* (Berlin, 1991), p. 44.

36. Esther Dischereit, "No Exit from This Jewry," in Gilman, ed., *Reemerging Jewish Culture in Germany: Life and Literature since 1989*, p. 281.

37. The Mylius affair is described in detail in Burgauer, *Zwischen Erinnerung und Verdrängung*, pp. 209–221. For the hopes the community had for the young Mylius, see Mertens, "Schwindende Minorität. Das Judentum in der DDR," in *Juden in der DDR*, p. 153.

38. *B.Z. (Berliner Zeitung)*, July 20, 1992.

39. Richard Koch, "Das Freie Jüdische Lehrhaus in Frankfurt am Main," *Der Jude* 7 (1923): 119.

Index